OBJECT RELATIONS
AND THE
FAMILY PROCESS

Object Relations and the Family Process

RANDALL S. KLEIN

PRAEGER

New York
Westport, Connecticut
London

Library of Congress Cataloging-in-Publication Data

Klein, Randall S.
    Object relations and the family process / Randall S. Klein.
        p.   cm.
    Bibliography: p.
    Includes index.
    ISBN 0-275-93268-0 (alk. paper)
    1. Object relations (Psychoanalysis).   2. Family—Psychological
aspects.   I. Title.
BF175.5.024K44   1990
158'.24—dc20   89-16226

Library of Congress Catalog Card Number: 89-16226
ISBN: 0-275-93268-0

First published in 1990

Praeger Publishers, One Madison Avenue, New York, NY 10010
A division of Greenwood Press, Inc.

Printed in the United States of America

The paper used in this book complies with the
Permanent Paper Standard issued by the National
Information Standards Organization (Z39.48-1984).

10 9 8 7 6 5 4 3 2 1

Copyright Acknowledgments

To the fond memory of
Ron Ruble

Contents

Preface

This book is an essay on the psychoanalytic theory of object relations and its application to the study of marital and family interaction. The conceptual premise on which this effort is founded is that the object relations theoretical model is one of many comprising the psychoanalytic paradigm as evolved since Sigmund Freud's revolutionary introduction of a new way of viewing the world and its people. The object relations model lends itself well to the integrated study of internalized object relations and external interpersonal relations, both of which by necessity coalesce in an intertwined and interdependent configuration to provide a comprehensive and inclusive investigation into the processes of marital and family transactions. Marital and family processes, in reciprocation, provide the most immediate and intimate relational focus in which the unified construct of object relations, incorporating both the internal and the external spheres of entity, can be most thoroughly studied and tested.

Chapter 1 presents an introduction to the object relations model and its inherently salient principles as I conceive them in reference to and in collaboration with the theoretical formulations of many psychoanalytic investigators. Chapter 2 describes the process whereby the human neonate acquires the concept of the object of both permanence, a substantial thing, and libidinal strivings, a loved person. Jean Piaget's (1952, 1954) theoretical constructs of cognitive and intellectual development emphasize experiential coordination with the external object world as the precipitator and facilitator of the acquisition of the object concept.

Chapter 3 represents the arduous attempt to define the concept of libidinal object, including its origins and functions. Chapter 4 provides an overview of the psychoanalytic theory of object relations, wherein due homage is paid to the British school of object relations. This overview presents the object relations hypothesis that the human being at birth is inherently embedded in both relations with and relatedness to the libidinized mothering object.

Chapter 5 addresses the prevailing issue of discrepancy in conceiving of object relations theory as an intrapersonal or interpersonal model. An attempt is initiated to integrate the perceived dichotomy into a unified and complementary model. An expansion of this conceptualization, described in more detail in chapters 6 and 7, respectively, is the intrapersonal and interpersonal spheres of object relations.

The remaining chapters comprise the presentation of a hypothetical model in terms of specific interactional processes that transpire in the two systems of marriage and the family. The marital and family groups are the most immediate and significant of all human systems, within which the most personal and intimate relationships take place. It is within the relational context of the marital and familial processes that the intrapsychic and the interpersonal manifestations of interdependence are more pronounced and dynamic, and therefore have greater influence on the evolution of both domains. It is my sincere hope that the presented hypothesis might play an integral role in the problem-solving activity of the psychoanalytic profession. If the present hypothesis has merit and the presented theoretical model has value in solving the dilemmas of the human person, the solution to dilemmas of the family group will transpire concomitantly.

It is within the social embeddedness of the family group that, as the reader will discover, the individual's internal struggles are born and, reciprocally, the intrapersonal conflicts foster and perpetuate the family's dysfunctional processing. The end result is that the family becomes stuck in its defensively and adaptively perpetuated struggle to sustain itself as a system in the face of a perceived threat. The reader will note that the scheme has a consistently strong flavor of general systems theory as founded by the biologist Ludwig von Bertalanffy (1968) and used in the study of marital and familial process by Becvar and Stroh-Becvar (1982). It is my contention that systems theory provides the most useful explanatory means of exploring and delineating the interactional and transactional processes inherent in any social group, particularly in the family group. In its broad and multivariable application, general systems theory constitutes a scientific paradigm unique and valid in itself and complementary to the psychoanalytic paradigm; however, it is of a differing scientific magnitude of discipline.

In the attempt to follow the progressive stature of the family group in both relational function and dysfunction, the present study was initiated with the forging of the marital bond as the origin of the new family system. The path that the study traverses is from the initiation of the family system with the forging of the marital bond, through the trials and tribulations of the marital process, to the expansion of the family group with the introduction of children and the developmental tasks confronting the family as a whole. I capitalized on a variety of theoretical contributions in this process—individual and family developmental theory, psychology of the self, ego psychology, and classical psychoanalytic theory—culminating in a well-diversified and contributory anthology of theoretical constructs complementary to and supportive of the object relations model.

The unconscious motivations governing marital partner selection set the stage for a process of marital relations dominated by defensive and adaptive mechanisms. As addressed in chapters 8 and 9, these object relations can take the form of either function or dysfunction, as determined by the unique interplay of earlier internalized object relations with current relational patterns. Chapter 10 highlights the causality of potential marital object-relational breakdown and perpetuated defensive interaction. Examples of specific relational patterns conducive to the breakdown of the marital system are provided in Chapter 11. Narcissistic personality disturbance unique to the individual partners facilitates a dyadic narcissism as manifested with myriad transactional patterns.

The solidification of marital relational patterning sets the stage for the solicited involvement of the children in the expanding family system, and this transactional quality is illuminated in the interface with developmental tasks confronting the family as a whole. Separation and individuation in adolescence, as discussed in Chapter 12, is one such shared task that necessitates the facilitating involvement of the entire family. Chapter 13 investigates the specific relational transactions that typify the family's defensive need for assigning stereotyped roles to its membership. The subtle and profound manifestations of family object relations conducive to the perpetuation of stereotyped delineation and the elicitation of members' collusive participation are outlined in Chapter 14. Chapter 15 describes the entrapment of the family group as they cling desperately to the unconsciously employed mechanisms of defense, misguidedly and unwittingly falling prey to the synergism of the intrasystemic process.

Chapters 16 and 17 describe patterns of narcissistic interpersonal transactions that transpire in the course of familial object relations. The family's utilization of its members as narcissistic objects to enhance individual self-definition and self-esteem, as well as to protect the inviolability and sanctity of the family as a systemic group, entraps the family in its self-perpetuated morass of overinvolvement and enmeshment. Within this familial narcissistic organization, as described in Chapter 18, members contribute to the formation of an intensely emotional process of relatedness, within which family members fail to differentiate and promulgate their individual selves. Chapter 19 provides the reader with a synthesis of the marital and family object relations model, underscoring the principle that object relations, both internal and external, take form in the process of both ''normality'' and ''abnormality.'' While this research emphasizes dysfunctional intrapsychic and interpersonal organization and processing at the relative expense of placing the normative process in the background, the intention is to present the psychoanalytic paradigm in its utility for solving problematic human, experiential phenomena while acknowledging that normality and abnormality are two sides of the same coin, both identifiable only in their humanly perceived distinction and differentiation, yet inextricably tied to their necessarily interdependent existence.

Acknowledgments

I acknowledge and deeply appreciate those theoreticians and clinicians to whom I have made reference throughout this volume because it is they who have provided the impetus and the groundwork from which I formulated my conceptual model of object relations in the marital and family process. I wish to thank Professor Thomas Evans, Ph.D., who introduced me to marital and family theory and therapy, and Professor Raphael Becvar, Ph.D., whose genuine and ceaseless appreciation for and knowledge of family systems theory and therapy have both humbled and inspired me. To the late Ronald A. Ruble, Ed.D., my professor and graduate adviser, who very subtly provided a holding environment when I was in great need, I thank you so very much. Thank you to my psychoanalyst, Barry Hiatt, M.D., of the St. Louis Psychoanalytic Institute, who has facilitated the expansion and affirmation of my self. Above all, a loving thank you to my mother and father, Amy and Vernon, with whom I have formed very healthy, lasting, and precious identifications.

===1===

The Marital and Family Object Relations Model: A Conceptual Base

Professional disciplines undertake the task of designing scientific theories as a framework from which to formulate acquired data into a coherent and substantiated set of facts. Insofar as the facts themselves may approximate logical validity, as Gedo and Goldberg (1973) pointed out, they are not, however, acknowledged as representational components of truth. As a means of comprehending the intricacies and complexities of scientific findings, we devise descriptive and analogous models that permit us to organize such findings into an ideally well-integrated and adaptable "fit." From the fit we may draw inferences, form hypotheses, and make predictions. With the guidance of such models and the theories associated with them, science assumes a smooth continuity of direction. Gedo and Goldberg suggest:

In contrast to such theories which grow out of the observational data, there are "hypothetico-deductive" propositions, theories which take a leap of the imagination away from the observables in order to postulate their causation. (p. 3)

This type of theorizing takes form around the venture into the unknown in an attempt to acquire new data and knowledge that might serve to create new "ways of seeing the world and of practicing science in it" (Kuhn 1962, p. 4).

The explanatory function of models enables scientists to unify their efforts in a benevolently constructive attempt to discover the truth. Insofar as such models continue to furnish scientists with a consolidated means of achieving this arduous task, we have effected what Kuhn (1962) called a "shared paradigm," "a fundamental unit for the student of scientific development" (p. 11). Though he noted that scientific research can proceed without the operation of a paradigm, as in the case of venturing into the unexplored and unknown, Kuhn asserted that the "acquisition of a paradigm and of the more esoteric type of research it permits is a sign of maturity in the development of any given scientific field'' (p. 11). Kuhn assigns to his concept of a paradigm two differing scopes of definition:

On the one hand, it stands for the entire constellation of beliefs, values, techniques, and so on shared by the members of a given community. On the other, it denotes one sort of element in that constellation, the concrete puzzle-solutions which, employed as models or examples, can replace explicit rules as a basis for the solution of the remaining puzzles of normal science. (p. 175)

Kuhn (1962) believes that the attainment of truth via scientific research and application of theory is not fully possible; it is attempted achievement that lacks necessity. Rather, the purpose and goal of scientific study are to make progress—progress identifiable and measurable through the discovery of solutions to identified problems. Scientific progress is not secured by a continuous flow of problem-solving engagement; rather, forward movement proceeds in discontinuous spurts. Radical shifts in paradigmatic relevance and influence, including the epistemological assumptions to which proponents of a given paradigm adhere, characterize the advancement of science. The perceived reality of the world is modified to a significant degree with the advent of each scientific, paradigmatic revolution. Perceived anomalies eventually pervade the universally accepted paradigm confronting its constituency with a problem unsolvable from within the confines of the given paradigmatic frame of reference.

Benevolent attempts may be made to assimilate newly discovered data into the existing schemata, thereby establishing an accommodation. However, insofar as this is only temporarily achievable, radical shifts in epistemological set are of necessity. Kuhn thinks that in a paradoxical manner the confirmation of a given paradigmatic set, solidified in its universal acceptance and methodological process of research activity, necessarily and simultaneously produces its own anomalies that must be reckoned with. Kuhn comments:

Normal science does not aim at novelties of fact or theory and, when successful, finds none. New and unsuspected phenomena are, however, repeatedly uncovered by scientific research, and radical new theories have again and again been invented by scientists. History even suggests that the scientific enterprise has developed a uniquely powerful technique for producing surprises of this sort. If this characteristic of science is to be reconciled with what has already been said, then research under a paradigm must be a particularly effective way of inducing paradigm change. That is what fundamental novelties of fact and theory do. Produced inadvertently by a game played under one set of rules, their assimilation requires the elaboration of another set. After they have become parts of science, the enterprise, at least of those specialists in whose particular field the novelties lie, is never quite the same again. (p. 52)

If there is to be progress, a shift in paradigms is a necessity. New scientific discovery does not present us with new realities; rather, it induces us to shift our paradigmatic framework to fit the new discovery, effecting a revision in the way we perceive our world. Kuhn (1962) explains:

Discovery commences with the awareness of anomaly, i.e., with the recognition that nature has somehow violated the paradigm-induced expectations that govern normal science. It then continues with a more or less extended exploration of the area of anomaly. And it closes only when the paradigm theory has been adjusted so that the anomalous has become the expected. Assimilating a new sort of facts demands a more than additive adjustment of theory, and until that adjustment is completed—until the scientist has learned to see nature in a different way—the new fact is not quite a scientific fact at all. (pp. 52–53)

Sigmund Freud made such a discovery in the face of a perceived anomaly. Insistent on developing a psychology of the mind that would support his contention that human nature is psychically determined, he set out to acquire explanatory conceptualizations of unconsciously derived emotions and cognitions as the very source of human behavior. Because his conceptualizations of the structure and process of the mind are by necessity purely speculative, and therefore are not objectively verifiable, his postulations comprise a metapsychology, by nature a metaphorical rendition of the organization and functioning of the intrapsychic.

Freud was indeed a revolutionary—the initial proponent of a new paradigm unacceptable to the loyal advocates of the then current paradigm, and presenter of new data and concepts incongruent with the beliefs staunchly upheld. Yet Freud's psychoanalytic paradigm has flourished through expansion and variation. Post-Freudian psychoanalytic theories, though divergent in theoretical construct, in light of Kuhn's (1962) conceptualization do not comprise true paradigms apart from the foundational prescriptions of Freud's metapsychological scheme. Cooper (1985) concurs, in his statement concerning Freud's central themes: "It is my suggestion that these core ideas form the agreed upon base for any set of propositions that should go by the title, 'Psychoanalysis' '' (p. 6).

Erik Erikson and Harry Stack Sullivan are among those who have diversified their thinking from that of Freud's in an attempt to bring into confluence the psychologies of the individual and of the society. The resulting theoretical focus is not merely on man's internal conflicts but also on man's struggle to adapt to his environment. Recognition of the natural physical and personal environmental context sheds new light in the study of the nature of man in terms of his psychology, sociology, and philosophy. The idealist philosopher and educator Herman Harrell Horne (1927) maintained:

The individual is a whole and he is also a part of a larger whole. It is the nature of an individual to be both himself and a *socius*. Individuality is not a narrowly circumscribed sphere, but is a larger circle inclusive of one's fellows. (pp. 142–143)

In this conceptualization, intrapsychic and interpersonal factors coalesce to provide explanatory propositions and postulates based on a set of core epistemological assumptions concerning man and his experience. Sarason (1981) is among those who support the belief that man and his social environment are inextricably tied in influence:

Built into psychology, part of its world view, is the polarity man *and* society. Call it a polarity or a dichotomy or even a distinction, it makes it easy for psychology to focus on one and ignore the other, to avoid dealing with the possibility that the distinction is arbitrary and misleading, that it does violence to the fact that from the moment of birth the individual organism is a social organism, that social means embeddedness in patterned relationships that are but a part of an array of such relationships rooted, among other things, in a social history and a distinctive physical environment. (p. 175)

Sarason's claim is that unless we acknowledge this artificial dualism as inhibiting our scientific striving for solutions to our problems, we unwittingly promote a *Psychology Misdirected*.

If the field of psychology in general provides a functional, conceptual integration of psychic factors of the individual and interpersonal relationship factors of both the immediate and larger contexts of society, it of necessity acknowledges and highlights the inherent phenomenon of interactional experience between the individual and significant objects, both animate and inanimate, of the external world. The pragmatic philosopher, educator, and psychologist John Dewey (1929) regarded experience as being the essence of human existence. The reality of the external world takes form around, and only around, the experience that the individual has in relations with the object world. The reciprocal interaction between subject and object comprises the very heart of experience, and it is through such experience that the individual explores the depths of the environmental world as well as of the sense of the self. In Dewey's view, experience is a continuous, ever-expanding, and reflective phenomenon, through which current experience of interaction with the environment is the direct result of, and acquires its characteristics from, preceding interactional experiences.

Piaget's (1952, 1954) sensorimotor theory of intellectual development complements this experiential conceptualization. He devised a conceptual framework from which the cognitive organization and functioning of the individual follows a continuous and progressive linear series of stages and substages culminating in the acquisition of mature thought processing. The transitional advancement to each successive stage takes effect with the confrontation with and "assimilation" of increasingly complex and sophisticated external-world information. The assimilation of new data into the existing schemata of the internal psychic world permits the individual to "accommodate" new, incoming information to facilitate adaptation to the environmental world. The ever-expanding internal schematic structures are formed through the direct experience that the individual has with the external world of both animate and inanimate objects. Even though the stages of Piaget's scheme progress in linear and forward direction, each stage and substage is characterized by spiral configuration, wherein the individual and the environment interface in revolving and recursive interaction as the two entities, in synchronicity, progress in the upward climb to a more sophisticated and expansive relationship.

It is by learning through experience with the vastness of the object world that the self matures and refines. The self emerges not merely in confrontation with new objects but also in the experience of more elaborate relations with current objects. Once again, the experience with current objects is contingent on the quality and nature of previous experiences with the same objects. The individual builds on previous interactional experiences, permitting the discovery of new objects and the revelation of the self in relationship to such objects. Loewald (1980) comments:

I say new discovery of objects, and not discovery of new objects, because the essence of such new object-relationships is the opportunity they offer for rediscovery of the early paths of the development of object-relations, leading to a new way of relating to objects as well as of being and relating to oneself. This new discovery of oneself and of objects, this reorganization of ego and objects, is made possible by the encounter with a "new object" that has to possess certain qualifications in order to promote the process. (p. 225)

The reader has been given, albeit briefly, a presentation of two models of conceptualization (the intrapersonal and the interpersonal) regarded here, in concurrence with others, as being legitimate theories in their own right; yet they are functionally interdependent, in that they provide a comprehensive explanation of the nature of the human person. Brevity and generality are adequate for this introduction, since it is my aim to provide a convincing constructional framework from which the reader can discern and clearly delineate an organized conceptualization of the relationship between the intrapsychic an the interpersonal. It is my purpose to punctuate the specifics of the marital and familial interactional processes that lend their experiential existence to the conceptual, albeit metaphorical, metapsychology of intrapersonal and transpersonal phenomena.

It is my contention, as the reader will soon understand, that neither the intrapsychic nor the interpersonal in confrontation with the other presents an anomaly. They are not two opposing factions and embodiments of purpose and intention venturing into the unexplored in separate and uninfluential directions; rather, they comprise one system of organization, one paradigm that in generated process becomes in and of itself the epitome of systemic "equifinality." Both lines of thought have their origins in distinct theoretical principles and follow their own paths; yet both processes culminate in the same shared ends and results: to attain the closest approximation to the ultimate truth of human nature (why we feel, think, and do the things we do). The founder of general systems theory, Ludwig von Bertalanffy (1968), described the term "equifinality" as "the tendency towards a characteristic final state from different initial states and in different ways based upon dynamic interaction in an open system attaining a steady state" (p. 46).

Three components of von Bertalanffy's (1968) definition invite further comment and expansion because they epitomize the designed crux of this volume. The "dynamic interaction" in which the intrapsychic and the interpersonal worlds coalesce and coordinate has been alluded to in the above conceptualization of one's experience with the external world of objects as invariably forming the very core of the conceptualization of both the object world and the self.

The "open system" to which von Bertalanffy (1968) alluded represents the crux of my position that the psychoanalytic paradigm, comprised of distinct yet interrelated theoretical models, takes the form of an open system in structure, organization, and process. As mentioned previously, the two dimensions of the intrapsychic and the interpersonal are not diametrically opposed. Rather, they comprise two elements of an open system formed in shared intention to solve human problems. It is through the concept of equifinality that the system of the psychoanalytic paradigm assumes its validity and legitimacy as an open system in its own right.

The third component of von Bertalanffy's (1968) definition of equifinality is that of "attaining a steady state," a balance necessary to the functional maintenance of the system. As has been noted, scientific discovery leading to the introduction of an anomaly to the current paradigm meets with variable oppositional force as the united advocates of the current paradigm, in an attempt to thrive, either assimilate the information from the new discovery into their existing paradigmatic framework or discard and renounce the merit or validity of the information. The shifting of the shared paradigm and the associated epistemological assumptions to a new level of organization is the natural and only means by which the system can maintain a regulatory balance and survive. Fortunately the shift usually effects a progressive scientific movement in the directional pursuit of problem solving. Disruption of the internal homeostatic state of the system threatens it with eventual dissolution; therefore epistemological assumptions must be periodically revised to meet the induction of new data and ideas. However, as Gedo and Goldberg (1973) explain:

Such changes should be, however, so as not to disturb the internal consistency of the whole system. The entire set of theories must not be treated as a rigid and fixed system; on the other hand, it is equally sterile for a science to regard its theories in an offhand or amorphous manner. (p. 169)

Also threatening to the equilibrium of the paradigmatic system is the prevalence of contradictory theories within its internal organization. Though there may be numerous theoretical models inherent in a given scientific paradigm, the system holds potential for functionally integrating the diversity into a coherent and solidified position in scientific endeavor. Gedo and Goldberg (1973) comment:

This principle of several concurrent and valid avenues for organizing the data of observation we shall call "theoretical complementarity." This principle operates so long as no internal contradictions arise among the various parts of the theory. However, it requires that the proper sphere for the utilization of each portion be stringently defined. (pp. 4–5)

The psychoanalytic scientific paradigm is an open system comprised of subsystemic, component theoretical models. Freud's revolutionary impetus in the development of a new perspective of human nature has been followed by subsequent theories of object relations, ego psychology, self-psychology, and developmental theory, some of which adhere to the mainstream of Freud's conceptual thought, others of which diverge to variable degrees from its centrality. All of these theoretical models belong to the psychoanalytic paradigm as initiated by Freud and play an integral role in its evolution. Freud's main premise—that psychic determinism is the main thrust and is at the core of human emotional, cognitive, and behavioral experience—underscores the basic tenet of the psychoanalytic paradigm. Interpersonal theoretical models, while they do not renounce the deterministic nature of the intrapsychic, do focus their scientific study on the interpersonal experiences of individual personalities and the relational processes inherent in the sustenance of a given social system. Both lines of thought, the intrapsychic and the interpersonal, represent separate directional means to the same end: the solutions to human problems. This process, once again, epitomizes the phenomenon of equifinality characteristic of the paradigmatic system.

The anomaly perceived and the problem that I am attempting to help solve here are that the two lines of thought, the intrapsychic and the interpersonal, have yet to meet in confluence in the ultimate attempt to understand human nature. The goal here is not to bridge the two schemes, which can be described as running parallel to one another; rather, it is to coalesce the two schemes in an intertwined configuration wherein each model becomes inextricably tied to and dependent on the other in a systematic organization of conceptualization comprising an open, paradigmatic system internally consistent and functionally equilibrated. Within this theoretical construct the two lines of thought retain their respective punctuational perspectives of intrapersonal and interpersonal, psychic and relational, manifestations. Each of the two models presents itself in an undeniably and consistently strong, valid, and reliable status as a theory in and of itself, and one that holds securely and resolutely in the position of explanatory power. As metapsychological frameworks, both lines of thought have thus far withstood the test of usefulness and internal consistency, thereby warranting, in Gedo and Goldberg's (1973) reasoning, sustainment as viable models of conceptualization.

Neither of the two models, respectable in its own right, has the fullest and lasting capacity to withstand the tests of usefulness and internal consistency throughout the rapid advancement of conceptual, theoretical, and philosophical human thought. This assertion is augmented with the conclusion that if psychoanalysis, either in theory or in practice, were not to integrate the intrapsychic with the interpersonal, it would in short order experience confrontation with an anomalous impact of such force that the breakdown of the hitherto promising paradigm would inevitably ensue. The result might be the formation of a radically new paradigm of vastly different concepts, principles, laws, and perspectives of the world well beyond our current conceptual capacity. It would behoove one to support the argument that this progression, culminating in the overhauling shift of paradigms, should be left alone to evolve as it would naturally. It is firmly suggested, however, that the natural course of scientific evolution at present is a structural and organizational shift within our present psychoanalytic paradigm conducive to the facilitation of a comprehensive view of man and his interaction with his environment.

Within this shift to a higher intraparadigmatic level of awareness, the two models almost imperceptibly intertwine to effect a change in the epistemological foundation held by the advocates of the psychoanalytic paradigm. The epistemological assumptions change from perceiving either human beings or their social context in isolation to perceiving human beings in their social world as a unitary entity. To study individuals or their interpersonal relationships independently does not in and of itself constitute an error in epistemological assumption, since each conceptualization has merit, albeit limited, when considered separately. However, this type of directional study does pose a vast and recognizable limitation to our conceptual scope. In other words, each line of thought, while not incorrect, is markedly and influentially incomplete. Bringing the two into confluence—an integration of reciprocal influence and interdependence—forms a single and whole conceptual picture; and because the whole equals more than the sum of its parts, a gestalt is formed in the organization of a comprehensive, intensive, and unified schematic structure, dynamic in its provision of explanatory conceptualization. Human beings and their social world are inseparable!

The purpose and function of this volume is to present a schematic conceptualization of a psychoanalytic paradigmatic model of the aforementioned characteristics. The theoretical formulations on which the conceptualizations are based are by no means of my design; rather, the theoretical concepts have been borrowed from numerous psychoanalytic investigators and compiled into an organized schematic framework from which the reader can representationally "visualize" the dynamic and conceptually abstract quality of intrapsychic and interpersonal interplay. The conceptual, theoretical model presented here is of psychoanalytic object relations. Object relations theory as conceived by the psychoanalytic paradigm has a significant shortcoming in its ill-defined basic premises and principles. Discrepancy pervades the model in terms of whether object relations is a theory of internal objects and object relations or a theory of external interpersonal relations. The gist of the hypothesis employed in this work is that neither is correct; rather, the psychoanalytic object relations theory is a theory of intrapsychic development as processed by the internalization and sustainment of external objects and the relationship of the self to those objects, and as directly determined by and reciprocally determinative of relationships with significant real and external others. In this light, the discrepancy dispels as both schools of thought acquire the fullest merit via incorporation of and coordination with one another.

===2===

The Acquisition of the Concepts of Permanent and Libidinal Objects

Psychoanalytic theory concentrates on the individual's adaptive functionability in relationship to the physical environment. Although the primary focus of the subject-object interactional study is on the developing infant's interface with objects of significant persons (libidinal objects), Piaget (1954) suggests that the concept of libidinal object is acquired through a process analogous, albeit accelerated, to the conceptualization of the permanent, inanimate object, the latter being the subject of Piaget's psychological studies.

Piaget (1952, 1954) described the process of acquisition of knowledge through the first 18 months of life as a continuously developing and unfolding growth of sensorimotor intelligence. Such growth is accomplished by means of adaptation through coordination of actions within the subject-environment domain. The child proceeds through Piaget's sensorimotor intelligence stage from an almost total lack of knowing in an initial phase of undifferentiation, through a phase marked by and fostering of the ability to recognize the object world as a continuation or result of its own personal activity, to the capacity to objectify its immediate world through the mastering of end-by-means relations, exploration of differing features of objects, and anticipation of proximate events.

The child's world at the end of the sensorimotor stage presents the character of spatial homogeneity. This world of space and substance is necessarily composed of permanent objects guided by principles of causality in the form of relationships between objects without changes in form or presence. The child has acquired the intellectual capacity to differentiate the external and stable universe from the internal world in which it recognizes itself as but one term among all other terms. This achievement is made possible by the development of the object concept, identified by the child through interlocking mutual coordinations, reaching the point of intellectual or cognitive development marked by the formation of a thing "out there," existing separately from the child and its own actions.

Furth (1969) spoke of the child's first acknowledgment of a clear distinction between the known object and the knowing subject: "Knowledge, in the full sense of its human meaning, is found right between these two terms; for knowledge is but our way of expressing the mutual relation of the knower to the known" (p. 44)

Piaget (1954) suggested that the known object is a thing that is "conceived as permanent, substantial, external to the self, and firm in existence even though . . . [it does] not directly affect perception" (p. 5). He added that it maintains its identification in spite of positional changes. Thus, even though the object has left the immediate field of the child's perception, it still conceives of the object as remaining in existence. When the child continues to search actively for something it can no longer see, hear, smell, touch, and so forth, it obviously believes that the object is still extant, somewhere to be found. Throughout the sensorimotor stage of intellectual development, the various steps through which a child progresses in pursuit of the hidden object will serve to measure the development of the object concept.

Piaget's (1954) permanent object is maturationally conceived not solely via normal bodily and psychic development but also, more significantly, in the accumulation and expansion of sensorimotor components of the subject-object experience. Spitz (1965) explains:

In the setting of normal somatic functioning and of a relatively stable environment (both tacitly implied by Piaget), object attainment is inextricably tied to experience, specifically to motor action which makes for the accretion of ontogenetic elements in the psyche in the form of memory. The acquisition and accumulation of experiential elements is conceived by Piaget as a buildup of schemata. (p. 326)

Implicit in the idea of psychoanalytic objects is that they necessarily are presented as subject to a given person's directed emotions, cognitions, and behaviors. There is a direct correspondence of object concept to subject-object interaction, be it in thought or in behavior. According to Dorpat (1981), "Subject, action, and object are different but related aspects of a description or explanation of experience. Any description of experience must refer to the totality subject-action-object" (p. 154). In reference to Piaget's (1952, 1954) theory of sensorimotor intelligence, we again acknowledge the subject-object domain and the interaction that transpires therein. At birth the human child is a helpless being, requiring consistent and adequate mothering to sustain life. The newborn infant is endowed with inherent capabilities to engage in a few reflex movements and other self-regulating physiological activities, but it is not equipped with intelligence or a sense of knowing. The newborn does not perceive of anything external to its own self. Its world is one comprised of things, or what Piaget (1952) referred to as "sensorial pictures," which are mobile, formable, and dissolvable, and lack stability, permanence, objective space, and constant dimension.

During this preobjectal stage the perceptual or sensory pictures are not yet differentiated from the pleasurable stimulation the infant may attain from its experience with them. At a later stage of Blatt's (1974) "sensorimotor representation," the infant is able to discern the source of the gratifying stimulation and invest itself in the cathexis of the object source. As Blatt notes, however,

the object still remains relatively undifferentiated and is cathected and represented primarily, if not exclusively, in its function of providing gratification. Although there is an awareness of the object, the object is still not fully separated from the context of the experience and the event. At this level the object is experienced in terms of its activities, its representation being an extrapolation of the action pattern. The object is recognized and valued only in the specific limited context of need gratification, and it has little meaning or existence beyond providing comfort and alleviating pain. The first representations of the object are indicated by the infant's capacity to search for the object, first after visible, and later invisible, displacement and by the imitation of the object's sensorimotor actions. (p. 143)

Although the object may still be inanimate, the infant's increasing cathexis of the object with all of its gratifying and pleasurable qualities will more likely be at the hands of the animate, human object. The human (e.g., mothering) object is inherently endowed with the capacity for providing pleasure and reducing tension, and therefore, in Wolff's (1960) words, the infant's "relation to them becomes the prototype of his interactions with the environment at large" (p. 81).

It is through the experience of need gratification and tension reduction that the concept of object emerges; and those objects most suitable for facilitating these relational experiences, the human objects, become more intensely cathected by the infant, while the inanimate objects serve as secondary replacements more functional to the infant in states of quiescence. Therefore, the concept of the human object is acquired parallel to, though earlier than, the concept of the permanent, inanimate object. The human object is referred to as the libidinal object, in recognition of the libidinal energy with which the infant cathects the object.

The first and most significant libidinal object becomes the mother, or otherwise mothering object. Mothers have the capacity and function of gratifying their infant's early oral wishes and demands, and they can stimulate a multitude of their infant's schemata simultaneously as they respond to their infant's cues by moving in and out of its perceptual range in response to its needs. Wolff (1960) explains this phenomenon in Piagetian terms:

All objects, animate or inanimate, become aliment to the extent that they can be assimilated to sensorimotor schemata; and the child's eventual discrimination between the human and the physical object is attributed to the fact that human objects are aliment for many schemata at once, tend to disappear and appear frequently, and are usually assimilated under "interesting conditions" such as feeding, cleaning, bathing, etc. (p. 80)

Spitz (1965) suggested that the hallmark of true object relatedness is the capacity of the infant of approximately six months to perceive the libidinal object clearly. Prior to six months of age, during the anaclitic stage, beginning at three months, the infant only tenuously perceives the object as the source of gratification. At this phase of the infant's psychic development, the external world is divided into objects of pleasure and unpleasure, with the parallel subjective experiences of pleasure and unpleasure. Even though it has experienced communication with these two objects, the infant as yet has no regulation of them. Sandler and Sandler (1978) explain:

These initial differentiated responses to the two major classes of experiences, the two primary "objects" of the child, are, in the beginning, biologically based. They are not under the (conscious or unconscious) voluntary control of the infant, although his responses immediately affect the state of his sensorium and lead to the development and construction of further mental representations which come to be linked with the different feeling-states. (p. 292)

It is at this juncture, with the developing "mental representations," that the concept of libidinal object takes firm hold. The increasingly articulate mental representations, or internal images, and their associated, experienced affective states strengthen the infant's perception of the mothering object as the distinct source of gratification, and hence the true libidinal object. Thus the image of the libidinal object emerges from stimuli emanating from within the infant's own body as well as from stimuli generated from the external object. As Spitz (1965) explains,

The first image of the object derives from exteroceptively mediated sensory impressions *whose permanence and intensity are due to a set of contemporary and complemental mnemic traces of interoceptive and proprioceptive origin.* (p. 328)

Memory traces of early relational experiences with the mothering object collect in the construction of the perceived libidinal object. The libidinal object becomes conceptualized via the significant role it plays in interaction with the infant in eliciting affective states within the latter. Arlow (1980) suggests that the libidinal

mental representation grows out of mnemic image, a recollected set of sensory impressions accompanied by a pleasurable feeling tone which, according to the dominant pleasure principle, one wishfully attempts to reconstitute as a sensory impression. (pp. 112–113)

The acquisition of the concept of libidinal object is necessarily facilitated by the infant's acquired capacity, at approximately six months of age, to fuse libidinal and aggressive drives into a single drive directed to the mothering object as the one and only mothering object, one comprised, in the infant's perception, of both "good" and "bad" components. Spitz (1965) explains:

The percept "mother" becomes a single one, will no longer be equated with any other person playing her role in identical situations. From now on she will focus on her person the infant's aggressive as well as his libidinal drives. The fusion of the two drives and the fusion of the good and bad object into one, namely, into the libidinal object, are therefore two facets of one and the same process. (p. 169)

. . .

Now that the two drives are directed toward the one single, emotionally most strongly cathected, object we can speak of the establishment of the libidinal object *proper* and of the inception of true object relations. (p. 170)

The concept of the mothering object in its gestalt, in conjunction with the totality of affective experience in interface with the libidinal object, provides the infant the required resources with which to engage in genuine object relatedness.

=====3=====

Toward a Definition of the Object, Its Origins, and Its Functions

The concept of object is used quite extensively and comprehensively in psycho-analytic theory. As previously noted, the object may refer to an inanimate thing, as well as to an animated person, the primal and most significant of the latter being the mothering object. The libidinal human object is the primary focus of psychoanalytic theoreticians and clinicians in the investigation of the development of the human intrapsychic within the realm of interpersonal object relations—relations with real external others. The concept of object refers, therefore, to objects of actual people as well as to objects of internalized images of them sustained within the intrapsychic. The two object domains are inextricably intertwined in a reciprocal, ongoing interchange of mutual influence. The study of object relations necessarily involves the developing subject's relationships with both internal and external objects.

Both internal and external objects assume changeable qualities as the subject's experiences with these objects inevitably evolve and transform not only in the earliest years but throughout the life cycle. The influential power of the objects over the subject's experiences fluctuates greatly, just as the subject's influence over the characteristics of the objects and its experiential nature in interface with them is readily observable in the therapeutic situation as well as in the subject's natural context.

Psychoanalytic theory of object relations has historically—rather vaguely with Freud initially and expanded with further clarity by such theorists as W. R. D. Fairbairn (1954) and Edith Jacobson (1954, 1964)—postulated that the groundwork for the development of internalized object relations is laid by the mnemonic images of external objects of real persons with which the individual transacts and which he subsequently internalizes into the intrapsychic domain. Psychoanalytic theory draws a clear distinction between the objects of the real external world and the images of those objects comprising the internal representational world. Goldberg (1985) explains: ''For most analysts 'object' seems to mean something outside of an organism designated as a subject; for others, however, 'object' refers to a diametric opposite—something mental and only mental, not to any material thing'' (p. 167).

Speaking of the latter, Greenberg and Mitchell (1983) note that

although in the phenomenology of the patient's experience "internal objects" are felt actually to exist, our use of the term does not imply the physical reality of such objects. These are certainly not entities, or homunculi within the mind. (p. 14)

Bierley (1951) speaks of the "subjectivity" of internal "mental objects" (quoted by Novey, 1958):

Mental objects are invariably mental and the objects of experience, as constituents of experience, are subjective. There is thus no difference in subjectivity between the object identified with the conscious self and the object distinguished form this self, wherever the latter may be localized; the difference is not one of subjectivity but of endopsychic economy, i.e., of mode of relationship. (p. 72)

Sigmund Freud, as a precursor of the object relations model, conceptualized the object as an integral component of his instinctual drive theory. In the psychoanalytic scheme, the object refers primarily to the libidinal object of another person—an object that serves as the target of an instinctual drive. However, as object relations theorist Balint (1958) said, "*object* is used here in the psychoanalytic sense, which includes people, ideas, sentiments, in fact everything that might be cathected by an instinctual urge" (p. 89).

Arlow (1980) suggested that it is actually the representation of the perceived external object, which is subsequently internalized, that is cathected, and that "whatever it is that is represented mentally as instinctively cathected constitutes an object" (pp. 113–114). He further acknowledged that the targeted object of cathexis may well be an object in its whole or in part:

Instinctual wishes of an aggressive or libidinal nature may center on mental representations of parts of one's own body, parts of someone else's body, or on mental representations of one's own or some other person's whole body. Any one of these may be taken as an object. (p. 114)

He augments this conceptualization by suggesting that

the object may be the representation of something which is part of one's own person— the lips, skin, mouth, or anus, for example—or it may be the mental representation of something inanimate which at a certain stage of cognitive development is still regarded as part of one's own person. (p. 113)

The inherent value of an object lies within its potential either to relieve or to intensify the instinctual drive tension. The subject will, and more intensely in early infancy, categorize the objects with which it interfaces as either good (tension reducing) or bad (tension intensifying). Even though it is innately, inextricably tied to the instinctual drive concept, the object is flexible and interchangeable. A given object may serve as the target of more than one drive, and any given drive may utilize a variety of objects as its targeted source of gratification. The infant manifests its natural tendency to discover and traverse the most direct path to the gratifying, tension-relieving object and avoid objects that fail to provide such supplies.

The human organism holds within its potential functioning the ability to maintain a homeostatic balance. When in states of experienced drive tension, the organism will attempt to alleviate the tension by dispersing affective (libidinal and aggressive) energies to the interior of its body (Jacobson 1954, 1964; Wolff 1960). In the event that this process serves inadequately to reduce tension, the individual will seek external objects for anticipated service of tension reduction and need gratification. Wolff explains further: "The absence of the drive-gratifying object in reality, or an obstacle on the way to it . . . induces an imbalance, and . . . determines the direction of development" (p. 78). However, the human organism holds potential for disrupting its own homeostatic balance in interface with experienced drive tension, just as the external object holds potential as the mechanism for reestablishing the homeostatic balance via tension-reducing and gratifying services. Thus we acknowledge the inherently inextricable tie among the three domains: the self, the object, and the drive.

As Goldberg (1985) maintains, "The term object has no valid meaning by itself; it is always inseparable from the self, from the drives, and from the external world" (p. 173). The self and its affective and cognitive experiences in cathexis of the object, in all of the latter's potential for drive reduction and need satisfaction, highlights the nature and vicissitudes of its object relations. Blatt (1974) referred to this inseparable bond among subject, object, and drive, as manifested during the sensorimotor phase of development, and summarized as follows:

In the sensorimotor stage, relationships are immediate and involve reflexlike physical reactions, which can be motoric or affective and are often directed toward satisfying biological needs. Some aspects of an object or situation impel particular stereotyped reactions on the basis of which the object or situation becomes known. Self and object are fused and there is no mental representation of the object independent of the concrete and immediate reaction. The object is defined by the affective and motoric reactions and has no special identity other than the specific sensations of need satisfaction. (p. 135)

The infant seeks an object in the external world in hopes of acquiring gratification of needs. In the event of inevitable instances when the object is not available or is blocked or thwarted in its service of supplies, the infant will evoke a memory of an earlier experience when gratification was attained. The hallucinatory fantasy of gratification and subsequent tension relief will maintain the infant's equilibrium for a variable amount of time until the fantasy can no longer sustain. The accumulation of these repetitive experiences of gratification and their associated pleasurably toned memories serve as the foundation for the infant's construction of the concept of object. Arlow (1980) explains:

Object seeking is predominantly oriented by the need to try to achieve the identity of pleasurable perceptions remembered but not independently attainable by infants. . . . Subsequently the memory traces of pleasurable sensory impressions connected with an external person become organized into a coherent memory structure, a mental represen-tation of a person which we call "object." (pp. 117–118)

The infant's acquisition of object concept is once again acknowledged in ref-erence to an ongoing, experiential relationship with the external world. Arlow further believes that "the term, object, therefore, represents a concept pertain-ing to a persistent, that is, a structured experience" (p. 118). As Arlow main-tained, the concept of the bad, nongratifying object is acquired via the same experiential process.

   Freud also conceived of the buildup of associated sensory perceptions in the formation of the concept of object. As Freud (1953a, quoted by Modell 1968) said, the internal representation of the object

is a complicated concept built up from various impressions, i.e., it corresponds to an intricate process of associations entered into by elements of visual, acoustic, and kin-esthetic origins. However, the word acquires its significance through its association with the "idea" (concept) of the object, at least if we restrict our considerations to nouns. The idea, or concept, of the object is itself another complex of associations composed of the most varied visual, auditory, tactile, kinesthetic, and other impressions. Accord-ing to the philosophical teaching, the idea of the object contains nothing else; the ap-pearance of a "thing," the "properties" of which are conveyed to us by our senses, originates only from the fact that in enumerating the sensory impressions received from an object we allow for the possibility of a large series of new impressions being added to the chain of associations. (p. 74)

   In reference to the experiential element of the ongoing, increasingly sophis-ticated conceptualization of the object, we comprehend the process as being one of creating the object as opposed to merely finding it. Winnicott (1965) suggests:

[I]n health the infant creates what is in fact lying around waiting to be found. But in health *the object is created, not found*. . . . A good object is no good to the infant unless created by the infant. Shall I say, created out of need? (p. 181)

   Even though the libidinal value of the object is in essence created by the infant via experience with it, Rangell (1985) warns that the universality of subjective distortion should not lead us to lose sight of the fact that the object existed prior to its encounter with the subject self, and continues to exist, however changed, after this interaction has ceased. (p. 324)

The creation of the needed object makes it all the more amenable to assimilation into the schematic framework of the infant's psyche; and this experience need not necessarily proceed within conscious awareness.

Lichtenberg (1979) theorized that the existence of innately endowed schemata, which, when triggered by inevitable environmental cues emanating from subject-object interaction, "enable the infant to organize his experience gradually into units having elements of self and of object, of affect and of cognition" (p. 376).

The creation of the object for the purpose of satisfying the subject's need illuminates the characterization of subject-object interaction. The significance of the object lies in its function of maintaining the subject's internal equilibrium as characterized by the state of well-being. As Edgcumbe and Burgner (1972) suggest, "The relationship is not to a specific object (or part object) but rather to the *function* of having the need satisfied and to the accompanying pleasure afforded by the object in fulfilling that function" (p. 299). Furthermore, this function continues beyond the early infantile, anaclitic stage of need satisfaction to the higher organizational level of the infant's intrapsychic development, the level at which object constancy is achieved, and therewith the object assumes a more diversified and aesthetic role (Burgner and Edgcumbe 1972; Edgcumbe and Burgner 1972; Joffe and Sandler 1965). Joffe and Sandler explain the inherently intricate connection between object and self:

[T]he value which any object has is directly connected with its genetic and functional relation to the self. This would appear to be so even after the attainment of object constancy, when the object has developed "uniqueness" and has become an indispensable key to states of well-being. . . . Object love, like the whole development of the ego, can be seen as a roundabout way of attempting to restore the ideal primary narcissistic state. (p. 398)

At the point of conception of object constancy, the external object, in conjunction with its primary functions, has been formed into an internal mental representation. This phenomenon is facilitated by the concomitant growth of ego functions. The functions of the internal object and of the ego system expand and diversify under reciprocal influence. As an "autonomy-furthering function," Stierlin (1977) postulates,

inner objects . . . contribute to the relative autonomy of the individual. They enable him to fall back on himself by relating to some part within. They constitute inner resources and facilitate an inner dialogue. (p. 132)

Expanding on this conceptualization, he notes that

the cognitive mastery of reality—requiring, among other things, the ability for sharp and rapid discrimination, for the differentiated handling of memories and percepts, for choice, and for task-appropriate dissociation—can be viewed as a manifestation of ego functions as well as inner-object functions. (p. 133)

This process is facilitated by what Stierlin calls the ''inner referent function'' of internal objects, in that the objects

allow us to tie a new percept to a familiar image. They provide a file for mental recall and make possible an adaptive intelligence which can rely on differentiated inner struc-tures. (p. 131)

Internal object functions are manifest in interpersonal as well as intrapsychic events. Subject-object interactional relationships formulate and transpire as based on the anticipated transactional modes mandated by the internal object (i.e., representation of the external object). Not only does the internal representation dictate the quality and characteristic of relational events with external objects, it also serves as the selector of external objects with which the subject is to interface. Stierlin (1977) explains:

Inner objects serve as guideposts for interpersonal relationships, present and future. In this sense they appear best defined as object images. They provide an inner anticipatory set which narrows the selection of possible outer subjects. This applies mainly to poten-tial partners in relationships. (pp. 131–132)

Sutherland (1963) expands on this phenomenon:

The objects sought are not individuals with mature independence but are realizations of the inner figures. . . . More often the inner object acts as a scanning apparatus which seeks a potential object in the outer world. The subego of this system then coerces these people into the role of the inner object. Such objects are not permitted to have any real independence or individuality; they have to fit the inner imago. (p. 117)

The significance of the inner object is formed in reciprocal influence where the ego system lies in its service as a facilitator of subjective experience of relationship between the self and its objects, as well as between the self and its constituent components.

=====4=====

Object Relations Theory

The most salient feature, in fact the heart and soul, of the object relations theory of personality development lies within its study of the nature of the human organism as developmentally unfolding within the environmental context of other human beings. Object relations theory lends itself uniquely to the study of man in a necessarily humanistic and experiential framework. As Sugarman (1977) explains:

If there is one basic premise upon which the object-relations model is based, it is that the appropriate level of inquiry and explanation for psychoanalytic theory is the personal one. The understanding of the human organism, and consequently of personality, must be in human terms. (p. 121)

Object relations theory is predicated on the assumption that it is within the matrix of human relationships from which the individual unfolds biologically and psychologically; it is therefore the human person who in essence becomes the object of the subject's interactional life. We thereby conceptualize, in Guntrip's (1969) words, "the study of man as a person whose be-all and end-all of existence is his relational life with other persons. For this, only object-relations terminology is adequate" (p. 391). The complexities and intricacies involved in the psychoanalytic explanation of individuals and the social world with which they interface transpire within a disciplinary inquiry of a truly individualistic yet human relational nature. Fairbairn (1955) points out that "as in the case of all forms of psychological research, the investigations of psychoanalysis should be conducted at the level of personality and personal relations" (p. 151).

The most original and significant object, that is, the person of the mothering object, inherently serves as the target of the infant's striving for need gratification, support, and confirmation. Winnicott (1965) highlighted *The Maturational Processes and the Facilitating Environment* in his conceptualization of this realm of mother-infant relationship. Ideally the infant matures via unfolding processes that transpire within an environment that facilitates this effect, an environment to which Winnicott referred as the "average expectable environment." The "good-enough mother," the person-object who can functionally serve as the target of the infant's striving for support, is an integral component of this environmental context. Implicit in this mother-infant relational domain is the object of a person who is both able and willing to assent to the infant's innate dependence while simultaneously fostering the gradual processing of adventure into autonomy, individuality, and independence.

Guntrip (1969) eloquently describes this object-relational transformation as one of

understanding how the psychosomatic whole human being, the biologically based infantile psyche, realizes its potentiality for becoming a "person," utilizing all its energies and capacities as they mature, in the good environment of maternal support; growing towards the "ideal" goal of a "whole" mature adult person, capable of fullness of living in personal relationships. . . . (pp. 405–406)

The "good environment of maternal support" comprises the gist of object-relational thinking, thinking that behooves us to conceive of the human organism as one inherently embedded in the indigenous context of external objects of significant other persons. In fact, as Fairbairn (1954) suggests, "it is impossible to gain any adequate conception of the nature of an individual organism if it is considered apart from its relationships to its natural objects" (p. 139).

To conceptualize the mother-infant matrix from which transpires the psychobiological development of the human being, we acknowledge the inescapable necessity for the infant to adapt to its environmental context. In the process of this adaptation, the infant-ego confronts its external object world and, via intrapsychic and interpersonal dynamic processing, coordinates with that world in recursive, interdependent interaction. Subsequently, born out of this interactional reciprocation, the whole, unified, fully functional human self emerges. Ego development and functioning owe their eventuation to this object-relational phenomenon. A. Balint (1949) notes:

The relation of mother-child has been at the centre of psycho-analytic interest right from the beginning. . . . As this is the earliest object relation the beginnings of which reach into the nebulous times where the frontiers of ego and external world merge into each other, it is of paramount importance both theoretically and practically. (p. 251)

Thus, we acknowledge, in Guntrip's (1969) words, *"the fundamental importance of ego-psychology as the psychology of the whole person in object-relations"* (p. 396). Guntrip (1961) defines "ego" as "the primary psychic self in its original wholeness, a whole which differentiates into organized structural patterns under the impact of experience of object-relationships after birth'' (p. 279).

The phenomenon of an organism's adaptation to its natural surroundings necessitates a complementary and mutually dependent interaction between organism and environment. Object relations theory presumes that the two components—those of the subject and the object—integrate and coordinate to facilitate a functionally ideal subject-object domain. Hartmann (1958) claims:

The observation underlying the concept ''adaptation'' is that living organisms patently ''fit'' into their environment. Thus, adaptation is primarily a reciprocal relationship between the organism and its environment. (pp. 23–24)

The earliest subject-object relationship significantly influences the infant's ability to maintain its psychobiological homeostatic balance as it matures via collaterally connective processes of morphostasis and morphogenesis.

The integration and coordination of the infant and its object initiate in the earliest postnatal period. These experiences are in part manifestations of the newborn's innately endowed capacity to initiate self-regulating physiological activities (e.g., reflex movements). Moreover, the infant's affective, sensorimotor, somatic, and impulse experiences present themselves in interplay with the mother-infant interactions, thereby serving to provide the infant with the capacity to organize its reality and to relate to that reality. The infant can relate to the external object without recognition and can remember the object as a cluster of proprioceptive and interoceptive, as opposed to exteroceptive, stimuli. This implies the presence of innately endowed capabilities of relating to things or objects desired or required. This is exemplified by the newborn infant's capability and tendency to turn its head in the nursing position to search for the mother's breast, to differentiate surrounding parts of the breast from the desired nipple, and automatically to initiate the sucking reflex. Piaget (1952) recognized this phenomenon not as a recognition of the object as a perceptual display but as relating to the mother as a source of the satisfaction of experienced hunger sensations.

From this point on, the maturational processes unfold in consistent interaction and transaction with the external object world. As Wolff (1960) says,

all development is due to the organism's need for active contact with the environment, because only contact with real objects will satisfy the need to function and will maintain structural equilibrium. Thus the organism actively engages the environment from the very first. (p. 60)

The infant's internal equilibrium, a balance of both a biological and a psychological nature, is regulated and maintained via the relational interplay between itself and its external objects. Hartmann (1958) remarks:

The first social relations of the child are crucial for the maintenance of his biological equilibrium also. It is for this reason that man's first object relations became our main concern in psychoanalysis. Thus the task of man to adapt to man is present from the very beginning of life. (pp. 30–31)

Hartmann acknowledges the infant's need for the object of the caretaking function from birth, which eventuates in "a state of adaptedness." However, he further asserts that the comprehension of the object as an object and the infant's interactional behavior toward it as such are not attained until the sixth or seventh month after birth. Therefore, Hartmann warns, "we should not assume, from the fact that the child and the environment interact from the outset, that the child is from the beginning psychologically directed toward the object as an object" (p. 52). He further implies that it is not the object as a perceptual display that the infant recognizes but, rather, that the infant has from birth the adaptive, inborn capacity to relate to its external environment, as exemplified, for example, by suckling at its mother's breast. He elaborates:

In this sense the individual has a relationship to the external world from the very beginning. The newborn is in close touch with his environment not only by his need for its continuous care but also by his reactions to its stimuli. (p. 51)

Balint (1960) also alludes to the dualistic nature of the child's innate biological as well as psychological relationship to the objects of its external world. He claims that "the individual is born in a state of intense relatedness to his environment, both biologically and libidinally" (p. 37). This relationship is indeed a primitive one—one that secures the foundation on which the early development of the ego system builds and to which Balint (1953) refers as "primary object-love." Balint (1958) comments on this primal object relationship:

This maintains that a healthy child and a healthy mother are so well adapted to each other that the same action inevitably brings gratification to both. Good examples are sucking-feeding, cuddling-being cuddled, and so on. Thus for some time a healthy infant feels that there is no difference of interest between himself and his environment, i.e., that he and his environment are mixed up. (p. 86)

Balint alludes to the reciprocal, mutually influential nature of the relationship between mother and infant. Mother and infant, both objects in their own right and each an object of the other's libidinal cathexis, coordinate to form the matrix characterized by the state of primary object love.

Klein (1975) concurs with the conceptualization of the object relation as initiating at birth—a relationship that illuminates its efficacy and ascendancy in the feeding situation. Klein comments:

My use of the term "object-relations" is based on my contention that the infant has from the beginning of post-natal life a relation to the mother (although focusing primarily on her breast) which is inbued with the fundamental element of an object-relation, i.e., love, hatred, phantasies, anxieties, and defences. (p. 49)

I found that object relations start almost at birth and arise with the first feeding experience; furthermore, that all aspects of mental life are bound up with object relations. (p. 138)

The gist of the infant's early experiences of affect, impulse, and instinctual importunity take effect in the infant's association with its relational object. Intrapsychic structural formation and interpersonal relations are born to this most primal and primitive of all object relations. Klein explains:

The analyses of very young children has taught me that there is no instinctual urge, no anxiety situation, no mental process which does not involve objects, external or internal; in other words, object-relations are at the *centre* of emotional life. Furthermore, love and hatred, phantasies, anxieties, and defences are also operative from the beginning and are *ab initio* indivisibly linked with object-relations. (p. 53)

In fact, as Balint (1953) suggests, "However deeply we are able to penetrate with all our analytic technique and observations into the history of a man's life, we have always, without exception, found object-relations" (p. 59).

The infant is born embedded in a world of objects with which it engages in interaction on contact. Bowlby's (1969, 1973) observational studies of the effects of the infant's attachment to and loss of the mothering object clearly illuminated the potency of the primary object relationship. The disruption of what Winnicott (1965) referred to as the "holding environment" triggers the infant's emotional imbalance, threatening its reality sense. Even in the mildest sense of this disruption, Balint (1953) reminds us that

little children, even infants, begin to whine and get disgruntled and troublesome if the good contact between them and their environment has been disturbed. Here, without doubt, it is a question of an object-relation. . . . (p. 58)

In the extreme sense, the results of prolonged mother-infant separation acutely exemplify the profound, passive dependence with which the infant thrives in early object relations (Bowlby 1969, 1973; Mahler 1968). Balint (1953) describes that object relation:

A very early, most likely the earliest, phase of the extra-uterine mental life is not narcissistic: it is directed towards objects, but this early object-relation is a passive one. Its aim is briefly this: *I shall be loved and satisfied, without being under any obligation to give anything in return*. This is and remains for ever the final goal of all erotic striving. It is reality that forces us to circuitous ways. (pp. 98–99)

Balint further suggests, however, that the inevitable separations from and frustrations with the mothering object, as mandated by reality, impel the infant to initiate active behavior, much of which is directed toward its object. He adds:

The human child has the wish to continue living as a component part of the mother-child unit (a dual unit); as this is frustrated—at least in our civilisation—by reality, it develops a number of instinctual substitutive symptoms, such as its sleeping position, a number of reflexes (Moro, etc.), many phenomena of sucking and hand erotism and, last but not least, the general tendency to cling to something in moments of threatening danger.

In all these instances we are faced with active behaviour on the part of the infant, even with an activity directed towards an object. (p. 99)

Balint concludes that, in fact, some activity is inherent in even the very earliest and most primitive of object relations, adding, "Contrary to common parlance, the child is not suckled, indeed it sucks actively" (p. 99).

The capacity and tendency to actively engage the object in interactive behavior is acquired through the vicissitudes of the reality sense. The "capacity to use an object" implies active behavior on the part of the infant—a behavior that is developmentally acquired at the hands of the "facilitating environment," as Winnicott (1969) explains:

To use an object the subject must have developed a *capacity* to use objects. This is part of the change to the reality principle.

This capacity cannot be said to be inborn, nor can its development in an individual be taken for granted. The development of a capacity to use an object is another example of the maturational process as something that depends on a facilitating environment. (p. 713)

Yet Winnicott notes further that actively using an object transcends a mere relating to the object. Making use of the object is a function emerging from a more elaborate, developmentally acquired maturational process involving unconscious, intrapsychically processed fantasies of destructive involvement with the image of the object. Thereupon the object survives the infant's unconscious fantasy of destroying it.

[T]he subject may now have started to live a life in the world of objects, and so the subject stands to gain immeasurably; but the price has to be paid in acceptance of the ongoing destruction in unconscious fantasy relative to object-relating. (p. 713)

In this scheme, according to Winnicott, there is a progression from object relating to object use, the latter being attained through maturational processing, contingent on a facilitating environment characterized by adequate holding and good-enough mothering. Having achieved the capacity to use an object, and hence to "live a life in the world of objects" (p. 713), marks a milestone in the ever-evolving sophistication and articulation of object relations. Winnicott (1965) says that "the term 'living with' implies object relationships, and the emergence of the infant from the state of being merged with the mother, or his perception of objects as external to the self" (p. 44).

The infant's acquired capacity to utilize the object in subject-object interaction is but one side of the coin. According to Winnicott (1965), of equal significance, and indeed a necessity, in the natural advancement of object relations is the infant's "capacity to be alone." Indicative of a paradox, the capacity to be alone is in fact a type of relationship in and of itself. Winnicott referred to this phenomenal relationship as one of "ego-relatedness" and stressed: "Ego-relatedness refers to the relationship between two people, one of whom at any rate is alone; perhaps both are alone, yet the presence of each is important to the other" (p. 31). Indeed, the presence of each is a necessity to the other's ability to sustain aloneness. In speaking of the infant's experience of being alone, Winnicott explained:

Although many types of experience go to the establishment of the capacity to be alone, there is one that is basic, and without a sufficiency of it the capacity to be alone does not come about; *this experience is that of being alone, as an infant and small child, in the presence of mother*. Thus the basis of the capacity to be alone is a paradox; it is the experience of being alone while someone else is present. (p. 30)

Winnicott suggested that it is in the state of aloneness, albeit in the presence of the mother, that the child develops its sense of selfhood—its unique existence as a person. In the state of acquiescence, wherein the infant or child is free from external impingement and active engagement with its environment, it is free to experience the very genuine, true, and personal sensational and impulse experiences that set the foundation for the emerging sense of personhood—the formation of the "true self." The mothering object's presence, albeit without requisition, will serve as the attending object to share in the infant's experiences of flourishing impulse and sensation emanating from its tranquil state. Winnicott maintains:

It is only under these conditions that an infant can have an experience which feels real. A large number of such experiences form the basis for a life that has reality in it instead of futility. The individual who has developed the capacity to be alone is constantly able to rediscover the personal impulse, and the personal impulse is not wasted because the state of being alone is something which (though paradoxically) always implies that someone else is there. (p. 34)

Thus the maturational expansion of object relations and the parallel development of personhood become possible as individuals experience their sense of self within the relational context of a significant other.

5

Internal-External Polarities in Integration: The Intrapsychic and the Interpersonal

Confusion and disagreement prevail among psychoanalytic theoreticians and practitioners concerning the focus of the study of object relations. One school of thought recognizes the establishment and functioning of internal objects and the relationship between the individual and these internal objects in the evolving construction of intrapsychic agencies and the functions thereof. The process of internalization of external objects, both real and fantasied, and the individual's unconscious interplay with these mental object representations—for example, further internalization and externalization processing—sets the course on which the ego, and later the superego, agencies formulate and operate.

The opposing line of thought maintains that the true object relations model is one of investigation of the external domain of individuals in which they actively engage in ongoing, real, interpersonal relationships with objects of other persons. The primary, innate purpose of man is to seek, in desire and need, sustaining relationships with other persons who will provide support, gratification, and affirmation. It is only in the study of the experiencing person within his natural, social-environmental context that one can understand the true nature of personality organization.

The ambiguity surrounding object relations phenomena is dispersed as some theorists and clinicians attempt to connect the aforementioned polarities in an effort to design a complementary and comprehensive model that necessarily includes the recognition and study of both the intrapsychic and the interpersonal domains—a scheme that acknowledges the uniquely individual subjectivity of the person in necessarily ongoing, recursive interaction with the phenomenological world. Tuttman (1981) describes this model and its inherent value:

Object relations theory involves metapsychological structures (i.e., the world of internal mental representations and the identifications which make up the psychic institutions). At the same time, object relations theory deals with the human world of subjectivity and the existential. Thus, an object relations perspective provides a meeting place for object and subject and the opportunity to study their origins and qualities. (p. 45)

Greenberg and Mitchell (1983) take this integrated position in their reference to the object relations model as one involving "individuals' interactions with external and internal (real and imagined) other people, and to the relationship between their internal and external object worlds" (pp. 13–14).

The integration of the two polarities of thought on object relations into a comprehensive yet composite perspective retains its utility only in acknowledgment of the reciprocal relationship that the two domains maintain in mutually dependent interaction and influence. Klein (1946) suggests that

the relation to the first object implies its introjection and projection, and thus from the beginning object relations are moulded by an interaction between introjection and projection, between internal and external objects and situations. (p. 99)

The object-relational processes of introjection and projection (types of internalization and externalization, respectively) facilitate the circular interdependency of the internal and external domains and the objects therein. Fairbairn (1954) reiterates this conceptualization of object relations theory:

The nature of the personality is determined by the internalization of an external object, and the nature of group relationships is in turn determined by the externalization or projection of an internal object. In such a development then we detect the germ of an "object-relations" theory of the personality—a theory based on the conception that object relationships exist within the personality as well as between the personality and external objects. (p. 153)

The dual connotation of object relations transpiring within the intrapsychic as well as within the subject-environment domain allows us to conceive of internal, intrapersonal object relations in interchange with ongoing interpersonal experiences. Object relations theories, Goldberg (1981) says,

attempt to categorize and explain by an exchange of phenomena that are intrapsychic in terms of the interpersonal; they attempt to understand what goes on between people according to an entirely inner or personal perspective. Thus, it is not surprising that a sort of miniature theater of the world becomes transferred to the inside of the skull. (p. 132)

The structural world of the psyche, Kernberg (1976) suggested, is a repository of the current interpersonal situations of reality. The intrapsychic not only contains the subject's interactional life but also sustains the object relations for future reactivation and utilization in external, interpersonal relationships. The intrapsychic structures influence the means by which, in instinctual need, the individual's striving to secure the object is procured. Reciprocally, the current interpersonal experiences of the individual will either facilitate or inhibit the expression of such needs and influence the development of intrapsychic structure. Kernberg defines object relations theory thus:

Psychoanalytic object-relations theory represents the psychoanalytic study of the nature and origin of interpersonal relations, and of the nature and origin of intrapsychic structures deriving from, fixating, modifying, and reactivating past internalized relations with others in the context of present interpersonal relations. Psychoanalytic object-relations theory focuses upon the internalization of interpersonal relations, their contribution to normal and pathological ego and superego developments, and the mutual influences of intrapsychic and interpersonal object relations. (p. 56)

The recursive way in which the internal and external worlds coalesce to form a matrix from which the infant-self evolves implicates a necessarily complex transformational procession from that which transpires phenomenologically on the "outside" to that which is perceived subjectively on the "inside," and vice versa. In this scheme, the objects of the external real world and those of the intrapsychic not only affect one another in ongoing transactional experience but also are responsible for one another's existential origination. This reality exemplifies the power with which these internal and external domains initiate and evolve in continual, relational existence. In Stierlin's (1977) words:

[T]he inner objects, as they are affected by outer objects, are constantly remodeled and restructured. But, to a degree, the inner objects, through the efforts of an actively adapting individual, also affect outer objects. This accounts for the dialectic, expanding circularity of the relationship. (p. 135)

Object-relational thinking may in constitution punctuate the transformation of the subject's perceived relationship with the primary mothering object into the subjective, intrapsychic position of the infant. This is in essence a process—one that transpires, however vaguely, primitively, and unconsciously, in the very earliest postpartum stage of life. Meissner (1979) suggests that "there is a supposition in the object relations view of development that the patterning of intrapsychic development depends on the sequence and quality of the infant's object experience" (p. 346). This transpires via the relational sequential process of internalization. It is the very nature of the mother-infant interaction that determines the qualitative posture with which the internalized object relation is established as an integral component of the infant's intrapsychic.

Loewald (1973) concludes that "early object ties may be viewed then as necessary antecedents, as foreshadowings and portents of intrapsychic relations and structures, of the character of a man, and of his interactions with the world of external reality" (p. 9). Characteristics of the external object, along with the subjective emotional experiencing of the relationship with these characteristics and of the object in general, transfer to the inner world of the infant, where

they reside and serve, however vaguely and loosely, as images of various formations and functions. Greenberg and Mitchell (1983) remark on these images
of the internal world:

What is generally agreed upon about these internal images is that they constitute a
residue within the mind of relationships with important people in the individual's life.
In some way crucial exchanges with others leave their mark; they are "internalized"
and so come to shape subsequent attitudes, reactions, perceptions, and so on. (p. 11)

Psychoanalytic object relations theory serves to bridge the gap between those
experiences that transpire in the external world of reality in which the subject
plays an integral role and those experiences that unfold within the internal subjective world of the same individual. Because the two domains are inherently
interdependent, the study of any one exclusive of the other renders the investigation not only incomplete but also misguided in the quest for the truth. Object relations theory thus presents a systematic and illustrative approach to the
understanding of human nature; it probes and illuminates both the intrapsychic
structure and functioning of the individual and the interpersonal transactions
through which the individual engages in the real external world of significant
others. The utility of the object relations model lies in its study of both the
psychology of man and the psychopathology of man; each focus of study may
stress one of the two realms of object relations—the intrapersonal or the interpersonal. Fairbairn (1954) comments on his view of normal and abnormal psychology in reference to object relations theory:

[P]sychology may be said to resolve itself into a study of the relationships of the individual to his objects, whilst, in similar terms, psychopathology may be said to resolve
itself more specifically into a study of the relationships of the ego to its internalized
objects. (p. 60)

Guntrip (1969) concurs with Fairbairn's conceptualization: "The psychoneu-
roses are, basically, defences against internal bad-object situations which would
otherwise set up depressive or schizoid states . . ." (p. 23). Guntrip acknowledged and stressed the inextricable tie between past and present external object
relations and past and present internal object relations, illuminating the gist of
Fairbairn's theoretical formulations in the conclusion of the immediately preceding quotation: "though these situations are usually re-activated by a bad
external situation" (p. 23).
    Individual psychopathology, as a result of both the specific workings of the
intrapsychic and the interpersonal object relations, is a phenomenon of which
the constituent elements are multiple and seemingly imperceptibly intertwined.
The significant external objects (e.g., mothering object and parenting objects)
are recognized as serving as the child's protective armor against the potential
dangers of the external environment and, via the empathic, emotionally laden

behaviors with which the significant objects respond to the child's cues and gestures, serve as agents between the child's ego and its inner world of objects (Horner 1979; Modell 1985). In this scheme both the real external object relationship and the associated internalized object relationship (though they are both subjectively perceived) play a necessarily integrative role in the formation of either psychological health or psychological pathology. In speaking of the genesis of the latter, Modell stresses:

To acknowledge the influence of trauma at the hands of the "actual" object in the etiology of psychopathology does not minimize the importance of the subjectively created object. Object relations theorists . . . have not suggested any simplistic equation correlating environmental trauma with psychopathological outcome. (pp. 87–88)

The formation of the internal object world lays the groundwork for the specific intricacies of psychopathological manifestations; however, the intrapsychic domain is contingent on, and the reflection of, the external world of object relations.

=====6=====

The Internal World of Object Relations

Object relations theory as thus far defined involves the developmental process of transferring relationships with external objects to the internal, intrapsychic world of the subject. The internal derivatives of the interpersonal relations constitute the internal world of object relations. Along with the internalization of the external object relation, the transplantation, so to speak, of the external object to the intrapsychic also takes effect. The internalized object takes the form of an object representation and, in conjunction with its associated internalized relationship with the subject, it transposes into intrapsychic structures. Sugarman (1977) describes this phenomenological process:

These internal representations of external objects take on the role . . . of providing a comprehensible internal and, therefore, active source of motivation. These internalized objects become more than just fantasied representations of external objects . . . they contribute to relatively enduring and stable patterns of behavior. . . . In other words, these internalized objects take on intrapsychic reality and . . . constitute some degree of object relatedness in all individuals, if only internal. (p. 125)

Horner (1975) believes that the original interpersonal relationship between the infant and its mothering object determines the organization of the individual's internal world. She quotes Phillipson (1955, p. 7):

This inner world of objects—more strictly object relations—is basically the residue of the individual's relations with people upon whom he was dependent for the satisfactions of primitive needs in infancy and during early stages of maturation. . . . (p. 100)

Horner concludes that the mothering object serves not only to facilitate a functional coordination between the infant and its external world, thereby helping the infant organize its reality and relate to that reality, but also becomes, through the internalization process, part of the infant's internal organization.

The individual's relationship with the internal object representation of the significant external object constitutes an internal object relation. It is the quality of the actual interpersonal, interactional relationship and the way in which the individual perceives this relationship that determine the quality of the internal- · ized object relation that becomes established as a constituent of the ego system. It is within the ego system that the internal world of object relations resides and activates. In this scheme, the ego system develops and expands in func- tionability as a result of the relationship of its own structure to its internalized object. The ego and the object coordinate to form an object relation. Sternbach (1983) defines object relations:

What is meant by object relations is the relation of the self-image or of the ego (the concepts are never consistently distinguished) and object images. Self images and object images are said to be formed by "introjection" of their relationship, which means by the formation of a mental image of this relationship. . . . These introjected object relations . . . are the medium in which all psychodynamic growth of the person takes place. (p. 404)

The internal object relation is one consisting of two representations within the ego, that is, that of the object and that of the self in perceived relationship to the object. The significance of these two internalized representations derived from the infant's relations with the mothering object is stressed in Stolorow's (1978) partial definition of object relations theory as focusing on

the "internalization" of interpersonal relations and, in particular, the contribution of early images of the self and others (objects) and their associated affects to the develop- ment of normal and pathological personality structures. The . . . constellations of self- images, object-images, and affects constitute the basic building blocks in personality development. . . . (p. 32)

Stolorow emphasized the significance of the emotional context in which the infant experiences its relationship to its object as an integral factor in the for- mation of the internalized object relation.

The mother-infant relationship and the infant's affective experience therewith set the stage for the internalization of that relational experience to the psychic domain of the developing infant. Meissner (1979) posited that the structurally evolving intrapsychic world follows a blueprint, so to speak, designed by the nature and quality of the actual mother-infant relationship and the sequential progression with which the relationship evolves. Though the blueprint reflect- ing the cuing and response transaction between the infant and its mother estab- lishes a foundation in the immediate postnatal state, it nonetheless is rendered in continual transformation of quality and patterning because its evolution is contingent on the vicissitudes of ongoing experience in reality. Meissner noted:

A fundamental element in the theory of object relations has to do with the supposition that the quality of object relations influences and gives rise to internal modifications within the experiencing subject. This supposition draws particular emphasis in the object relations perspective on development, but also finds its appropriate role in the understanding of ongoing experience. . . . (p. 345)

Once again we acknowledge the recursive nature with which the internal and external worlds transact in interdependent evolution, because not only does the quality of external object relations influence the development of intrapsychic structure and relations but also the evolving subjective experience of the infant does affect the quality of the mother-infant relationship and the subjective experience of the mother. Reciprocity is the earmark of object relations theory.

To punctuate the development of the intrapsychic in early infantile experience, the object relations model presents a theoretical explanation for the genesis of an internal world of objects in relation to the subjective self. Given the painful and trying fact of reality that a bountiful, growth-enhancing, and growth-facilitating environment in its purest sense simply does not exist, as exemplified by the inherent incapability of the mothering object to fulfill her infant's every desire and demand, the infant is inevitably faced from primacy with the experiential realization that tension and pain do exist. It is in interface with this actuality that the infant finds itself in a quandary (albeit a primitively experienced state) as to what to do to alleviate its experienced condition. The infant's stance, as facilitated under the auspices of universal genetic endowment, is to internalize its unsatisfactory external world to its inner domain, where it can be more easily scrutinized and influenced. Modell (1968) explains this universal phenomenon:

The pain experienced in relation to external objects is dealt with by a symbolic re-creation in the inner world of the relation between self and objects, a re-creation that is altered in accordance with defensive and instinctual needs. An element of magic is retained. . . . By symbolic manipulation, an illusion of control and mastery is created—an illusion that the original objects in the external world can be controlled by means of the symbolic representation in the internal world. (p. 129)

Thus the process of internalization is one dictated by the universal laws of human nature and immediately affected by the defensive stature of the struggling infant. This internalization process, be it facilitated by magic, fantasy, or illusion, becomes the vehicle in which the infant's external world is transported to its inner world.

Balint (1968) also remarked on the infant's need to internalize the perceived insufficient external environment. *The Basic Fault,* as described by Balint, refers to the state rendered by the individual in the experience of a perceived void within himself—a void that theoretically exists as a result of a failure of functional coordination in the early mother-infant relational experiences. The cuing-response transaction fails either to develop or to sustain adequately. The infant's response to this dilemma is to create an internal arena of object relationship in which

the individual creates objects or artistic products in a private internal way to try to make something more satisfying than the real objects. The basic fault is also a precursor to the emergence of two types of object relations: *ocnophilia,* in which objects are cathected with great intensity and so clung to for security, and *philobatism,* in which the inner world is cathected to provide a degree of independence from the precariousness of objects. These object relations are thus for Balint a defense against the effects of the failure of the environment. (Sutherland 1980, pp. 832–33)

In this scheme the infant's construction of an inner world serves as a substitute for an unsatisfactory external world. However, it is not solely under unfavorable conditions that the object and the experiences of the self with the object are internalized. As previously noted, the infant in early postnatal life is involved in a relationship with its mothering object; this object and the relationship of the self to it are internalized in all its satisfactory goodness or unsatisfactory badness. Klein (1975) addresses the establishment of the initial good object in the infant's psyche:

I have already mentioned that the mother is introjected, and that this is a fundamental factor in development. As I see it, object relations start almost at birth. The mother in her good aspects—loving, helping, and feeding the child—is the first good object that the infant makes part of his inner world. His capacity to do so is, I would suggest, up to a point innate. (p. 251)

The first good object with which the infant interfaces in external reality (i.e., the mother's breast) is taken in by the infant, who establishes an internal object relation with the good breast. Klein (1948) speaks in general of the process of the internalization of external object relations:

Along with the child's relation, first to his mother and soon to his father and other people, go those processes of internalization on which I have laid so much stress in my work. The baby, having incorporated his parents, feels them to be live people inside his body in the concrete way in which deep unconscious phantasies are experienced—they are, in his mind, "internal" or "inner" objects, as I have termed them. (pp. 312–13)

Children have the capacity to modify these unconscious fantasies at their own discretion to suit their own needs and desires, and they will do so if the external world of objects and their relations to them are deemed unsatisfactory. In this scheme, the internalization of external objects and object relations serves as a defense mechanism as well as simply a means of relating to the external world. Concerning the latter purpose, Guntrip (1971) sees the external world becoming "a highly personal inner world of ego-object relationships, finding expression in the child's fantasy-life in ways that were *felt* even before they could be *pictured* or *thought*" (p. 59). Again, both the good and the bad elements of the external world are internalized. As Klein (1948) remarks, there are

innumerable objects taken into the ego, corresponding partly to the multitude of varying aspects, good and bad, in which the parents (and other people) appeared to the child's unconscious mind throughout various stages of his development. Further, they also represent all the real people who are continually becoming internalized in a variety of situations provided by the multitude of ever-changing external experiences as well as phantasied ones. (pp. 330–31)

The infant's earliest experiences in object relations are greatly influenced by the powers of fantasy and illusion, wherewith the infant's experiences of omnipotence determine the nature and quality of internal object relations. As a defensive means of alleviating anxiety, in early object relations the infant will split the external objects, and subsequently internal objects, into good and bad objects—introjecting good objects and associated good feelings and projecting bad objects and associated bad feelings. The infant's unconscious fantasies interplay with the external reality of objects and object relations, and as maturation proceeds in time, the child's internal world of object relations increasingly coincides with the external world of reality (Klein 1948, 1975; Segal 1974). Segal explains:

The earlier the introjection, the more fantastic are the objects introjected and the more distorted by what has been projected into them. As development proceeds, and the reality-sense operates more fully, the internal objects approximate more closely to real people in the external world. (p. 20)

As the reality principle strengthens and primary-process thinking subsides, the ego functions mature and expand, and the personality organization of the child is less influenced by the omnipotent and omniscient fantasies characteristic of early object relations. The child is thus more easily able to establish and maintain functional and pleasurable object relations without the employment of excessive defensive and primitive object-relatedness mechanisms of splitting, introjection, and projection.

Klein's (1948) conceptualization of the internal world of object relations stressed the element of unconscious fantasy in the organization of the personality. Internal objects, in Klein's scheme, are comprised essentially of such fantastic, illusory phenomena. Following Fairbairn's (1954) theoretical formulation of internal objects as structures in and of themselves with energy sources of their own, Ogden (1983) expanded on this conceptualization. He postulated that the internalized object can be described as a dynamic organizational component of the ego, which provides its own energy, direction, and experience vis-à-vis emotion, cognition, and perception. Ogden believes that

the ego is split into parts each capable of generating experience and that some of these subdivisions of ego generate experience in the mode modelled after one's sense of an object in an early object relationship while others generate experience in a mode that remains fixed in a pattern congruent with one's experience of oneself in the same early object relationship. The two parts of the ego remain linked and when repressed constitute an unconscious internal object relationship. (p. 227)

The internal object thus is a derivative of a split-off part of the originally whole ego. One subego component is qualified by its experience with the external object in the self-object relationship. This dual identificatory formulation, as presented by Ogden,

accounts for the dynamic nature of the internal object and also defines the relationship between the concept of ego and the concept of internal objects. In brief, internal objects are subdivisions of the ego that are heavily identified with an object representation while maintaining the capacities of the whole ego for thought, perception, feeling, etc. (p. 234)

There exists an inextricable tie between object and self as they necessarily evolve in mutual influence and inclusiveness.

=====7=====

The Interpersonal Realm of Object Relations

We have noted that the capacity for two individuals to experience one another in relatedness is contingent on the parallel phenomenon of the capacity to be alone, and that this sense of aloneness is subject to the experience of being alone within a relationship, that is, in the presence of another (Winnicott 1965). As one can surmise from our investigation of object relations, the structuring and developing of an internal world of object relations is facilitated by, and necessarily so, the existence of an external, contextual world of object relations. Because the human being is a social being, it is only in the context of other individuals that a person's existence holds significance. Object relations theory is predicated on the assumption that the individual is engaged in object relations upon birth; equally important, object relations continue to unfold and expand throughout one's life span. The person is an integral component of his own environmental context. Mendez and Fine (1976) comment on this conceptualization:

With mature ego relatedness, one does not feel alone even if one is literally alone. One's whole psychic makeup is permeated by relations' experience. Absolute independence is never reached because of the interrelatedness and interdependence of the person and his environment. Actually, the question of absolute independence need not even arise if maturity is considered to be self-possession as an experience saturated by object relations. (p. 365)

Indeed, the crux of object relations theory holds that the person is a social being—one naturally embedded in an environmental context of other persons (objects). The concept of object relations necessarily includes that of social relations. Spitz (1965) suggests:

All later human relations with object quality, the love relation . . . and ultimately all interpersonal relations have their first origin in the mother-child relation. Our investi-

gation therefore provides a starting point for the understanding of the forces and conditions which make a social being out of man. . . . The ability of the human being to
establish social relations is acquired in the mother-child relation. It is through this relationship that the channeling of the fused drives onto the libidinal object is accomplished
and the templates for all later human relations laid down. (p. 296)

Again we acknowledge the inherent interconnection between the intrapersonal
and the interpersonal as well as between the earliest mother-infant object relations and the ongoing interpersonal relations at present. Object relations theory
is essentially this. The interconnection and interdependency are highlighted as
we punctuate the interpersonal realm of object relations in the present discussion.

The interpersonal realm of object relations denotes the actual interactional
and transactional relationships that transpire between two or more individuals
in the real external world. The experiences of each individual in interaction
with the other(s) carry a subjective quality unique to the individual; however,
these experiences contribute to the ongoing procession of the continually dynamic, conscious and unconscious, verbal and nonverbal, cuing and responding
that transpire within the relationship. Though object relations in this scheme
can be properly regarded as but one of many ego functions, the recursive nature
of self and object development commands that we acknowledge the existence,
at birth, of an object relation—that is, an interpersonal interaction (albeit a still
primitive and archaic one)—and that the ego develops in conjunction with the
unfolding of increasingly sophisticated object relations. Object relations and
ego system develop under mutual influence and in mutual inclusiveness. Neither is subordinate to the other; the two progress hand in hand.

Interpersonal relations transpire within the realm of reality, that is, two or
more people engaging one another as separately perceived individuals in their
own right, each acknowledging the other's unique experiences of emotion, cognition, perception, and behavior. However, this acknowledgment will vary in
degree and will be clouded by the unconscious experiences of the individual.
The thrust of the object relations model is the investigation into the unconscious, subconscious, or, at best, tenuously conscious motivations behind the
mode and quality of current object relationships. These motivations, as previously noted, stem from the nature and quality of early mother-infant and mother-
child object relations. Schafer (1972) explains the nature and source of interpersonal interaction:

Interpersonal, finally, refers to what the objective observer sees, that is to say, two or
more people interacting. Insofar as the subject is realistic, he will be the objective
observer of his interpersonal situation. We know, however, how often it is the case that
when the subject is ostensibly dealing with another real person, he is found on analytic
examination to be dealing more or less with a fantasied version of that person; and that
version is likely to include details of significant figures from the subject's childhood.
(p. 418, footnote)

The "fantasied version" of the object and the relationship therewith in the present, real interpersonal interaction is fundamentally a derivative of the earliest mother-infant and mother-child interactions. These early object relations, as previously noted, serve as the foundation for the construction of the internal world of object relations, and hence the intrapsychic structural organization. As Arlow (1980) suggests, "Fundamentally, it is the effect of unconscious fantasy wishes, connected with specific mental representation of objects, that colors, distorts, and affects the ultimate quality of interpersonal relations" (p. 114). The way individuals perceive, feel and think about, and behave toward their significant objects is determined by the nature of the same experiential processes that transpired in relation to their early psychological objects.

The object representations—which become established subsequent to the child's internalization of the external, significant object and the relationship of the self therewith—serve to guide the individual in later life in the striving for increasingly mature object relations. Their functions, in Greenberg and Mitchell's (1983) words, are to serve

as a kind of loose anticipatory image of what is to be expected from people in the real world; as becoming closely entwined with the individual's experience of who *he* is; as persecutors, fulfilling the function of a kind of critical fifth column; or as a source of internal security and resource, invoked in times of stress and isolation. (p. 11)

The individual, in interpersonal interaction, seeks others who will fulfill these early-established expectations. The internal object representations, according to Gordon (1983), "act gyroscopically to seek out others who fulfill our wishes and fears," and "who provide sufficient reality justifications for their transferences and projective identifications" (p. 329). He adds that the relational "partner is sought out to fit the internal representations of past processes and original bad objects" (p. 332). In this scheme, past object relations reactivate to manifest themselves in current, ongoing interpersonal relationships. Such experiential and relational phenomena arise in the analysis of both the subtle nuances and the more overt dissentions and disparagements in marital and familial interactions.

The internal world of object relations holds potential for being so rigidly set that such relations reemerge from repression in the unconscious to manifest themselves with varying degrees of conscious awareness in later relational experiences of the individual with significant external objects; the individual is rendered subject to limited control over such phenomenological events (Stierlin 1977). Too deeply entrenched in the interpsychic makeup of the individual, early battles with bad internal objects will rage on in part on the battlefield of the external world of object relations. Stierlin remarks of the individual's vain attempts to change these bad internal objects in current interpersonal relationships:

[T]he subject feels driven to match his unchangeable inner objects with outer objects which are perceived as equally unchangeable. This condemns the individual to tread a rigid and narrow relational path with only scant hope of reaching his goal. For this subject will have only very limited object choices available to him. He appears committed to chase an unalterable ideal. His inner gyroscope sets his course too rigidly. (p. 136)

In parallel fashion, an ''inner gyroscope'' set too loosely will lead the individual aimlessly into the external world of object relations, having no guidelines to influence functional object choice. Stierlin describes these individuals:

They have then too little gyroscopic valence and are too unspecific as anticipatory sets. They fit themselves effortlessly into a wide variety of outer objects. Thus they no longer steer the subject effectively towards a manageable range of suitable partners. Such a person appears rudderless in his (or her) relational quest. (p. 136)

At either extreme the individual's internal world of object relations has strict influence over the nature and quality of external object relations. Stierlin continues, ''Whether the inner gyroscope is set too rigidly or too loosely, a circularly unfolding and yet enduring dialectic with external objects will be impossible in either case'' (p. 137).

For those individuals whose intrapsychic development is stable enough to foster a functional dialogue with external objects, the internal and external worlds reciprocate in influence as internal object relations and external interpersonal relationships maintain a relatively close match, the two spheres complementing one another in mutual recognition and validation; internal world and external reality correspond and concur. This person is consistent in the quest for external objects and relationships therewith, which will facilitate the continued maturation of an already healthy ego system and stable sense of self. Open and functional communication transpires between the components of the individual's intrapsychic world as well as between the self and the significant objects with which it interfaces in the external world. Sutherland (1963) further describes this healthy individual:

In the healthy adult, the main needs are sufficiently ego-syntonic and of such a character that a manifold set of personal relationships is sought and maintained. The relatively free transactions between the need systems themselves (greater communication) in the healthy person also means that he responds more as a whole, is more integrated in assessing inner and outer reality. The central ego in such a person is therefore being enriched throughout life and this *constant enrichment provides a motivational growth and support.* (p. 116)

Because of the mutually supportive facilitation of concomitant growth between individuals and their chosen object, the individuals' internal world of object relations is subject to continual modification at the hands of a fertile environmental context of interpersonal relationships. Arlow (1980) notes:

[I]t is not just the experience with the object, but what is done with the experience, that is decisive for development. This has some bearing on the development of the capacity to love. Later experiences in love relationships may modify the effect of earlier object ties. . . . (p. 129)

This modification of internal world organization exemplifies the ongoing dynamism with which individuals and their environment evolve in mutually inclusive dependence.

Thus the structure of the internal world of object relations, as determined by the nature and quality of early object relations (e.g., mother-infant and mother-child interactions), is not in normality permanently set and maintained. Though the core of the individual's personality organization may be established during the early stages of development, various components of the healthy personality continue to alter in adaptation to its environment. Those components that affect object choice and the nature of the relationship therewith, for example, are continually flexible enough to be subject to adaptability to the vicissitudes of object relations at various stages of the life span.

New forms of object relations—from the initial vague sense of object relatedness at birth, to primary object love of the mothering person, to the triangular relational configuration and the oedipal situation, the expansion of object relations to siblings, peers, teachers, and so on, to the ever-advancing mature object love—do not subjugate and replace old forms of object relations. Rather, increasingly sophisticated object relations integrate with previous ones to create a higher form of object relations organization. Earlier forms of object relations retain their existence, albeit in altered form. Sandler, Holder, Kawenoka, Kennedy, and Neurath (1969) explain this phenomenon:

[W]e probably do not ever get a real replacement of one type of relationship by another. What we see is rather the addition of various new types of object relationship developing collaterally, being integrated with and dominating the old, but not necessarily replacing them. (p. 643)

Thus some basic elements of our earliest object relations (e.g., those based on illusory wish fulfillment and omnipotent control) sustain and color subsequent relationships and affect object choice to some degree. Sandler et al. further suggest:

Thus even in the person who has attained the most mature type of object love, the infantile aspects, for example, the pure need-satisfying aspects, remain, although they may be subordinated to the higher-level developments. (p. 643)

Arlow (1980) concurs with this theoretical formulation:

A hierarchy of stages of object relations culminating in a so-called "mature" relationship is essentially an idealizing concept. Clinical experience underscores the fact that in
every love relationship the individual acts out some form of complicated unconscious
fantasy rooted in early vicissitudes of drive and object experience, a fantasy that ultimately determines, but only in part, the pattern of loving and the specific person or
types of persons that will correspond to the object choice. (p. 127)

Indeed, object relations in childhood, adolescence, and adulthood provide the
means by which one seeks to fulfill needs of both primitive and more advanced
types.

Unconscious, wish-fulfilling fantasies, according to Sandler and Sandler (1978),
seek actualization, as manifested in current interpersonal relations. Two individuals in relationship are in continual interchange of cues, signals, and messages, some of which are to a degree conscious; however, the general affective,
cognitive, and perceptual experiences of each member are rooted in the unconscious. Each partner finds subtle and covert means of only partial awareness
by which to lure or coerce the other into responding in a manner that can be
assimilated into and reinforce the wish-fulfilling fantasies of the first partner.
These transactions, for the most part, remain outside the arena of conscious
awareness, purely for defensive purposes. The unacceptable wish or impulse
emanating from the unconscious would prove to be too anxiety-producing should
it reach consciousness, and is therefore acted out in disguised form: "All the
defensive displacements, reversals, and other forms of disguise, can enter into
the way in which we repeat or attempt to repeat wish-fulfilling early relationships" (Sandler and Sandler 1978, p. 287).

Each partner, either implicitly or explicitly, attempts to cajole the other into
assuming the position in the relationship that would complement the initial
partner's behavioral stance in an interchange conducive to the initial partner's
acquisition of gratification. The person will employ a variety of defense mechanisms to avoid emergence of the wish or impulse into consciousness (e.g.,
splitting, projection, and projective identification) as a way of achieving this
goal. The person attempts to entice the partner into assuming the assigned role
and responding in accordance with his desires (Sandler 1976). Sandler and
Sandler (1978) explain:

This reflects what has been called his "role-responsiveness." . . . The idea of "testing
out" the role-responsiveness of another person brings together the concepts of object
choice and object relationship, inasmuch as we make rapid trial relationships until we
find someone who fits the role we want the "other" to play and is prepared to allow
himself to respond according to that role. (pp. 288–89)

The medium through which this transactional phenomenon transpires is referred to as "transference." Sandler and Sandler further note: "Transference

can be said to include the attempt to bring about a situation which would be a disguised repetition of an earlier experience or relationship, or be a defence against the repetition of such a relationship" (p. 288). In this scheme, the wish-fulfilling fantasy may not necessarily be of repeating experiences of gratifying mother-infant interaction but perhaps of avoiding in current object relations the reenactment of unpleasant early object relations. Nonetheless, of whatever nature it might be, the transference phenomenon exists in all interpersonal relationships, though it may or may not elicit the desired response. As indicated, an amalgam of emotions, cognitions, perceptions, fantasies, desires, and expectations permeates the unconscious realm of interpersonal relationships.

The internal world of object relations plays a powerfully influential role in the processing of ongoing, external object relations. While we acknowledge the inertia with which the unconscious intrapsychic is manifested in current interpersonal relationships, it should be noted that the *real* relationship that transpires in conscious human interaction is of equal significance in the understanding of human nature. Modell (1985) stresses:

I would not depreciate the importance of internalized objects, but the internalized object and the actual object are not equivalent concepts and we cannot evade the problem by describing actual objects by a notational system of object representations. What occurs in a relationship between two people is not simply something that can be described in the mind of the subject. (p. 87)

Whereas object relations in the traditional psychoanalytic scheme may be defined simply as "the libidinal cathexis of an image which represents the object in the mind" (Hendrick 1951, p. 53), more recent thought places equal significance on the ongoing interpersonal interaction that transpires in reality. The simple cathexis of an object, or its internal representation, provides an incomplete picture of the complex nature of human beings in interactional relationship (Joffe and Sandler 1967; Sandler and Sandler 1978). We would do well to recognize that the potent existence and significance of the internal world of object relations acquires its efficacy only with the integral role it maintains in the analysis of human interaction. Equity is highlighted in the significance with which the internal world and the external world coordinate in mutual influence and interdependence in the unfolding of the fully integrated, whole, enriched human self.

=8=

Object Relations and Marital Partner Selection

The marital object relationship is sustained and energized by the early acquired capability of partners to evoke and maintain an internal object representation of a significant other. In the absence of the spouse, individuals are able to draw on the internal image of the partner as well as on the representative quality and nature of the object relation. This phenomenological application of object constancy renders individuals capable of predicting, in a sense, what their spouse is experiencing in terms of emotion, cognition, and behavior even when the spouse is not in direct contact with them. This ability of individuals to foretell the experiences of one's spouse and their own gestalt experiences in interface with the spouse's experiences is the hallmark of a flourishing, functional marital object relationship.

In face of the fortunately inescapable reality that they are not capable of entirely predicting a spouse's emotional, cognitive, behavioral, and overall perceptual experiences, individuals will inevitably meet periodically with marital relational experiences that cannot be readily assimilated into their existing schema. A spouse's presented behavior will at times be incongruent with the expectations that individuals have derived from their mental representation of the object and the relationship of that object representation with their self-representation.

Brodey (1961) suggests, "To the extent that this unexpected behavior is discovered, given meaning and valued, a new aspect of the other's personality has emerged to be incorporated into the inner representation" (p. 70). To the extent that this newly discovered behavior is not acceptable, and therefore not assimilable to the existing mental representation, individuals will be faced with a dilemma that will penetrate the marital relationship and subject it to the plight of discordance. In the former situation, Brodey adds, "this feedback between inner image and outer substantial reality allows the inner image of our loved one to grow and unfold'' (p. 70). Hence the marital relationship in its essence and totality will likewise flourish.

The ability of individuals to acknowledge, accept, and affirm the real, true personality of their spouse and therewith develop their own personality in relation to that of the spouse's, is determined greatly by the level of separation and differentiation that they have achieved from their earliest parental object ties. In essence, the more integrated and whole their personality or sense of self, and the more their identity is experienced as being separate and distinguishable from significant external objects, the more readily they will be open to, and the less they will be threatened by, the emergence of the spouse's identity.

Marital couples whose individual identities are as yet diffuse and unstable will relate to one another with a certain degree of dysfunctional fusion. This fusion will cloud the perceptions that the partners have of each other and of the relationship as a whole. Expectations permeate the very core of the transactional and interactional patterns, subjecting both partners to inevitable frustrations and hurts when the other cannot and does not meet those expectations.

In this type of marital relationship, the partners expect one another to conform to and fit the internal mental representation of the object and of the self's relationship to the significant object. The partners attempt to modify the external object and coerce it to match their internally derived expectations. The nature and quality of interaction in the marriage is thus based on internalized objects. The residues of the earliest experienced object relations and the resulting internalizations, which freeze as stable introjects, serve as the foundational elements with which the partners build their identity or sense of self and in essence mold the internalized role model to that which the partners expect one another to conform.

Meissner (1978a) discusses this potential for either functional or dysfunctional marital relationship:

[T]he new relationship can be contaminated by the effects of the pathogenic introjects inherent in the personality organization of each partner and their intermeshing. As already mentioned, if the personalities which enter the marital relationship are relatively individuated and differentiated, the potentiality exists for positive and constructive identifications that enhance and enrich the personality structure of each partner. Where the personalities are dominated by pathogenic configurations, however, the intermeshing internalizations in such a couple will take place in terms of the organization of such pathological introjects. (pp. 46–47)

Partners bring to the marital relationship healthy and/or pathological introjects that have greatly influenced the degree to which their respective identities have formed in differentiation from the significant external object and that affect the degree to which the partners' identities can be integrated into a healthy, growth-enhancing, shared marital object-relational experience.

The acquisition in early childhood, suspended and reinforced through maturation, of a clearly separate and autonomous sense of identity is facilitated by a productive parental marriage comprised of two functionally separate yet interdependent persons. The best general indicator of a functional and constructive marriage is that in which partners have originated from a family system wherein the parents' marital relationship was characterized by individual separateness and ego autonomy within a relational context of mutual sharing, support, and affirmation. Whereas not all problematic marriages produce a problematic child who may later engage in a dysfunctional marital relationship, a young child does indeed internalize the object relations of the parental marital partners and form an internal relationship between the self and such internalized external object relations. Mahler and Rabinovitch (1956) comment on this phenomenon:

While the imprints of marital discord do not always lead to manifest neurotic symptoms in the child, they affect his attitudes and outlook on life. Later these appear as unconscious patterns which impair his own choice of a sexual and marital partner. The child now grown to adulthood may repeat in a similar or complementary way traumatic situations which the marital discord of his parents stamped on his pliable personality structure as a child. (pp. 55–56)

The parental introjects that sustain as internal objects within the psychic structure of the child reemerge in subsequent, later-life interpersonal relations (e.g., the marital relationship) in disguised, unconsciously motivated interaction and transaction. These internal objects and the relationships therewith reflect the quality of the marital and parental relationships of the partners' family of origin, as well as the relationship of the self to these marital and parental objects.

The internalized objects and object relations play an integral role in the process of ongoing interpersonal relations. As previously mentioned, partners will attempt to coerce or cajole each other into assuming the expected internal role. They relate to one another not only as consciously perceived real persons but also unconsciously as "good, gratifying" and "bad, ungratifying" internalized parental objects to be either loved or scorned. Throughout the life span individuals internalize significant external objects, which are assimilated into existing, earlier formed object-relational configurations of both good and bad qualities. The encountered, real external object (e.g., the marital partner) is perceived in part as fitting into these configurations, wherein the partner serves as the idealized recipient of the individuals' libidinal strivings or as the recipient of the disavowed, split off, and projected aspects of the individuals. In this scheme, the external interpersonal relations are perceived and colored by the subjectivity of the internal object world.

Framo (1982d) illuminates this concept:

The relational environment is manipulated such that others are maneuvered into being chastising parents, monitors, or expressors of one's sexual or hostile impulses, faithful servants, oppressors, or what have you, in order that more primitive conflicts will not come to the surface. People are constantly "acting out" old conflicts, and they seek through marriage . . . the supporting responses which will enable the relationship with the internal role models to continue, and prevent the anxieties and fears associated with those internal relationships from emerging. That is to say, they avoid painful symptoms by interpersonal choice. The reciprocal roles are formed with exquisite accuracy. . . . (p. 39)

Partners attempt either to correct or to avoid an earlier intolerable, bad object relation in their family of origin. Framo (1982b) believes that "each partner unconsciously attempts to maneuver the other into some earlier relationship pattern in the family of origin; each has the disquieting feeling that some old, tormenting ghost has risen to haunt him" (p. 142). In this scheme, the interplay of conscious and unconscious motivations produces a clouding effect that obscures the real relationship between partners in a marital relationship.

Boszormenyi-Nagy (1965a) acknowledges the effect that the internal object world has on ongoing interpersonal, marital object relations:

Internal relatedness can intrude into seemingly unconnected external situations and produce deceptive effects. Real and transferred relational attitudes can overlay in a complex pattern. What appears to be a true feedback between two partners may actually be programmed by their internal relational events. Many marriages are essentially lived between each partner and their respective introjects. (p. 122)

Efforts toward reparation of inner conflictual object relations or the denial and avoidance of such relations illuminates, however disguised in presentation, the processes of external-world, real interpersonal relationships. These actualized interpersonal interchanges, as exemplified in the marital relationship, are nonetheless real in nature and exert a variable degree of influence on the evolution of the organization of the internal world of the partners. However, to the extent that the internal role model with its gyroscopic functioning is rigidly sustained in the intrapsychic, individuals will be impelled to subjugate their partner into fitting the given role model.

Individuals are rather adept at, for the most part unconsciously, selecting a mate with whom they can achieve this subjugation rather readily; and because of the reciprocal nature of both unconscious and conscious marital transactions, equity in interactional motivation and contribution sustains throughout the relational process; partners are willing to accommodate each other. The dynamics of the reciprocally influential relationship can take many forms of patterning in the process of mate selection. Individuals may appeal to one another by overt or covert acknowledgment of similar neurotic fears and anxieties. Because of their mutual recognition, the partners can join force in the united attempt either to confront such fears and anxieties or, more likely, to deny or defend against their presence. Solace is found in shared experience and mutual support (Lansky 1980–1981). These fears and anxieties may often revolve around actual or perceived losses in past experience.

Paul (1967) notes that such experiences of object loss may linger unresolved and incompletely mourned through the life span, only to resurge within the matrix of the marital relationship:

Such fixity, though present for many years, appears to be rooted in maladaptive responses to both real and imagined object- and part-object-loss. Furthermore it appears that such losses and associated sense of deprivation lead to deposits of such affects as sorrow, anger, grief, guilt, bitterness, despair, and regret. These affects, timeless as experienced internally, appear to dictate a restitutive response characterized by the emergence of a perceptual set leading to mate selection. It is as if the prospective mate seeks, in the mate to be selected, both what he had and didn't have in his object relations. (p. 188)

The object loss and its associated affective experiences are denied, disavowed, negated, or in some form externalized, as dictated by a couple's shared defensive organization. The relinquishment of employed defense mechanisms, bringing the pain to the fore, would necessarily elicit the fear and anxiety perceived as being threatening to the individual ego as well as to the shared ego of the marital relationship. The loss experienced by either or both marital partners may not necessarily be of a distinct, separate part or whole object. The loss may be one of an aspect of one partner's self. In this case, the individual seeks in the choice of object those cherished aspects of the self that are deemed missing. The lost aspects are split off from the self in its earliest insufficient object relations with the mothering and, later, the fathering objects.

Framo (1982a) believes that partners choose one another in hopes of recapturing lost split-off aspects of early object relations. In parallel fashion, individuals may split off currently disavowed aspects of their personality, such as perceived inadequacies, insecurities, weaknesses, defects, or otherwise "bad" characteristics, projecting them onto their partner and either vicariously acting out such badness through the partner via projective-identificatory defense mechanism or chastising and punishing the self safely and indirectly through persecution of the partner. Early internal splits and the resulting continued conflictual experiences thrive not only within the internal world of individuals but also seek reenactment on the available battleground of current, external interpersonal relationships.

Dicks (1963) comments on this phenomenological aspect of marital object choice and object relations:

I visualize the obscure process of mate selection . . . as largely based on unconscious signals or cues by which the partners recognize in a more-or-less central ego-syntonic person the other's "fitness" for joint working-through or repeating of still unresolved splits or conflicts inside each other's personalities, while at the same time, paradoxically, also sensing a guarantee that with that person they will not be worked-through.

Thus they both hope for integration of the lost parts by finding them in the other, and also hope that by collusive "joint resistance" or mutual defence this painful growth can be by-passed. (p. 128)

The unconscious fear of successfully resolving the internal conflicts is strong enough in both partners in conjoint alliance to prevent such reparation from happening. Individuals cling desperately to their bad internal objects and object relations out of uncertainty of what individual and relational experiences exist otherwise. Feared depletion or annihilation of the self, as well as feared loss of the loved object, are at the basis of such tenacity.

The marital object-seeking process is unconsciously patterned in efforts to alleviate the fear of self-loss and/or object loss. However, an equal fear of self-object merger, as well as perceived engulfment, may also elicit the anxiety that dictates the choice of the loved object. Unconscious infantile fantasies of blissful union with the primary love object, inasmuch as they derive from the earliest mother-infant relations, are preserved and manifested throughout the life span—perhaps to reach their fullest expression in the intimacy of the marital bond. The fear of recognition and expression of such infantile fantasies in simultaneous conjunction with the equally luring desire for their gratifying actualization elicits an ambivalence experienced in a very real yet vaguely recognized mode of existence. The conflict-producing ambivalence highlights the very subtle yet definitive process of mate selection—one based, again, on the effort to avoid what one fears most.

Eidelberg (1956) suggests that such unconscious motivation induces an individual to

select someone who helps to gratify and partly to deny the presence of infantile wishes. In other words, whenever neurotic choice is made, the patient, instead of choosing a person with whom he could be happy, has selected an object he needs in order to avoid recognizing what he is afraid of. (p. 58)

The fear of object loss and/or object fusion will be intensified to the extent that individuals have failed to acquire in early childhood, and sustain through the life span, adequate self-object differentiation, mature ego functioning, and functional narcissistic regulation. These acquisitions are contingent on the experiences of healthy object relations and positive, growth-enhancing ego and superego identifications and introjections.

To the extent that self-object differentiation fails to develop properly and pathological internalizations of identificatory and introjective types permeate the internal object world, the individual will experience difficulty in regulating its narcissistic equilibrium. Unable to maintain a stable and functional narcissistic balance, individuals will look to external objects to guide the self's tenuous perception of its value and worthiness as a person among persons. Individuals who experience difficulty in maintaining their self-esteem without the excessive elicited feedback from external others are subject to the experience of intense conscious and unconscious fantasies of narcissistic gratification. Even though narcissistic needs characterize all individuals in their quest for the gratifying love object, it is the extent to which such needs are manifest that determines whether object-seeking and intimate love is of functional or dysfunctional processing.

Meissner (1978a) suggests that

falling in love is a multidetermined result of a number of dynamic factors, but involves in some significant degree the operation of intense narcissistic needs. The intermeshing of and the responsiveness to such needs play an important part in the choice of marital partner. Each of the partners, then, seeks—with varying degrees of conscious or unconscious intention—for a mate who promises to provide optimal gratification of such usually unconscious and predominantly narcissistic needs. (p. 42)

The more precariously individuals maintain a narcissistic equilibrium, and thereby find it necessary to elicit feedback from external objects to illuminate their self-perception, the more likely they are to seek a marital partner from whom they not only can easily elicit such cues but whom they also can consciously or unconsciously dominate to secure the desired responses to facilitate the gratification of their narcissisticly wishful needs. The dynamic process by which this is accomplished is facilitated by the employment of primitive introjective, projective, and projective-identificatory mechanisms, and is characterized by complementary, reciprocal interplay, which maintains not only the narcissism of the individual partners but also the narcissistic homeostatic behavior of the couple as a system.

=9=

Marital Object Relations in Process

Dictated by both the external reality of interpersonal transaction and the unconscious domain of internal-world object relations, marital couples engage one
another in interaction of a mutually invested and, however unwittingly, stylized
nature. Couples unite in their armamentarium against shared fears or in joint
striving for shared, elusive wishes. It is precisely because these predominantly
unconscious fears and wishes are shared by individual partners that they have,
seemingly imperceptibly, attracted one another and consciously accepted one
another in matrimony. Ongoing overt and covert marital interaction of both
functional and dysfunctional qualities exemplifies the purely reciprocal, complementary influence that the partners collusively maintain as they harmoni-
ously synchronize their efforts in confrontation with their internal and external
worlds.

The unconscious fears and wishes that the partners typically share in union
are based on the correlated sharing of similar levels of self-object differentiation, maturity, and personality structure in general. Persons attract one another
on the basis of such characteristics because they find security and solace in
familiarity and shared experience. Meissner (1984) elaborates:

[T]here is a tendency for partners of relatively equivalent degrees of immaturity and
self-differentiation to be attracted to each other. . . . . The tendency for marital partners
to be operating at equivalent levels of immaturity or to manifest similar degrees of lack
of self-differentiation is sufficiently general to put us on guard; when we find signs of
such pathology in one marital partner, we keep an eye open for indications of a similar
level of personality organization in the other partner. (p. 391)

Bowen (1978) suggested, however, that the defensive organization of the
partners typically takes an oppositional form, although each partner's defensive
stature complements that of the other in the overall homeostatic regulation of
the marital system. Slipp (1984) further explains:

In the terms of object relations theory, if one spouse has a developmental arrest and employs primitive defenses as a way of relating, the spouse generally does so also, or at least is willing at an unconscious level to accommodate. Otherwise the relationship cannot sustain itself. . . . Thus, a complementary transference-countertransference relationship, in which defensive structures mesh, can become established that stabilizes one or both of the personalities. (pp. 68–69)

Willi (1982) concurs with this finding:

In an unresolved couple conflict there is an equivalence of neurotic structures. *Both partners display similar basic disturbances in relation to marriage, but they play them out through contrasting roles.* (p. 52)

Some individuals may manifest flagrant, dysfunctional symptoms while their partners may present a seemingly functional appearance. As Giovacchini (1984) explains:

The superficial adjustment, in terms of behavior, defenses, and general adaptations, may appear markedly different in each partner, for one may present a picture of relative calm and equanimity, while the other may seem markedly disturbed. (p. 226)

It should be noted, however, that such phenomenological presentation in marital relationships is not restricted to the interplay of so-called disturbed partners, since the same basic object-relational pattern transpires within the realm of two healthy partners as they may complement each other's ego-autonomous, maturational development and identity formation within the context of the marital bond.

It should also be noted that all persons experience internal object-relational conflict and externalize the conflict to the sphere of interpersonal relationships. Individuals are adept at securing the marital partner who shares a similar, albeit differently manifested, conflict. Willi (1982) and Dicks (1967) conceptualized the ongoing marital interaction, including inevitable conflict, as playing on a consistent theme that encapsulates the couple's shared unconscious motif. Willi comments:

[C]ouples usually carry out their conflicts in continuing variations on a constant theme. The daily incidents leading to disagreement always echo the refrain of a similar "song." Looking beyond the specific circumstances of a conflict, one discovers a narrowly defined basic theme which disturbs the couple. This constitutes their *common unconscious.* (p. 45)

The partners engage one another in interaction based on the "common unconscious," in a collusive attempt either to resolve or to avoid their similar conflicts. Couples in collusion become enthralled in the experienced turmoil of their respective internal object worlds as well as the external dissention and disparagement in which the turmoil becomes manifest. The meaning of such interactional engagement is beyond the conscious awareness of the individual partners; yet the same theme is carried throughout the transactional patterning of couples. The sustained, unresolved conflict shared in union is acted out through two seemingly oppositional positions taken by the respective partners, although it is programmed by the one consistent theme.

Willi (1982) conceptualized couples' conflicts as being the result of neurotic disorders experienced in commonality by the partners. Being basically of the same personality structure, neurotic individuals magnetically attract one another as they mutually reinforce the shared object-relational conflict. Mahler and Rabinovitch (1956) poignantly describe this phenomenon:

The subtle immanent capacity of man to react to his fellow man's unconscious (empathy) and to seek out those toward whom he has, so to speak, unsaturated affinity (unconscious attraction) is especially important in the case of neurotic partners. The unsaturated affinity of neurotics is particularly strong, and they complement one another in their neuroses. (p. 44)

Attraction to others by means of empathic responses is based on the unconsciously experienced identification with the emotional, cognitive, and behavioral experiences of the persons to whom individuals are attracted. Individuals can in a sense mysteriously and unconsciously seek out and identify with an internal, object-relational, conflictual experience of another and find relief, security, and/or strength in the empathic identification.

Even though the conflict revolves around early object-relational experiences, such conflict sustains through the life span, resurging during periods of external crisis and developmental transitional points (e.g., the forging of the marital bond and the advent of parenthood). When these stressful events occur (e.g., in the marital relationship) and cannot be resolved because of the defensive stature of the partners individually and of the relationship as a whole, couples are propelled into neurotic collusion. As Willi (1982) sees it:

Collusion means to me that a couple engages in neurotic warfare. By "neurotic" I mean that the partners are unable to objectively evaluate and resolve their differences because of unconscious fixations on conflicts experienced in childhood. (p. 162)

. . .

The neurotic game of collusion can be assumed to take over when both parties become caught up in a formalized fighting ritual which drains them of mental energy for long periods and thus prevents them either from reaching a solution or from escaping the trap. (p. 163)

In this scheme, an experienced marital conflict is not necessarily the result of neurotic collusion; rather, it may resolve itself in the conjoint working through of the couple in everyday transaction. It is when the conflict perpetuates in the generation of destructive and depleting interaction that the couple is deemed to

be in collusion. Collusion is not the purposeful end of either conscious or unconscious pursuance; rather, it is the result of benevolently motivated yet faulty
adaptation to the marital system. Willi (1982) explains:

Since collusion arises in the course of a mutual process of adjustment, *it is not a predetermined phenomenon. An individual with a neurotic relationship disturbance is not
necessarily compelled to seek a partner with whom to develop a corresponding collusive
connection.* (p. 166)

As Willi (1982) suggested, the essence of the collusive process wherein the
partners embroil in neurotic defense entails a complementary coexistence in a
bipolar pattern of relationship. Seemingly dichotomous positions assumed by
the respective partners integrate to form a recursively patterned relational process of an acutely interdependent, complementary nature. Individuals assume a
position in regression, wherein they retreat into immature, dependent, and
seemingly inferior behavioral presentation, while their partner assumes the progressive position of the mature, independent, and seemingly strong and supe-
rior person.

While both positions may be punctuated to present a picture of isolated,
problemed individuals, the gist of the picture in its gestalt illuminates a shared,
mutually dependent, complementary, object-relational configuration of marital
partners in collusive transaction—a configuration characterized and generated
by the partly conscious, yet mostly unconscious, interplay of reciprocated defensive mechanisms. The recursive and perpetually reinforced processional pattern of regressive-progressive role interplay is seen, on closer inspection, to be
a shared facade of pretensive personality presentation, designed and implemented by the relational system to provide the partners with an assumed identity, be it of a genuine or a pseudo nature.

Individuals can take solace in assuming the position of the regressed, infantile character, insofar as that role is at least covertly acknowledged by both
partners as necessarily an integral component of a higher-level systemic organization, balanced by the equally acknowledged need for the complementary
role of the "together," pseudo-integrated partner. Both positions are incomplete—indeed, unattainable—without the other. Individuals will find neither
identity nor value in the "tower of strength" without a significant other of
whom to be supportive; and, in parallel fashion, they will find neither identity
nor value in "the mild and the meek" without a significant other on whom to
lean.

The unconsciously determined purpose of this polarized transactional dynamic is to provide couples with a shared defensive stature in opposition to the
underlying shared conflicts and fears that permeate relationships. By partners'
collusively denying, disowning, and projecting those consciously and unconsciously experienced fears, couples in amalgamation build an organizational

system sufficiently durable and strong in structure to subdue the insidiously impinging fears and wishes. Willi (1982) explains:

The bond of the similar, central conflict causes one partner to seek a resolution through progressive (overcompensatory) behavior and the other through regressive behavior.

This progressive and regressive behavior is a major reason for the mutual attraction and the resulting bond. Each hopes that the other will release them from their central conflict. Both believe themselves now to be protected against the things they fear most and expect that their needs will be met more than ever before. (p. 56)

It is within the context of mutually shared fears and the experienced conflicts therewith that couples mobilize their defenses in a unified maladaptive attempt to secure freedom from the treachery of the internal conflict, thereby lending themselves to relationship pathology. The regressive and progressive behavioral stances assumed by couples in marital relationship are by no means necessarily indicative of a dysfunctional dyadic system. On the contrary: regressive and progressive role presentations are a necessarily inherent component of the healthy marital transactional bond. Psychoanalytic object relations theory postulates that the intimacy of the marital bond is acutely akin in nature to the mother-child bond of early object-relational experience.

The unitary matrix of the marriage, from which the partners experience a sense of fused oneness, is perhaps truer to the nature of the symbiosis spoken of in object-relational conceptualization than is Mahler, Pine, and Bergman's (1975) symbiotic relationship of the mother-infant dyad. Characteristic of the marital relationship are partners who are equally dependent on one another for the sustenance of the relationship system and, to a significant extent, the sustenance of the individual partners embedded in the natural context of the relational configuration.

In this scheme, it is inevitable that under variable circumstances, and ideally in alternating patterning, partners will revert to a more helpless, dependent, infantile state wherein they assume an inferior role to the complementarily stronger role of the protecting spouse. The healthy marital relationship is one that facilitates the vacillation of behavioral stances wherein partners are granted the right to display elements of weakness and neediness. Dicks (1963) expands on this phenomenological aspect of the mature marital object relationship:

Marriage is the nearest adult equivalent to the original parent-child relationship. Thus its success must revolve around the freedom to regress. The freedom to bring into the adult relation the deepest elements of infantile object-relations is a condition of growth. To be able to regress to mutual child-like dependence, in flexible role exchanges, without censure or loss of dignity, in the security of knowing that the partner accepts because he or she can projectively identify with, or tolerate as a good parent this "little needy ego" when it peeps out—this is the promise people seek when they search for the one person who will be unconditionally loving, permissive and strong—who will enable one to fuse all part-object relations into a meaningful whole and be enhanced by it. (p. 129)

Paradoxically, the oscillatory patterning of regressive and progressive behavioral positions wherein the fragility of the ego is permitted to show in dependence on the stability of the partner's ego becomes possible only in the context of a mature relationship comprised of equally mature, ego-autonomous persons with respectively secure identity formations. Well-integrated and -delineated couples are able to facilitate their own growth and productivity in the process of periodic regression. Thus, as Willi (1982) says, "Each partner expects deep, human understanding from the other and achievement of real personal fulfillment" (p. 22). The recursive nature of marital object relations fosters natural empathy, support, caring, and love.

The magical sense of symbiotic merger and perceived oneness with which couples experience their bond continues to operate throughout the evolution of the marital relationship. Residues of early object-relational experiences sustain within the internal world and, as these internalized object relations expand and mature as the ego system develops in autonomous functioning in interface with external objects, they provide the framework from which current interpersonal relations take form. The nature of the blissful union between marital partners is in essence a derivative of the early mother-child object relationship, although the unified relation is of a more mature and sophisticated type.

However, the presence of the temporary regressive element of the marital relationship is not necessarily contingent on the presence of a complementary progressive element in counterbalance. Rather, as indicative of healthy, productive marital relationships, the partners can, temporarily and in cooperation, simultaneously regress to the infantile state. The act of copulation exemplifies the ecstasy with which lovers regress in concert to the blissful state of temporarily mutual envelopment and incorporation. The temporary regressed states in which partners are permitted to revert to infantile dependence on the other partner paradoxically foster the very ego differentiation, autonomy, and maturation required of a healthy, constructive, and productive marital relationship.

The capability and opportunity to revitalize the residues of early object relations strengthen the maintenance of ego structure and integration. Individuals form an identity partially by means of experiencing in vacillation a spectrum of states or conditions in which they are able to perceive differences in the subjective experiences of themselves as well as of themselves in relation to others. The capacity to learn and grow from these changing ego states and concomitant qualities of object relations determines the nature of ongoing internal and external world experiences as well as the degree of intrapsychic and interpersonal health.

The degree to which individuals do not learn from the vacillating regressive and progressive states and occasional fused experiences is indicative of the degree to which marital partners are unable to functionally integrate their separate ego systems into a single, unified ego system of the marital relationship. The ability to form and work within a marital ego system, while maintaining individual identities, is the hallmark of a healthy relationship. In essence, however, individuals perceive their partner to some degree as an element of themselves. Framo (1982d) comments on this phenomenological aspect of close human relations:

Multi-person systems, whereby one person carries part of the motivations and psychology of another person, are only beginning to be understood; the close other can become a structural part of the self. *Whenever two or more persons are in close relationship they collusively carry psychic functions for each other.* (p. 39)

One marital partner can be strong while the other is weak; one dependable while the other is undependable; one healthy while the other is unhealthy; and so on. The two complementary positions maintain the marital system in equilibrium while the psychic economy of the system is such that at least one partner is free to experience temporary regressions without jeopardizing the integrity and maintenance of the system. Dicks (1967) remarks that this is a

need for unconscious *complimentariness,* a kind of division of function by which each partner supplied part of a set of qualities, the sum of which created a complete dyadic unit. This joint personality or integrate enabled each half to rediscover lost aspects of their primary object relations, which they had split off or repressed, and which they were, in their involvement with the spouse, re-experiencing by projective identification. The sense of belonging can be understood on the hypothesis that at deeper level there are perceptions of the partner and consequent attitudes toward him or her *as if* the other was part of oneself. (p. 69)

In this scheme, Nichols (1984) suggests that "at an unconscious level a marital pair may represent a single personality, with each spouse playing the role of half self and half the other's projective identifications" (p. 202). The intrasystem functions are divided and delegated to respective partners who individually contribute a variety of characteristics to the marital system. The relationship's unified ego, or personality, allows individuals to disown and project certain undesirable qualities in themselves or allows their partners to recapture earlier disavowed, split-off aspects of themselves by projectively identifying with them in their spouse.

The enactment of these modes of interaction and transaction in the marital relationship can take the form of either function or dysfunction, adaptability or maladaptability. Dicks (1963) sees the two forms in contrast:

The marriage—the dyad—here represents a total personality with each partner playing the role of "one-half" of the unrecognized conflicting polarization, instead of a complementary growth toward individual completeness and enhancement such as is possible in the healthy marriage by acceptance of the ambivalence of a "mixed" person. (p. 128)

Stewart, Peters, Marsh, and Peters (1975) suggested that the marital relationship pattern characterized by mutual and perpetual denial, splitting, blaming, projection, and projective identification is a result of a deeply entrenched collusive arrangement by which the unified ego of the marital system serves to constrict the otherwise healthy differentiation of individual ego systems. The separate egos become so intertwined in collusive arrangement that the perceived distinction of persons diminishes and the partners become the container and embodiment of certain elements of the other's self. The diffusion of ego boundaries becomes a natural consequence, as exemplified in the persistent cat-and-dog, antagonistic relationship of individuals, each with an ego deficit, in marital interplay.

Stewart et al. (1975) noted that partners within the confines of the marital relationship may seek to repair their respective ego deficiencies, albeit with great ambivalence for fear of loss of the needed and loved, however seemingly oppositional, object. Efforts at reparation will succeed only to the extent that partners are able to differentiate effectively their respective egos and identities while simultaneously integrating into a unified marital ego system wherein they are able to coordinate functionally in mutual sharing, empathy, respect, and affirmation.

=====10=====

Marital Object-Relational Breakdown

The formation of a functional, well-integrated, and delineated marital ego system within which partners maintain a stable sense of self and identity is characteristic of the healthy marriage in evolution. Couples in interchange of separate personalities construct firm yet permeable ego boundaries within the marital system as well as between the system ego and the external world. Because individuals establish a sense of identity through comparison and contrast with external objects, it is necessary that the ego boundaries retain fluidity, fostering a functional interchange and sharing of ideas, beliefs, attitudes, values, and otherwise experienced emotions, cognitions, and behaviors.

It is precisely by means of this marital process that couples establish their intrasystem and intersystem boundaries, thereby developing and strengthening their individual and unified identities. The dynamics involved in this process hold potential for guiding couples into either shared growth and productivity or collusive relational breakdown. The dynamic process by which partners attempt benevolently to establish ego boundaries and concomitant identities involves elements of defensive and adaptive mechanisms of disavowal, denial, splitting, blaming, projection, projective identification, and idealization.

The establishment of ego boundaries and a sense of individual and unified selves is typically facilitated by the partners' continued search within themselves for the ideal self. The ideal self is that wished-for person in which the individual identifies with the all-good, gratifying, pleasurable mothering object of early object-relational experiences. In face of the experienced ambivalent emotions of love and hate toward the significant external object, infants purge the self of the experienced "bad" feelings toward their loved object by thrusting them into repression, while the "good" feelings in the object relationship are maintained in consciousness and partly projected onto the idealized external object as well as partly contained within the ego to form the ego-ideal, or idealized self (Fairbairn 1954).

The defensive and adaptive mechanistic process is sustained throughout the life span and played out in the interpersonal sphere of individuals' lives. In the context of the marital relationship, according to Dicks (1967), it is manifested as the principal defense mechanism by which partners attempt to organize their individual identities and stabilize their relationship system:

The unreal expectation that in their marriage the partners must be "all in all" to each other, make good all defects and offer perfect gratification of all needs is, of course, idealization. I described it as the main defence mechanism in marital relations. (p. 71)

Thus partners repress the perceived bad, ungratifying aspects of the marital relationship, allowing only the good, pleasurable, need-satisfying aspects to be experienced by the individual and to be attributed to the partner. Dicks further notes:

This permits an unalloyed "pure" love to be felt. Biologically idealization serves the reproductive drive well during the courtship and mating phase, making love "blind." Reality-testing that follows the honeymoon may activate the return of the repressed. . . . It is the return of the repressed that causes the trouble. *It breaches the idealization.* (p. 71)

The idealization will sustain and serve its purpose inasmuch as the repressed bad aspect of the object relations is prevented from reemerging into consciousness.

However, according to Fairbairn (1954), the repressed tends to return. In fact, the more intensely an internal object or object-relational representation is thrust into repression, the more sharply and strongly it surfaces to consciousness, to be played out in intrapsychic experience and interpersonal transaction. The marriage provides fertile ground for the reexperiencing of early object relations. Willi (1982) believes that every early object-relational experience that has never been permitted to formulate naturally, and thereby remains as unrealized potential, permeates the essence of later object choice and object-relational experience. Dicks (1967) suggests: "Deeper-lying and hitherto repudiated relationships of the ego to earlier objects are activated and brought into at least partial awareness in the disturbed marriage" (p. 71).

The intensity with which the mechanism of idealization is maintained in the marital relationship is indicative of the degree of anxiety with which one or both partners experienced the insufficiency of early mother-infant relations. The unfulfilled potential that resurges in current object relations provides the tools with which the marital relationship can gratify unfulfilled early needs or the weapons with which the relationship can augment the embattlement that led to the early repressive defensive stature at its origin. Inasmuch as the shared idealization serves to prevent the reexperience of the bad aspects of early object relations, as well as the current experience of similarly bad aspects of the marital relationship, couples become entrenched in an interactional pattern conducive to the denial of experiences of anything other than expression of caring and concern. Denial of any wrongdoing on the part of the spouse limits partners to the relational experience of all-goodness wherein all overt and covert disagreement and dissention are prohibited. Dicks (1967) describes this idealized transactional pattern:

At one level are the conscious expectations of the ideal union already mentioned. These have the aim of keeping all "bad" feelings out of the marriage. Here the partners have to do a lot of unconscious work "to let the sleeping dogs lie," to deny and keep inner realities out of sight. There develops what might be called a collusive or joint resistance to change, a smooth facade of "happiness," of perpetual sunshine without a shadow. Such unions often endure if there are inner resources (e.g. rational insight or secure repression), and living conditions to keep the fiction in being. (p. 73)

Provided couples can collusively deny or disavow the internal and external reality sense, they can maintain a relational pattern characterized by what Wynne, Ryckoff, Day, and Hirsch (1958) refer to as "pseudo-mutuality," wherein couples can maintain a facade of blissful togetherness in presentation to the external world as well as to themselves. However, a price must be paid for the maintenance of such a system, not only in terms of the denial of reality but also, as Dicks (1967) suggests, in terms of the denial of genuine loving feelings that may otherwise transpire within the relationship:

Since the idealization . . . covers the relationship between the ideal object and a central ego purged and weakened by splitting off of all disturbing elements, the egos will defensively repudiate manifestations of forbidden libidinal or other "primary" behaviour in the real partner, who quickly becomes the scapegoat and image of the forbidden object-relation. (p. 72)

As a result of this defensive stature wherewith the individual partner, or both partners, feel depleted in their sense of selfhood and thus are reluctant to invest in libidinal strivings, sensual feelings and sexual relations may be individually or jointly prohibited.

In this scheme, as noted by Klein (1948, 1975) and Fairbairn (1954), the dynamic process of repressing the bad, ungratifying aspects of the external object and the relationship therewith necessarily entails prerequisite splitting of that object in its internal representative form as well as of the self's ego structure in relationship to the internalized object. Because the ego continues to cathect even the bad components of the external object and its internal mental image, a part of the ego splits off and follows the bad split-off object, with continued cathexis, into repression. Following Fairbairn's conceptualization, Dicks (1967) postulated that in current, ongoing object relations (e.g., the marital relationship) the ego may be so drained of cathectic energy that individuals may feel unequipped to contribute to a sharing, intimate relationship:

What is essential about this way of looking at mental life is that it is not feelings, not impulses as such, but affective relationships between the self and some figure outside the self which are repressed. This splitting necessarily involves a portion of the reacting self, which thus becomes less, if at all, available to the central ego. . . . Therefore, if my split-off internal relation to a forbidden or dangerous object takes up its quota of ambivalent cathexis, and preoccupies part of me unconsciously, I have that much less investment of self to offer to an adult relationship. (p. 70)

Splitting, as a precursor of the defense mechanism of idealization, manifests itself in other ways within the marital object relationship. Partners may split off a disavowed aspect of themselves, which is deemed intolerable, and subsequently attribute that personality characteristic to the other partner, who may act it out under the vicarious scrutiny of the attributing partner. Conversely, partners may assume the unwanted badness perceived as part of themselves, totally absorbing the badness while attributing all goodness to the spouse. The former is done out of motivation to protect oneself from intolerable self-perceptions, while the latter is done to protect the investment one has in the spouse and the relationship therewith.

As noted earlier, couples unite in the formation of a joint ego or personality within which each partner embodies and displays certain mutually and unconsciously determined characteristics in presentation to the extrasystem world. Thus, as Dicks (1967) explains,

they defend the stability of the joint legal-social personality that they have created in marrying one another. In protecting the image of the partner (for example as a "drunk" or as "sexually inadequate" or "slovenly," and so forth) they are in the other secretly cherishing the rejected, bad libidinal ego with its resentments and demands while *within* the dyadic system they can persecute it in an inter-personal framework. (pp. 122–23)

It is out of desire to maintain the homeostatic balance of one's own internal world as well as the equilibrium of the marital system that one employs the defensive maneuver of splitting.

In this scheme, as Stewart, Peters, Marsh, and Peters (1975) point out, the intrapsychic and interpersonal realms of experience intertwine to reinforce the stability of each:

The internal process . . . can be acted out in interpersonal relationships where, for instance, a spouse is seen as all "bad." . . . The spouse is seen as all bad and therefore cannot be related to except in a negative, often abusive way. (p. 162)

Preserving the bad object (the marital partner) as external to oneself by continuously persecuting it and thereby maintaining the self's illusion of all-goodness, the narcissistic equilibrium of the self is maintained while simultaneously balancing the marital system in terms of dichotomous goodness and badness.

The perseverance with which couples collusively maintain this pattern of marital relationship in spite of experienced pain and turmoil is comprehensible when we acknowledge the extraordinary efforts of individuals to adapt not only to the external environment of which they have become an integral part but also to the internal world they have constructed in an effort to deal with the inherently unsatisfactory elements of early object-relational experiences. It is by means of protecting themselves and simultaneously adapting to the external world that marital partners attempt so steadfastly to manipulate each other into assuming a complementary role. Failing in the effort to subjugate and coerce their partner into fitting the internal object-relational model leads to experienced anxiety. Punishment and persecution become the final armament in the urgent attempt to seek security and belongingness.

Fantasy world illusions and the subsequent expectations based on those illusions form the core of the processional breakdown of marital object relations. One or both partners who are unable to acknowledge and respect the other's identity and sense of selfhood are subject to desperate attempts to mold the other into a preconceived model of, however ill-fated, emotional, cognitive, and behavioral expectations. The source of the ill-conceived internal role models is found in the maturational development of the individual as facilitated by the original family system. Internal object-relational conflicts, which stem from the nature and quality of transactional patterns existent in the family of origin, behoove the individual to make reparative efforts in current, intimate interpersonal relations (e.g., the marital relationship) in hopes of resolving such internally suspended conflicts.

Insofar as the partners are able to bring their respective interpretative sets into a functionally integrated new system of interpretations, anticipations, and expectations, they are likely to accommodate one another in assimilation of one another's perceptions and establish a functional relationship. However, as Paul and Paul (1975) explain, incompatible family backgrounds can, and do, breed conflict:

It is in this original family field of interactions and interplay that an individual develops his values about life, which contribute to an image of what he or she desires in a prospective mate. This image, often embodied in daydreams, naturally tends to idealize the image of the projected spouse. It is in the uncompromising determination that this image must be realized, coupled with one's difficulty in being able to understand both the sources of such images in oneself, and in the other, that the seeds for future incompatability are sown. (p. 29)

Failure of partners to coordinate functionally their respective interpretative sets in mutual adaptation results, as suggested by Paul and Paul (1975), in a variable degree of incompatibility. In interface with this incongruity, couples are likely to succumb to, out of defense and benevolent attempts to adapt to one another's frame of reference and personality style, one-sided but often mutual blaming and projection. In a healthy sense, projection of experienced emotions, cognitions, and personality traits in general onto the partner can liberate the projector from anxiety-producing internal experiences, providing sufficient relief from conflict for the self to grow and expand. Inasmuch as recipients of the projections are not excessively subsumed and controlled by these attributes, they can maintain the sense of self and identity hitherto established and brought into the marriage. Projectors who disavow those aspects incompatible with their ideal self and attribute them to the spouse can benefit from such a defensive and adaptive process only to the extent that they negate or deny those self-aspects short of distorting reality sense in regard to perception of themselves, their partner, and the entire relational context.

Lansky (1980–1981) addressed the unhealthy employment of blaming and projective tactics as couples collusively and continuously reenact early object-relational disturbing experiences. The nature of this collusive interchange not only exemplifies the anxiety the partners experience concerning dependency and fusional fantasies but also, in more specified and current terms, serves the purpose of acquiring, however misguidedly, omnipotent control over them-selves and their loved object. In speaking of the original, inadequate object-relational experiences that are internalized and played out in current marital relations, Lansky (1980–1981) states:

What was internalized is a traumatic, intensely dependent and, above all, precarious relationship. Subject to constant withdrawal and abandonment, it is replayed as a mas-terful act of self-righteousness. Presumably, what was experienced in a passive victim-ized role is replayed actively in a verbal role involving blame. (p. 443)

Control and mastery through current blaming transaction diffuse the essence of helplessness with which individuals experienced early object relations and currently experience interpersonal relationships:

Infantile fears of loss of the relationship, loss of omnipotence, being let down, and being helpless are still in evidence in the background but in the forefront are well-ordered verbal attacks, with the self-assuredness and exhilaration that one sees in the accusatory state. (p. 443)

The act of blaming—in essence an expression of the experienced fear of aban-donment and object loss, and a process that permits the expression of rage in response to these fears—can persist only to the extent that couples collusively engage one another in a unified front against the awareness of feelings of in-adequacy and helplessness. In this scheme, couples, through mutual blaming and projection, are able to effect functional marital distance regulation by sep-arating one another through harsh verbal attack out of fear of abandonment, while simultaneously preventing that abandonment through the maintenance of a collusively unified dyadic bond within which the partners feel secure and strong in their sense of oneness.

Blaming and projection, Lansky (1980–1981) believes, allow the couple "to avoid intimacy, involvement and risk, and at the same time serves to replay anxieties about object loss and loss of fantasied special entitlement" (p. 449). The attending conflict surrounding mutual blaming and projection persistently and firmly holds the relational pattern in a locked position wherein partners cannot attempt, without retaliation and sabotage by the other partner, to break away from the system and seek autonomy. The fear of object loss and the acknowledgment of the partner's individuality induces dreaded feelings of aloneness and possible fragmentation and dissolution of the self.

Because one or both partners may feel so inadequate individually outside of the context of the safe, albeit maladaptive, relational matrix, and as a direct result of the lack of an acquired differentiated sense of self, couples are subject to blaming one another for the experiences of their own perceived sense of unhappiness and discontentedness with life. The need for individuals to subjugate their partner into assuming the responsibility for their joy or sadness, fortune or misfortune, rather than assuming their own responsibility for their position in life as a distinct person in their own right, is illuminated in the interaction of the marital relationship comprised of one or two undifferentiated persons. Because one or both partners may feel inadequate in assuming responsibility for their own behavior and internal and interrelational experiences, demands and expectations will be placed on the other. To the extent that partners are able to meet those demands, irrational as they may be, without losing their self-respect and dignity, the relationship may functionally equilibrate. However, as Meissner (1984) maintains,

such a system of interaction is perilously fragile and subject to the regressive pulls and vicissitudes of the neurotic needs that drive and determine it. If either partner decides to assert his or her own needs in the face of the demands of the other, to establish and differentiate his or her own self in the face of these regressive pulls and neurotic needs, that partner can expect the other to use every resource of manipulation, exploitation, pressure, rejection, and force to keep the partner in the position of compliant dependence and emotional involvement. (p. 396)

The intensity with which couples may become embroiled in collusive blaming and projective transaction, wherein neither partner is able to empathically relate to the other, can be so strong that the entire relational context changes during the blaming periods of interaction. The relationship is not only replete with overt and explicit verbal attack but also, at a more individual and deeper level, the blamer and the blamed both are subject to experiences of altered ego states in the projective process. Individuals lose their self, in a sense, in the fierce interchange of verbal accusations. Part of their ego structure splits off from conscious awareness during the blaming process, leaving an insufficient part of the self to perceive objectively the reality of the relational context. Lansky (1981) describes this phenomenon:

[L]ow level projective mechanisms accompanied by vengefulness and self-righteousness leave the blamer lost so much in the issue at hand that an observing ego is not available during the conflict. . . . (p. 167)

. . .

Blaming behavior or provocative blame-inviting action is difficult to get into therapeutic focus, because the ego state that blames or provokes blame by drinking, bungling, gambling, and so forth, is split off from the more usual state of consciousness, which is the one that presents to the therapist. At such times when a normal state of consciousness is present, the patient is bewildered by the behavior, oblivious to it, ashamed of it but, above all, not in control of it. This combination—split-off ego states accompanied by low-level projective defenses and actions—make appeal to an observing ego nearly impossible. (p. 169)

Entrenched in the process of mutual commanding, accusation, and defamation, partners are subject to confusion about their own perceptions and experience, and the resulting distortion of the relational context. Individuals are unable to respond empathically to each other or to identify their own experienced emotions revolving around the issue. Yet emotional content floods the marital relationship, laid out for both partners to feel hurt and rejected by each other, too frightened and paralyzed to communicate effectively their genuine feelings.

=11=

Patterns of Marital Object Relations: Dyadic Narcissism

From the matrix of a functional, growth-enhancing, and productive marital relationship develops an interactional pattern wherein partners are, at any given juncture, permitted and encouraged by their spouse to utilize the ego functionability, perceptual faculties, and empathic responsiveness of the spouse to carry them through stressful periods of time. These instances are typically eventful in intermittent periods of crisis during which, as a result of unforeseen trauma at the hands of environmental reality, individuals suffer an injurious blow, so to speak, to their self-esteem. Provided the marital relationship is based on the existing capability for and processing of mutual empathy, the relational system permits individuals to lean on and use their spouse as a mirror.

Through the mirror's reflection despondent partners can acquire perceptions of the self as being changeable through the processing of the perceptions via the internal faculties of their spouse. Narcissistically injured partners use the spouse as an extension of the self, exercising ego functions with the empathic assistance of the stable partner who lends his/her ego functionability to the despondent partners. This pattern of transaction is manifested only temporarily. Once the crisis has been resolved and the trauma that they experienced has been functionally integrated to the point of reestablishing the narcissistic equilibrium of the sufferer, the marital system is once again stabilized on the basis of equitable contribution to the ego system. This scenario, through transient, is often experienced by couples whose relationships evolve through the normal phases of the marital sector of the life span and confront the realities that the interphase transitional points present to their marital system.

The narcissistic element that permeates and pervades the dyadic relationship is reminiscent of earlier object-relational experiences wherein the young child develops the sense of self, organizing and structuring its intrapsychic world through interaction with the mothering object. The "self-object," in Kohut's (1977) terms, through nurturance, affirmation, and empathy, provides a "mirroring'' bridge connecting the young child to its significant objects, who facilitate the child's development of a sense of cohesion, permanence, and stability. The selfobject, perceived as an extension of oneself, serves the function of providing the young child with the necessary sense of grandiosity to establish a healthy narcissism—a narcissism that will become a self-regulated function of the emerging self.

To the extent that the external objects are deficient in their ability or willingness to serve as selfobjects by mirroring the emergence of the self, children will fail to develop, among other things, the capacity to regulate functionally their self-esteem and maintain a healthy narcissistic equilibrium. They will proceed through the sequential stages of their life span with experiences of object-relational failure and narcissistic injury, stunting the formation of a cohesive sense of identity. Lacking a cohesive and consistent self, these individuals enter a marital relationship wherein they, as yet unintegrated and undifferentiated, attempt to acquire and maintain a sense of identity through the mirroring provided by their partner. Their image of self, the self-representation, is colored strongly by the nature and quality of interaction with the significant object of their marital partner. Narcissistically incapable of establishing and maintaining an accurate self-image and a parallel degree of self-esteem, these individuals look to the spouse to strengthen and support the weakened self-representation.

As suggested by Rubinstein and Timmins (1979), the object may be sought to serve as an actual ''supplement'' to the perceived sense of self-inadequacy:

An individual may relate to an object's magic attributes and establish a narcissistic relationship with the object in order to supplement the deficiencies in the self-image. In essence, the object functions as a substitute for the missing or defective self-esteem. (pp. 125–26)

This marital transactional pattern serves to protect individuals defensively by preventing feared fragmentation and dissolution of the self. Poorly self-defined individuals capitalize on the availability of the marital partner to merge with the perceived strength and stability of the partner. The stronger object becomes an extension of one's poorly established self. Rubinstein and Timmins explain that, to the narcissist

the world and its objects are perceived as reflections of the self, belonging to the inner experience of the individual. Such a person interprets experiences with others only in terms of the emotional subjective world and as fulfillments or frustrations of narcissistic needs. The self is not encountered objectively, but is perceived as frustrating or fulfilling some preplanned expectation following a demanding ego-ideal. Therefore, in the world of the narcissist, object relations are not real, but are only a part of the self reactivated through relationships with others. (p. 126)

Narcissistic persons, within the relational context of the marriage, struggle to discover and maintain the wished-for, idealized self—a self that, in presentation to the external world, will be haughty, demanding, controlling, and grandiose, while internally these individuals feel inadequate, weak, and unworthy, though to a variable degree they defensively deny it. Narcissists fear disintegration of the tenuously organized self, defensively and desperately clinging to the loved object for the support and supplementation that they deem necessary to survive. One can readily predict the potential downfall of object relations and wonder how narcissists can sustain prolonged marital relationships.

As previously noted, however, individuals tend unconsciously to seek and marry another who is of approximately the same level of acquired maturity, differentiation, and ego functionability. Narcissistic individuals marry a person who has relatively equal difficulty in regulating a functional narcissistic balance. The partners tend to experience problematic object relations, though the narcissistic manifestations may differ in nature and quality. Couples become embroiled in a mostly unconscious, collusive pattern of interaction and transaction wherein mutual projections and introjections pervade the relational system as the partners desperately attempt to defend against feelings of inadequacy and fears of abandonment and self-dissolution. The marital relationship becomes one characterized by dyadic narcissism. The partners collusively and covertly agree to serve as objects of one another's projections, introjecting each other's disavowed split-off and externalized aspects of the self. Rubinstein and Timmins (1979) remark on this collusive, reciprocal dynamic:

[T]he narcissistic individual always functions in a dyadic relationship, and *narcissism is not exclusively an individual phenomenon.* The individual and his object do not establish a linear-causal relationship but a mutually contributory process which produces secondary gains in order to improve individual self-esteem in both partners. (p. 128)

The result is a haphazard, dysfunctional relationship in which the partners are individually self-absorbed, unable to relate empathically to each other as differentiated and distinct persons in their own right.

Meissner (1978a) noted that the lack of differentiation and autonomy creates, as emanating from the relational matrix, a primitive emotional climate that the partners cannot comprehend and embody within their personalities, and thus cannot learn or grow from the emotional, transactional experiences. Emotional communication remains unconscious and covert, seemingly emanating from nowhere, yet pervasively affecting both partners as they relate haphazardly to one another in a rather primitive and illusory manner. To the extent that the partners can successfully confirm one another's projections, allowing them to identify projectively with each other, the dyadic narcissism will sustain within the marital relationship.

Brodey (1961) refers to this narcissistically pervaded relational pattern as a "narcissistic relationship," emphasizing the reciprocity in which the two partners attempt benevolently to verify and affirm their respective identities. Brodey (1959) defines the narcissistic relationship as one that has two ingredients: one person relating to the other as a projected part of self, the fragment of self projected being unintegrated with a perception either of self or of the external object, and, second, the other person's becoming, within the specific relationship, symmetrical with the first person's expectations, validating them. (pp. 385–86)

Brodey (1961) conceptualizes the narcissistic relationship as an example of an "image relationship." The image relationship is the type of object-relational patterning that is unconsciously designed to prevent the actual, external object in its reality from altering the preestablished internal representational image of the same object. As previously noted, individuals will to a variable degree try desperately to manipulate their partner into fitting the internal role model. In Brodey's words, "The reality testing and prediction system specifically and profoundly operate to *reduce* the possibility of discovering aspects of the other's existence not fitting with the established expectation" (p. 71).

Conceptually, Brodey (1961) suggested that in opposition to the image relationship is the healthy "object relationship," wherein the partners use the reality of interpersonal relations to modify the inner object representation, providing for growth of the self and enhancement of the marital relationship. "The *object relationship* uses the unexpected as a device for correcting the inner gestalt" (p. 71). The narcissistic relationship does not represent a position along the continuum of the image and object-relational polarities; rather, it is

descriptive of two people *each making an image relationship to the other and each acting within this relationship so as to validate the image-derived expectation* of the other. Now we are moving toward a closed system. Both participants of the narcissistic relationship work at reducing the possibility of intrusions of the unexpected, using the devices of restriction and omission. (pp. 71–72)

Brodey (1965) stressed that partners locate and accentuate in each other those ego-dystonic aspects involved in their own internal-world conflicts. Insofar as this is successful and the partners accept each other's projections, the intensity of narcissistic involvement is established.

One of the significant functions of dyadic narcissism within the marital relationship is to afford partners the opportunity to externalize early object-relational conflicts sustained within the intrapsychic. By projecting those unwanted aspects of the self-representation as developed in relation to internalized objects, these couples collusively and unconsciously protect themselves from narcissistic injury to their respective ego systems. As Rubinstein and Timmins (1979) pointed out, externalizing internal conflict via splitting, projection, and projective identification, the partners are partially relieved of the experienced internal-world conflict and of having to confront a pervasively low self-concept. These mutually employed mechanisms of defense and adaptation leave these couples enthralled in a morass of perpetual verbal and sometimes physical assault—all in the desperate attempt to save face with their unfulfilled sense of self.

Lansky (1981) presented another significant function inherent in the "narcissistically vulnerable" marital relationship. The periodic flare-up of unconsciously arranged blaming and blame-eliciting behaviors serves to induce the perceivably needed discord to abort any overt or covert efforts by partners to separate and seek autonomy. Intense fear of abandonment and the resulting fears of narcissistic injury, a pervasive sense of aloneness, and potential dissolution of the self induce the fearing partners to cling to each other, even if by such maladaptive means as blaming and engaging in blame-eliciting behaviors. Lansky explains:

Moves of independence are met with behavior that reestablishes even an unsatisfactory dyad as the primary focus of its members' attention. The behavior is usually felt to be symptomatic, antisocial, or frankly psychotic: infidelities broadcast to the spouse, drinking, suicide attempts, and so forth, that give one party a chance to demand, uncover, and blame—preoccupied states offering much relief in themselves when the split-off state is allowed to express itself—and the other, a chance to inflict punishment by the behavior. (p. 168)

The marital system maintains its equilibrium and sustenance, albeit at the expense of the individual partners' misery and precarious adjustment. The partners are locked into a collusive stalemate in which the maintenance of the dyadic narcissism and the marital system is of unconscious priority. Lansky concludes: "Both resume an unpleasant union, attachment to which is disowned, but attention to which is undivided and unremitting" (p. 168).

Indeed, the individuals may employ a variety of maneuvers to subjugate their partner, thereby saving the dyadic system and saving the individual from having to face the perceived inadequacy, inferiority, and incompleteness of the self. Rubinstein and Timmins (1979) and Lansky (1980–1981, 1981) noted that alternating patterns of passive and aggressive behaviors employed by both partners are characteristic of the relational patterns that are manifest in the narcissistic marriage. In the desperate attempt to acquire the narcissistic gratification that the struggling self has sought since early life, individuals will seek to acquire and exercise power over their partners; it is through this power that the narcissistic needs are met. This power takes the vacillating form of both passivity and aggression in behavioral presentation to the partner. Because these narcissistic individuals continuously experience frustration at the hands of an ungratifying partner, as previously mentioned, they tend to blame their partner for their own experienced sense of unfulfillment in the world of plenty. Narcissists firmly believe that relief from the experienced frustrations at the hands of the withholding object is to come from the marital partner and that the partner belongs solely to them.

It is the effort to claim this sense of entitlement that induces narcissists to dominate their partner through passive or aggressive behavior. Rubinstein and Timmins (1979) described a resulting type of relational patterning that transpires within the narcissistic marital relationship: Partner A projects onto partner B those disavowed and split-off aspects of oneself that are incompatible with the ego-ideal toward which partner A strives and hence, projectively identifying with those internalized aspects, comes to persecute them in partner B. Partner B, feeling equally incomplete and inadequate, as well as attacked, may introject these projections, furthering the projective-identificatory process; however, in retaliation partner B may simultaneously project an increasingly perceived lack of worthiness onto the shortcomings of partner A. Rubinstein and Timmons add:

The process of *mutual hostility,* with alternation of passivity and aggressiveness, subserves the basic dyadic narcissistic process. It is still categorized as *narcissistic,* because functionally it serves to protect and maintain the structural cohesiveness of each individual's self-esteem and self-representation. (p. 131)

· · ·

Thus, in functional terms, "passive" and "aggressive" might have a narcissistic function because they both fulfill, gratify, or complement a deficient self-image. (p. 133)

Quadrio (1982) described a marital object-relational system wherein the narcissistic husband and the depressed wife engage one another in a similar passive-aggressive stance. Referred to as the "Peter Pan and Wendy syndrome," the dyadic narcissism inherent in this relational configuration is characterized by the unfaithful husband, Peter, who seeks his narcissistic gratification aggressively through his sexual exploits. The depressive Wendy passively acknowledges Peter's quests and attributes her experienced depression to the infidelity and immaturity of her husband. Fearing abandonment, Wendy chooses to negate passively her feelings of pain and anger. While Peter pursues his narcissistic conquests, Wendy remains at home, raising the children.

In essence, both Peter and Wendy experience dreaded fears of abandonment as well as of intimacy; both experience difficulty in regulating their respective narcissistic equilibrium without the aid of the other, onto whom each can project his/her dreaded fears. For Peter, sex serves as a substitute for intimacy, and his sexual encounters in conjunction with separating himself from Wendy and their children are a passive-aggressive behavioral stance in which he can acquire and maintain omnipotent control over his own devalued sense of self and associated fears of both abandonment and engulfment leading to disintegration of the self. Wendy, who fears being alone and no longer needed as the nurturing person she is, capable of raising Peter as a child, clings to her partner for security and a sense of identity.

The underlying dynamics of this relational pattern can be surmised as follows: Peter projects onto his wife his own disavowed aspects of inadequacy as a husband and father, blaming Wendy for shutting him out of his home, leaving him to flit from sexual partner to sexual partner. In the process, Peter is able to disown his fears of genuine intimacy and attempt to match his poor self-image with the grandiosity of his ego-ideal. Peter also passively negates the feelings of anger he experiences in relation to the controlling mothering object he had experienced as a child and currently projects onto Wendy. He fears his own dependency.

Wendy, in turn, disavows her feelings of inadequacy in meeting the demands of the real world, splitting off that part of herself and projecting it onto Peter. Wendy thus identifies projectively with that aspect of herself and induces Peter to act out her own fears of real-life involvement as well as her projected, forbidden sexual impulses. Peter's affairs are vicariously experienced by Wendy, providing her pleasure while simultaneously protecting her from actualizing such desires. Her depressive condition serves as a means of holding herself and Peter together as a dyadic unit.

Both partners employ alternating patterns of passive-aggressive behavior as they become embroiled in a symbiotic relationship protecting both from feelings of inadequacy and incompleteness and fears of intimacy perceived as potential engulfment, as well as from abandonment perceived as potential emptiness and disintegration. Both have difficulty maintaining a functional narcissistic balance without the aid of the complementary role. This type of object-relational patterning typifies the dyadic narcissism that characterizes the narcissistic marriage. Lansky (1981) explains:

The vulnerable marriage, perhaps best characterized by the full-blown chronically conflictual or blaming couple, is not organized around satisfaction, enjoyment, or desire. Such marriages are organized around the containment and expression of massive rage, by the collusive exchange of projective defenses warding off the experience of inadequacy and the humiliating realization that abandonment (or even the threat) results in debilitating anxiety and fragmentation experiences. The security operations in the marriage may come entirely at the expense of satisfaction. (pp. 168–69)

The narcissistic interchange that takes place via dynamic marital transaction, as thus far described, is recognized clearly by the narcissistic qualities of the partners' personality organizations as they engage one another in mutual pursuit of their respective ego-ideals. The partners are used as the medium through which they struggle to secure the embodiment of integrity and self-sufficiency. Misguidedly, they strive to find themselves, so to speak, through the mirroring of the other by which, in order to establish the self, the partners refuse to acknowledge each other as a significant object. Couples subject themselves to mutual offensive and defensive transactional maneuvering through which they encapsulate themselves in perpetual degradation and open warfare. Neither can empathize with or substantiate the other.

The schism that this pattern of marital object relations generates, and with which the relationship is symmetrized in seemingly infinite embattlement, behooves one to observe with awe the resiliency and longevity of the relationship system. Precariously self-perceived individuals struggle in benevolence to find the ideal self within the context of a complementary partner relationship in which neither objectively perceives the other as anyone or anything other than an extension of himself/herself. Although the contextual relationship remains the same, the narcissistic dynamism described by Willi (1982) illuminates a varied pattern of transaction in which the partners complement one another in their mutual striving for their respective ego-ideals. The element of complementarity inherent in this relational configuration is indicative of the indomitable skill with which individuals unconsciously select their prospective marital partners and collude in ongoing relationship.

Willi (1982) believes that frequently one encounters a marital relationship in which the "narcissist" and the "complementary narcissist" share in the narcissistic element of their respective personality organizations, although the manifestations of the pathogenic narcissism present are diametrically opposed yet are defensively and complementarily congruent. The partners narrowly perceive the relationship in terms of necessitating that either partner lives through, or is lived through by, the other. Mutually and unconsciously chosen partners of low self-concept and tenuous narcissistic balance seek to improve and dignify their self-perceived inferiority through the object of complementary narcissists.

Narcissists come to admire themselves with fervent grandiosity as complementary narcissists sacrifice themselves to substantiate that glorified image. Complementary narcissists explicitly and overtly, albeit implicitly and covertly in collusion with the narcissistic partner, sacrifice their individuality and personhood to their partner. Complementary narcissists project their own unattainable ego-ideal onto the narcissist, forming an identification with, and living through, the idealized substitute for the empty self. Narcissists willfully introject the partner's idealized image and live it out for both the partner and themselves. Willi (1982) notes:

> The partners complement each other in terms of an ideal. The narcissist experiences the idealizing of the complementary narcissist as decisive self-development and can feel grandiose. The complementary narcissist is happy to be able to identify with the narcissist. Both feel sure of their defenses. (p. 73)

The partners need not worry about the remaining unwanted, inferior aspects of themselves, since they may easily be repressed, denied, or externalized through the mechanism of projection onto a third party (e.g., the children or the extrafamilial world at large).

In this collusively designed and processed pattern of marital interaction, complementary narcissists identify solidly and projectively with the idealized self-image that they have failed to attain, and hence attribute to their partner. Narcissistic partners in turn identify with that same idealized image projected onto them by their partner. Thus the partners form an identification with the same ego-ideal, however illusive and elusive the ego-ideal may come to be. Willi (1982) summarizes this conceptual scheme involving narcissists and complementary narcissists:

Both manifest the same disturbance, namely a weak definition of the self and a sense of inferiority. It is only the defense mechanism or the means to come to terms with the weak self that is different: the narcissist tries to upgrade his inferior self through the partner, while the complementary narcissist tries to appropriate an idealized self from the partner. (p. 71)

In this scheme, the partners feel precariously self-enhanced in their subjection to the otherwise inferior and unfulfilled aspects of their identities.

Within the confines of the recognizably distorted and unbalanced interchange, as workable as it may to a certain degree be, the balance of power appears to favor narcissists. Narcissists entice their partner to relinquish their individuality in service to their own depleted self. This maintains insofar as narcissists willfully contain and live out the ego-ideal that they have internalized through an introjectory mechanism from the complementary narcissist. However, as typically ensues in this pattern of relationship, the balance of power almost imperceptibly reverses to favor the complementary narcissist. Insofar as the narcissist's newly discovered grandiose self is contingent in quality on the nature of the partner's idealizing projections, complementary narcissists have acquired control over the emotional, cognitive, and behavioral experiences of their narcissistic partner. As Willi (1982) explains, the complementary narcissist

merges with the narcissist, penetrates him and exercises strong control over him precisely because, paradoxically, she forfeits her own self-image. Finally, it is no longer clear whose self-worth is being enhanced and who is borrowing a self-image from whom. (p. 72)

The once-shared ego-ideal comes to be more under the influence of the complementary narcissist, who may restrain the narcissist from the autonomy that the latter once enjoyably maintained:

[The narcissist] . . . may try to differentiate himself from the complementary narcissist but he is becoming steadily more imprisoned in his partner's imagined ideal. He may try to defend himself by degrading, rejecting or destroying her. (Willi 1982, p. 74)

As narcissists reproach the increasingly restrictive confines of the idealizing partner for fear of being engulfed by the powerful loved object, complementary narcissists seek to merge with the partner with whom they identify worthiness, to be at one with the idealized, loved object. Narcissists feel frightened and angry; complementary narcissists feel hurt and dejected. Both fall prey to their own individual and systemic defensive organizations.

=12=

Familial Object Relations and the Task of Separation-Individuation

The normative psychological and psychosocial procurement of individuation and autonomous function transpires within the first three years of the human life. The "separation-individuation" (Mahler, Pine, and Bergman 1975) process is characterized by the gradual, sequential unfolding of the human child as a distinct and acknowledgeable person, or self, psychologically perceived as being separate from the object of the mother. From within the matrix of the mother-child bond, the child acquires the capability of forming and maintaining a mental representation of both the self and the object, facilitating the acquisition of object constancy, wherewith the child is able to evoke by the thirty-sixth month of life a mental image of the libidinal object in the physical absence of the object. Blos (1967) contends that the conceptually parallel process of identity formation in adolescence, culminating in the disengagement from previously maintained family ties and the formation of extrafamilial object relations, is in essence a "second individuation process." Recapitulating the first course of individuation, adolescents liberate from the infantile objects of the internal world and establish new external object relations of both libidinal and aggressively tinged qualities with significant others of the adult world. Blos compares the two normative processes of individuation:

What is in infancy a "hatching from the symbiotic membrane to become an individuated toddler" (Mahler, 1963), becomes in adolescence the shedding of family dependencies, the loosening of infantile object ties in order to become a member of society at large or, simply, of the adult world. (p. 163)

In the first separation-individuation phase of intrapsychic and interpersonal development, young children develop stable and differentiated self-concepts and object concepts through the process of internalizing the mothering object's empathic concern and soothing services, leading to, in Blos's (1967) words, "formation of internal regulatory capacities which are assisted and promoted by maturational—especially motor, perceptual, verbal, and cognitive—advances" (pp. 163–64). Children, throughout the early years of life, rely on the ego systems of the parents for support and nourishment of their as yet underdeveloped and weak ego structure. The parents serve as supportive extensions of their ego, aiding children in functionally regulating their narcissistic equilibrium, in controlling experienced tension and anxiety, and in leveling mood vacillations.

In the second separation-individuation phase of adolescence, the internal regulatory faculties of the ego system are ideally developed and sophisticated to the extent that adolescents are capable of relinquishing the aforementioned infantile object ties in favor of the formation of extrafamilial object relations and the attainment of genital primacy in heterosexual relationship. As the adolescent ego consolidates and the opposing "good" and "bad" ego states coalesce in collateral connection with the internal "good" and "bad" objects (Kernberg 1976), identity formation is finalized. As Blos (1967) maintains, "Not until the termination of adolescence do self and object representations acquire stability and firm boundaries, i.e., they become resistant to cathectic shifts" (p. 163). The construction of a fully autonomous, functioning self is contingent on liberation from earlier internalized infantile objects and object relations. Blos continues:

A growing capacity of reality testing went parallel with the repudiation of infantile ego positions, thus enlarging the scope of the autonomous ego.

The disengagement from the infantile object is always paralleled by ego maturation. The reverse is true, namely, that adolescent inadequacy or impairment of ego functions is symptomatic of drive fixations and infantile object dependencies. The accumulative ego alterations that parallel drive progression in each adolescent phase accrue in a structural innovation that is identified here as the second individuation. (p. 165)

Drive progressions characterize the pubertal experiences, and the newly attained genital primacy beckons the adolescent to seek extrafamilial libidinal objects with which to engage. Instinctual urge necessitates the formation of new object relations, since the impulses at the puberty stage revolve around earlier experiences of oedipal anxiety that, not fully resolved, lie dormant during latency, only to be unconsciously rekindled at puberty in accordance with psychobiological changes. In defensive stature, in confrontation with these incestuous stirrings, adolescents disengage from relationships with familial objects. Sandler and Freud (1985) suggest that "the general hostility to instinct is usually first directed against incestuous fantasies, and as a result the ego turns against the members of his family as though they were strangers" (p. 480).

The renunciation of familial objects is the normative process wherein adolescents acquire ego-identity and a place in the adult object world. However, this process presents adolescents with experienced ambivalence of potentially problematic proportions. Adolescents' diminished cathexis of parental and sibling objects is indeed faciliated by the fear of unconscious incestual strivings; yet adolescents are placed in a state of quandary in face of ambivalence concerning autonomy versus dependence. They entertain the fantasy of regression to a dependent, infantile state while simultaneously defending against the wish by repudiating parental objects. Sandler and Freud (1985) believe that "this puts the conflict between the wish to be an adult and the wish to be a child at the center of the adolescent's internal concerns" (p. 468). Ideally adolescents will be able to contend with the experienced fear of helplessness and proceed with the normative decathexis of familial objects in favor of other external object relations.

The process by which adolescents liberate themselves from the influence of parental ties and internalized object relations will come at a variable degree of expense for both them and their parents. Adolescents experience a certain degree of helplessness in the quest for independence. The parents will face their children's degradation and devaluation of them as adolescents defy the previously accepted parental authority and value system in the search for autonomy and self-definition. Prior to the advent of adolescence, children admire and idealize the attributes of the parents, which they proceed to imitate as well as internalize. The parents facilitate the children's idealization of them as the normative means by which the children progressively organize an image of the self and therewith formulate an identity (Kohut 1971). As children's ego-identity and sense of self emerge with increasing strength and maturity, their experiences of adolescence come to more or less equilibrate with the experiences of the parents. Skynner (1976) explains that the idealization of parents in childhood

is followed after a certain period by a phase of withdrawal, of separation, of more realistic perception of the other who appears to have lost the previous enviable advantages precisely *because* they have to some degree been obtained and a greater objectivity is therefore possible because the relationship is more equal, more on a level. (p. 157)

The parents are faced with the unenviable yet challenging task of withstanding their adolescent children's criticism and verbal attacks, physical and emotional withdrawal, and new object choices.

In this light, parents are subject to assuming the role of providing a supportive context within which adolescents can differentiate themselves functionally from their parents. Assuming that the parents were successful in providing a "holding environment" (Winnicott 1965) for their young children in early object-relational experiences, wherein the adventurous toddlers were supported in their quest for autonomy and independence, they are called on once again, in the second individuation process, to facilitate the emancipation of their adolescent children from the protective parent-child union. The adolescents' experiences of felt or actual parental failures in facilitating age-appropriate differentiation and independence with empathic support impede their maturation of ego functions and formation of an identity. Adolescents' psychosocial task of establishing an ego-identity, as conceptualized by Erikson (1956), is subject to great influence by the specific parent-adolescent interactional patterns that manifest during this potentially tenuous stage of family life. R. Shapiro (1967) notes that

the relationships within the family then become psychosocial events contributing to identity consolidation or diffusion, and these events can be observed with the hypothesis that they constitute important determinants of adolescent disturbance. (p. 223)

The parents' perceptions of and attitudes toward their adolescent children's bid for autonomy and self-definition become a significant factor in the success or failure of this vital task. Stierlin (1977) speaks of the profound influence that parents maintain on the potential development of their adolescent children's ego autonomy:

Perceptions and expectations bearing on separation, therefore, carry the greatest leverage because they determine [the adolescent's] susceptibility to all other parental perceptions and expectations. They entail a meta-message or meta-perception about these other perceptions. They convey to the adolescent how his parents perceive and judge his confidence and capacity either to heed or turn away from these parents themselves! They contain a message about his ability to liberate himself from his parents and thereby to immunize himself against what they—his parents—think, say, and want that might conflict with that message. (p. 173)

In recognition that "there are few situations in life which are more difficult to cope with than an adolescent son or daughter during the attempt to liberate themselves" (A. Freud 1958, p. 276), one also acknowledges the equally precarious position that adolescents maintain in their quest for independence. In mutual influence, adolescents and their parents engage one another as they collectively traverse this tenuous stage of family-life development. Stierlin (1977) stresses this reciprocity of influence:

We conceive of separation in adolescence as part of a continuous movement toward relative mutual individuation in which parents *and* children participate. The ultimate aim is mature *interdependence* of the parties. (p. 173)

One can transcend the constricted analysis of parent-child dyadic transactions, mutually influential as they indeed are, to broaden the scope of investigation to the family group in its entirety. Viewing the family system as a continuously evolving configuration—wherein each member plays an integral role in its dynamic process and wherein changes in any one element necessarily effect change in all other elements as new behaviors reverberate throughout the system—behooves one to acknowledge the propensity of the family either to facilitate its own maturational evolution or to impede the system in potentially dangerous stagnation. E. Shapiro (1982–1983) recognizes that

the failure of the holding environment, as defined by inaccurate or unresponsive parental empathic sensitivity to the adolescent's developmental needs, is determined not by one pathological relationship, but by a *shared* family regression. . . . In this regression, a re-creation of the failure of the early holding environment, family members respond to autonomous or dependent needs . . . or narcissistic needs . . . with withdrawal, retaliation, or empathic failure. (p. 212)

Adolescent experience recapitulates early familial object-relational experiences of separation and individuation, revitalizing issues surrounding autonomy and the family's ability to foster or inhibit the expression of independence. The task of separation-individuation does indeed belong to the family as a systemic whole.

According to R. Shapiro, Zinner, Berkowitz, and E. Shapiro (1975) the specific developmental, phase-appropriate task of the family is to foster adolescents' acquisition of competence and ego-autonomous functionability and to encourage psychological differentiation in a behavioral and emotional context "regulated by the reality principle and mediated primarily through secondary process thinking" (p. 90). Zinner and E. Shapiro (1975) summarize:

With regard to the evolution of an ego identity in the developing child, the family group as a group, not merely its component members, must provide a "holding environment" in which the group itself "survives" the instinctual demands and angry assaults of the child without, in retaliation, cutting off sources of gratification. (p. 106)

Insofar as the family system is capable of providing the holding environment necessary to facilitate functionally successful disengagement by its adolescent members from the familial orbit, while simultaneously maintaining the provision of emotional support and empathic concern, adolescents will acquire and maintain the necessary ego autonomy and differentiation essential for the solidification of an integrated sense of identity and selfhood and a functional position in the adult object world. As Zinner and E. Shapiro (1975) explain, the failure of the family system

to accomplish this task prevents the development of the capacity for ego autonomy, ambivalence, mourning, and concern (authentic guilt), all of which are contingent on integration of "good" and "bad" self- and object representations. (pp. 106–07)

Insofar as adolescents are able to consolidate an identity through the integration of contradictory self-images and parallel object images to which the ego attaches in relationship, they proceed through the normative developmental stages with an increasingly clear self-definition. Because this process is necessarily contingent on the facilitating role of the family system, the family in its entirety progresses through this arduous phase of the life cycle. The family as a group, not merely its adolescent members, evolves maturationally as a progressive, constructive, and productive system. Likewise, should the family fail to facilitate this growth of its own system, not only the adolescents but the entire family stagnates in a morass of defensive projections and introjections perpetuated mutually and collusively in the family's benevolent yet maladaptive attempts at restitution. Family interactional patterning therewith is characterized by primary-process cognitive processing and governed primarily by the pleasure principle.

The stagnation of object-relational patterning at the stage marked by the advent of adolescence and the vicissitudes it inherently presents assumes a characteristic colored by irrational and magical reasoning. Intrapsychic and intrafamilial cognitive processing is governed by shared family fantasies and assumptions, which for the most part remain unconscious to the family members. Parents who have processed their marriage in collusive, complementary transaction establish an emotional and cognitive interactional process within which children are induced to cooperate from birth. Meissner (1978a) claims:

From birth onward, these parentally derived pressures play upon the child's own instinctual needs to embed him in the family system as a collusive participant in the process of responding to and fulfilling unconscious parental needs. (p. 75)

The family history of object relations is built on and maintains adherence to this emotional and cognitive interactional process. This process plays a significant role in the object-relational configurations revolving around the first separation-individuation phase of toddlerhood, and the pattern is revived, based on the same family fantasies and assumptions, at adolescence. Meissner suggests that the family's interactive involvement emanates from an earlier object-relational climate, which maintains in continuous evolution. The foundation on which this object relational climate evolves derives from the unresolved intrapsychic conflicts of each parent, and their tendency to act out their internal-world conflicts in their external object relations. To the extent that children are subject to internalization of parental projections and projective identifications, their personality organization and ego functioning will be negatively influenced. R. Shapiro (1979) notes:

Unconscious assumptions are assumed to derive from the internalized developmental experience of both of the parents in their families of origin. An organization of motives and defenses evolves, then, in the marriage, which is operative throughout the development of the child and adolescent. Depending upon their centrality and coerciveness as the family develops, unconscious assumptions are powerful determinants of disturbance in the maturing child and adolescent. (p. 186)

Should the family have failed to provide the soothing functions of an adequate holding environment during the individuation of toddlerhood, the family will have difficulty in facilitating its now adolescent children's striving for autonomy and independence. Unable to establish a functionally integrated and consolidated sense of self, the children, throughout the maturational progression, will remain under the strong influence of the sustaining presence of the familial object-relational climate. The family's unconscious fantasies and assumptions inhibit its completion of developmental tasks, one of which is the liberation of its adolescent members. Behavioral and verbal communication within the family system may become so laden with powerful affective content, individually disowned and displaced onto other members, that the adolescents are rendered incapable of responding realistically to the parents' requests and demands, and are unable to convey effectively their needs and desires to the parents (E. Shapiro, 1982–1983). R. Shapiro et al. (1975) expand on the conceptualization of shared unconscious family fantasies and assumptions:

[F]amily behavior is determined by shared unconscious fantasies mobilized more by instinctual needs or defensive requirements within the family than by realistic developmental considerations. Family functioning determined by unconscious assumptions may be mobilized when behavior appropriate to a new phase of development is initiated. Anxiety, regressive and defensive behaviors, disturbances in communication, and interference in the family's reality functioning ensue, resulting in serious failures in family task performance with regard to the development of the child or adolescent. (p. 90)

In face of the group task of adolescent separation-individuation, the family governed by these unrealistic fantasies and assumptions succumbs to a regressive state, wherein the adolescent's ego fails to attain mature functioning, and the family ego fails to fulfill the developmental tasks of its membership.

Thus it becomes evident that each and every member of the family plays an integral role in the formation and evolution of the distorted reality of the system, just as the individual members and the family as a whole are affected by the system's internal workings. This phenomenon is likened to a dramatic play by Zinner and E. Shapiro (1975): "Within the family group the shared fantasies are played out by members who are both implicitly and explicitly assigned roles in the unconscious family drama" (p. 107). Brodey (1959) concurs, presenting this analogy between the family's dramatization and the medieval morality play:

The family drama is unlike the modern theater. It is more like the morality play of medieval times. Actors take allegorical role positions that are stereotyped and confined—one is Good; another, Evil; a third, Temptation. Though the interactions of these roles are rigidly ritualized and limited, still the play has an impelling quality which tends to drive the audience into complete involvement, sharing with the actors in forgetting the complexities of life, perceiving only in terms of Good or Evil, Power or Helplessness, Omnipotence or Infantalism, and losing entirely the breadth of perspective, shading, and sense of impinging reality which are a usual part of everyday life. (p. 382)

The very essence of the interactional climate is founded on the magical qualities of primary process wherein all perceptions are distorted as deemed necessary to rationalize and legitimize the pseudo reality with which the family collusively processes in a defensive, adaptive attempt to legitimize its existence.
Brodey (1959) comments:

Within the family circle *accurate* reality testing would chiefly reinforce the continued
cathexis of primitive primary-process mechanisms and give reduced reinforcement to
the development of ego functioning and secondary process as ordinarily conceived. (p.
394)

Because the family shares in the ongoing current of mutual denial, idealization,
splitting, introjection, projection, and projective-identificatory mechanistic interchange, and also shares in the design and perpetuation of a quasi-functional
unified synergy, Richter (1976) believes that the "inner structure is determined
by a *homogenous pathological principle*. Each member of the family shares in
a similar pathological fantasy" (p. 389).

The means by which the family system prevails in its dysfunctional, albeit
maintainable, pattern of object-relational transaction is the formulation of and
adherence to a similarly shared family value system. Relationships within the
family assume a very rigidly stylized manner wherein similarity and complementarity are mutually stressed to the exclusion of conflictual or contradictory
emotional, cognitive, and behavioral presentation. As Meissner (1984) says,
"Relatedness is maintained in a fragile and inauthentic form by the avoidance
of differences or by desperate attempts to convince the other of one's point of
view or to justify oneself in the other's eyes" (p. 417).

The family's transactional manifestations assume a flavor that Lidz, Fleck,
and Cornelison (1965) referred to as "masking," an interactional phenomenon
wherein family members collusively deceive themselves and extrafamilial others in a dire attempt to conceal a potentially disrupting event or situation within
the unmentioning confines of the family system. The matter is spoken of neither within nor outside the family. To facilitate the outright denial or disavowal
of the event or situation, the family behaves as if the system were a unified,
benevolently concerned, and need-fulfilling amalgamation.

The family picture is akin to what Wynne, Ryckoff, Day, and Hirsch (1958)
describe as "pseudo-mutuality"—a shared family fantasy based on the presentation of a conflict-free, harmonious, ever-so-caring, and loving group of individuals comprising a happy family. These types of shared unconscious family
fantasies, or "family myths" (Ferreira 1963), serve the function of maintaining
the system in homeostatic balance as it precariously confronts real-life crises
and normative family-life tasks such as the emancipation of adolescent children.

Insofar as the shared unconscious family fantasies and assumptions are conducive to the lack of differentiation of the members, differences of emotional, cognitive, and behavioral experiences will be avoided. Meissner (1984) notes:

[A]ny movement in the direction of individuation or of the acknowledgment of differences or any attempt at confrontation and authentic conflict may be labeled as betrayal of the inherent values of the family system—a radical form of treason the proper punishment of which can only be isolation and abandonment. (p. 417)

Insofar as the family system is comprised of functionally differentiated, fully autonomous, individuated persons whose reliance on one another is strictly of a healthy, interdependent nature, the family will not be subject to the necessity of selectively role-typing individual members in accordance with unconscious fantasies and assumptions. Disagreements, varying interests, and intrafamilial and extrafamilial conflicts are all freely acknowledged and confronted in a primarily democratic manner wherein each member is fully recognized, affirmed, and empathized with. The aforementioned shared, unconscious family fantasies and assumptions are the manifested results of two individuals, both unsuccessfully differentiated from their respective families of origin, joined in matrimony, and thereafter processing an intrasystemic array of defensive and adaptive interpersonal transactions.

Each and every induction into the family system is presented by the parents with an implicitly or explicitly determined complementary role with which the family system can sustain and equilibrate itself, however dysfunctional the sustenance and equilibration may be. The adolescent members of this system of familial object relations are susceptible to the growth-inhibiting influence of the family ego system in which they play a collusively integral role. The family system becomes stuck in its self-perpetuating dynamic array of defensive and adaptive interplay; and the adolescents are likely to bear the brunt of the family's manifest symptomatology.

The dynamic collusion in which each and every family member contributes to the family regression is organized and governed by the shared unconscious fantasies and assumptions historically evident in the family's ongoing operation and existence. The processing of such illusion and irrationality is powerfully maintained. A focalized family fantasy and assumption, as described by Brodey (1959), is that of the mystical and unquestionable presence of a supreme "force" or omniscience and nurturance that provides the very nourishment with which the family thrives:

It is as though the family relationship exists within a clearly drawn circle, enclosing a system of narcissistic relationships. It is a family myth that whoever steps outside this reciprocal system steps into outer space, to float abandoned outside the "life-sustaining" circle of family relationships. It is observed that the symptomatic family member, in his efforts to leave the family, may be defeated by his need to direct his efforts, primarily, toward the denial of this myth. (p. 390)

In this case, the life-sustaining nourishment is perceived by the family as emanating from within the very essence of the family—the ever-so-benevolently-concerned interrelationships. R. Shapiro (1979) noted that denial of the family's fantasy implies defiance of intrasystem authority, which remains unquestionable in its link to the omnipotence of the system. Denial of the family's fantasy, according to R. Shapiro et al. (1975), also implies the comparison of the inner family reality with the reality of the extrafamilial world—a world that the family vehemently fights or from which the family makes desperate flight. Zinner (1978) pointed out that aggressive action generated by the family—action that does not serve the purpose of protection from external reality—is promptly designated by the system as being potentially destructive and thus is promptly dismantled. The experience and expression of anger within the confines of the family unity are similarly deemed to be destructive to the integrity of the system and its caring internal transactions.

R. Shapiro et al. (1975) suggested that in this type of system the family members are sharing in the irrational assumption that the family in essence "exists for satisfaction of dependency needs and wishes (basic assumption dependency)" p. 91. E. Shapiro (1978) elucidated with a clinical example of a family family whose members mutually assume, and perpetuate in fantasy, that depression and its associated experiences of helplessness and hopelessness are unbearable and unsupportable in the relational context: "Family members protect themselves by localizing these affects in one family member and repudiating him" (pp. 370–71). So are the family members selected and renounced if they act out or, conversely, excessively restrain, experienced impulse. As Zinner and R. Shapiro (1974) put it, there prevail within the family "unconscious assumptions in which impulse expression is equated with messiness and sexual license, and loss of control and inhibition of impulse is equated with inadequacy" (p. 185). The family fantasy dictates that any deviance from the arena of commonality that the family presents to the external world must be thwarted and reintegrated into the family delineations.

In reference to families with adolescent members, faced with the task of facilitating supportive differentiation and independence of their maturing children and siblings, the system, inclusive of the adolescents, may succumb to the regressive group transactions that directly defy this natural developmental transition. Independent thinking and behavior on the part of the adolescents are viewed by the family as evidence of disclaiming the family and are taken as a personal affront to the integrity of the group. Zinner and E. Shapiro (1975) explain:

The loss through maturation of certain children is experienced by the family as a hateful abandonment. Independence is not seen, at levels of unconscious group fantasy, as a desirable goal for the adolescent but rather as a rejection and devaluation of the group. The youngster is experienced as leaving the family because he hates it. A fantasy evolves that if the family became more "good" or satisfying to the adolescent and purged itself of those "bad" qualities that cause him to wish to grow up, then perhaps he would, after all, remain. (p. 110)

Family fantasies and assumptions become self-perpetuating and increasingly irrational as the family falls prey to its own defensive and self-defeating mechanistic stature. Kolb and Shapiro (1982) describe the plight of the runaway adolescent who, in experienced ambivalence concerning dependency and autonomy, is confronted with a family that becomes

panicked by the adolescent's pseudoautonomous moves, because these are interpreted as evidence that the family is "bad." . . . The family's response to a runaway is to sacrifice the integrity of the family and to "get the adolescent back at all costs." This posture is one that meets the defensive needs of the parents but fails to acknowledge the conflicted state of the adolescent. (p. 351)

The family's task is to promote in its adolescent members ego-autonomous functioning and an integrated and stable sense of identity, wherewith the adolescent will develop a perception of the self as differentiated from and maturely interdependent with the familial system. The interdependence is hence characteristic of the contextual change with which the system sustains yet advances to a higher level of organization. Adolescents mature into an age-appropriate, object-relational configuration with parents and siblings in which they relate to the parents with an established sense of equity. Insofar as adolescents are supported by their evolving familial context in the establishment of spontaneity and assertion in object relations, they will command the respect and affirmation so deserved and earned. The family as a whole will reap its rewards through successful confrontation with yet another challenging developmental milestone.

=====13=====

Familial Object-Relational Role Typing

The dramatization of the family organization is dictated by the unconscious fantasies and basic assumptions that the family members share in collusive interchange and proliferation. The fantasies and assumptions are in turn generated by the instinctual tendencies primarily, though not exclusively, of the parents and the defensive organization of each member individually as well as of the entire family system collectively. These contributory factors form a design for a "hidden agenda" with which the family group implements the undertaking of developmental tasks. Zinner and R. Shapiro (1972) explain:

[S]mall group behaviour is determined both by shared unconscious fantasies and more reality-oriented secondary-process thinking directed towards the fulfillment of particular tasks.

We view the family as such a small group, and, more metaphorically, as the cast of the drama, the themes of which are some combination of adaptive and functional family "work" tasks and a variety of generally unconscious fantasies, or covert assumptions, often conceived of as if they were a "hidden agenda." (p. 523)

Each family member colludes in the attempt of the family system to realize its unconscious fantasies. The family members in cooperation implicitly and covertly determine specific role types for each member to assume and act out in the family drama.

The characterization of the family drama, as determined by the nature of the unquestionable unconscious fantasies and assumptions, is the result of early object-relational experiences of the soon-to-be parents as they initially forge their marital bond. Marital object choice and object-relational process are governed by the instinctual fantasied needs and wishes of each partner, as each strives to actualize these fantasies and acquire gratification via the complementarity of the other. This reciprocal and mutually dependent interchange establishes the foundation on which the hidden agenda is initially constructed. Each new induction into the membership of the family system is subject to the influence of the established yet evolving family drama, and the family drama is equally and simultaneously affected by the integral role that the new member assumes. Zinner and R. Shapiro (1972) elucidate this universal, object-relational phenomenon:

Prior to their birth, children are introduced into the covert assumptions of family life in their parents' fantasies, and from birth onward, a variety of parental coercions interact with the child's own instinctual requirements to fix him as a collusive participant in the family's hidden agenda. (p. 523)

The family drama is propelled into action with the advent of marriage, and it evolves in kaleidoscopic configuration, in which each member is assigned, often before joining the system, a given role that is played out actively in obligation to the ongoing object-relational current of the family process.

The intricacies of human communication and interaction that almost imperceptibly transpire within the dynamic realm of the family process render the family members, individually and collectively, unwitting participants in their collusive and potentially destructive transaction. To shed some light on these universal yet idiosyncratic intricacies, and therewith illuminate the salient features of the family synergism, one would do well to explore the intrapsychic and interpersonal elements inherent in personality organization and development. To punctuate as a reference point both the conscious and the unconscious meanings of parenthood and the associated interchanges of the parent-child dyad, we acquire insight into how and why the unconscious family drama originates and processes.

The vicissitudes of parenthood play a profound role not only in the psychological development of children but also in the evolving personality organization of the parent. Benedek (1959) conceived of parenthood as being a normative developmental phase inherent in the life-cycle progression of the human being. Schwartz (1984) concurs with Benedek's conceptualization:

Complex in itself, parenthood cannot be understood in isolation from the total personality with its various lines of development. Parenthood is an integral part of a parent's personality, influencing and influenced by all aspects of the parent as a person. (p. 358)

Benedek contends that the intensity, in quality and nature, of parent-child interaction is such that it triggers in parents earlier object-relational experiences with their parents in the same developmental stage. Current parent-child interaction effects a resurgence of both positive, healthy object relations and those characterized by conflict. Dysfunctional object relations, internalized during earlier experiences and sustained within the intrapsychic, emerge from suppression or repression in intensified form, to be externalized into the realm of parent-child interpersonal transaction. Insofar as the parents have failed fully to differentiate the self from the parental objects of early object relations and have failed to integrate conflicting good and bad aspects of the self and of significant others, they will relive the unresolved symbiotic tie of past experience in current relations with their children. Zinner and E. Shapiro (1975) state that "Early in their life, and often even before birth, certain children are 'chosen' by a parent to participate in a reenactment of the parent's own early object relations with his parent" (p. 110).

In this phenomenological process, according to Schwartz (1984), the parents form an identification with the children wherein the parents perceive the children similarly to the way they experience themselves as having been as a child at the same developmental stage. Concurrently, the parents also identify with their own parents and experience themselves similarly to the way they perceive their parents as having been during their parents' parenthood experiences. These two identificatory processes intertwine to generate a given emotional climate in the parent-child interaction. Meissner (1984) uses the example of past and present father-child object relations to explain this experience:

The emotional relationship of father and child thus derives from both the father's identification with the child and his identification with his own father. Normally, these two levels of internalization are complementary and are integrated into the fathering experience. Identification with the child serves as a basis for paternal empathy, while identification with the father's own father shapes the internalized norms both culturally and personally of what it means to be a father. (p. 402)

The internalization of conflictual object relations with one's parents will be, on the advent of one's parenthood, externalized via a projective mechanism onto the new parents' children, rendering the new parents incapable of, among other things, empathizing adequately with the children in a reality sense and providing an adequate holding environment. Schwartz (1984) discusses the inherent consequences for both the child and the parent:

Regressive identifications in the parent annul the conscious good intentions toward the child and the consequences for the child (and parent) are disturbances in self identity, self and object differentiation, and object relations in regard to dyadic and triadic levels of psychic organization, as well as neurotic solutions in regard to sexuality, aggression, guilt, and shame. (p. 367)

Effective parenting and the smooth procession through the progressive developmental phases of parenthood require in parents the capability of maintaining a healthy identification with their children—an identification from which the parents' internal representations of the children and of the self are differentiated enough to permit the intrapsychic conceptualizations of the children as selves fully differentiated from the self of the parent. Schwartz (1984) adds:

Intrapsychically the child is differentiated from the parent and other children, although the psychic representations of the child change over time. The parent integrates the representations of the child of the past with the child of the present and those images of the potential and wished for child. . . . (p. 362)

Schwartz states further that parents ideally are able to maintain a stable and consistent, albeit continually evolving and maturing, internal representation of the children. In addition, the parents ideally are able to maintain a distinction between their representation of the self in early object-relational experiences and the representations of the children in current experiences. Similarly, when parents are able to differentiate adequately the selves of the children from their own selves of the past, a potentially destructive transference reaction is prevented from transpiring in current parent-child relations.

In recognition that dysfunctional identifications and negative transference phenomena can, and do, pathologically infiltrate the evolving parent-child relations, which leads to defensive adaptation in the relational context, it would be well to acknowledge that healthy identificatory and transference reactions can equally and conversely enrich the quality and nature of the empathic relationship between parents and children. Effective ego and superego functioning can be transmitted from generation to generation via the facilitation of a selfobject as easily as can pathological defensive and adaptive ego mechanism be employed. In fact, the vicissitudes of parenthood can provide parents with the means by which to correct or resolve conflictual internalized object relations through current object-relational experiences with their own children. Elson (1984) explains:

[M]aturer forms of narcissism—as increased empathy with childhood needs, increased wisdom and creativity, and specifically the *ability to respond to the child as a center of perception and initiative*—now permit the parents to perform their caretaking functions without unempathic intrusion of their own conflicts. The parental self may be sorely taxed by intrapsychic or interpersonal events, but it is as parents offer themselves as precursors of psychic structure that the forming self of the child is supported and that parents may be able to fill in their own earlier deficits or distortions or manage more effectively with what they now learn about themselves. (p. 298–99)

The discussion thus far has investigated the identificatory processes by which the parents and their children can either learn and grow or stagnate in defensive relationship as a dyadic entity. However, of equally great significance, both the children and the parents identify with one another as integral components of the psychosocial context. Not only is the object of the single person identified with through the internalization process, but it is also the entire context of that person that is internalized by the subject. Framo (1982c) describes the internalization process of the child:

[I]ntrojects are not only based on a one-to-one relationship to the mother and father as individuals, but on the nature of the marriage relationship between the parents; on the *psychological* mother and father of the family; on the family itself, including the sibling system. In other words, a whole family system—its emotions, its codes, its style—is sometimes introjected. (p. 74)

The children's internally formed representations of the relational context of which they are an integral part constitute the identification from which ego strength and function are acquired. The mother, for example, serves as the external object with which the children identify, internalize into the representational world, and utilize as a provider of soothing, regulatory functions. "But," Stierlin (1977) warns, "more is involved here than the relation between two persons, for the way the mother relates to her child depends, in turn, on how she fits into the whole family and, in particular, how she relates to her husband" (p. 163). Boszormenyi-Nagy (1965b) provides an illustration of the internalization of the family relational system:

The growing child can respond to its parent's actions with either identificatory imitation and fusion or reciprocal complementation and differentiation. The little girl identifies not only with mother's femininity but also with her coquetry vis-à-vis her father or males in general. In other words, the little girl learns the feminine role vicariously through both an identification model and the latter's complementary role or relational context. Thus, according to the dialectical principle, each Self-referent agent depends on a conscious or unconscious Not-Self-referent as its context. Certain aspects of our person are grounded in a reciprocal or complementary relationship to a whole family's— not just to one person's—mode of functioning. (p. 42)

The emotional climate of mother-child object relations has been punctuated by psychoanalytic investigations in the quest for learning about the process in which children's ego, or sense of self, formulates and matures. Adding the fathering object to the mother-child matrix, and later the family system in its entirety, there is a new and more complex dimension in the object-relational configuration. Abelin (1975) investigated the role in which the father can either facilitate or impede the process of separation-individuation in toddlerhood. The father assumes a significant role in providing the toddler an organizing experience with which the child can functionally disengage itself from the mother-child symbiosis and therewith formulate a sense of identity and selfhood. Abelin (1975) clarifies:

To that experience I had given the name of *"early triangulation,"* indicating thereby that the toddler had had to apprehend and internalize the *relationship between* his two most cathected objects, father and mother. (p. 293)

. . .

Situations are thus bound to occur in which father and mother are experienced by the child as relating to *each other.* (p. 293)

The father provides the same dyadic, mirroring relationship to the adventurous and liberating toddler that the mother provides, permitting the child temporarily to replace mothering-object cathexis with cathexis of the fathering object, therewith facilitating differentiation of the child's self from the loved objects. The child transgresses the symbiotic orbit of the mother-child dyad, thereby coming to internalize not only admired aspects of the mother and its relationship to her but also gratifying aspects of the father and the relationship with him or, perhaps of most importance, the dyadic relationship between mother and father and the triadic relationship between self, mother, and father.

The indelible intricacies inherent in the internal processing of family life have been investigated. We have acknowledged the profound impact that the emotional experience of the marital and family systems has on the emergence of children's selfhood and identity as well as the reciprocal effects of the children and of parenthood on the evolving identities of the parental partners. Family members are acutely sensitive to the nuances and intricacies of the family emotional climate of which they are a part, and they internalize and process the object-relational configurations of the family system. The means by which this phenomenon transpires constitutes the hidden agenda with which the family maps its journey into the trials and tribulations of family life. Role typing and the assignment of functions become necessary components of the defensive and adaptive stature of the family members as they unconsciously and collusively design and implement fantasies and basic assumptions with which they can securely, though misguidedly and maladaptively, attempt to resolve internal conflict through intrafamilial relational transaction.

Framo (1982d) discusses the intergenerational transmission of the multidetermined emotional context that dictates the assignment of irrational roles within the family system:

Human needs operate most forcefully in the family setting, with struggles over love, hate, rejection, hurt, gratification, and jealousy having a continuous dynamic process from one generation to the next. The implicit or explicit irrational assignment of roles in the family (role being defined as a pattern or type of behavior which a person builds up in terms of what significant others expect or demand of him) reflects unconscious attempts by the parents to master, reenact, or externalize their intrapsychic conflicts about these powerful human needs, derived from relationship experiences in their family of origin. (p. 25)

The essence of the irrationality of role assignment takes form around the unconscious dimensions of the parents' internal object-relational worlds. Within this intrapsychic domain the parents are subject to the reemergence of repressed fantasied wishes and needs, eliciting the anxiety and ambivalence that revolve around such fantasies and rendering the partners collusively bound to their defensive positioning. Much of the unconscious internal conflict of both partners is, successfully or not, played out in the dynamics of the marital interaction. Intrapsychic conflicts wreak havoc in the interpersonal field. To the extent that the partners can equilibrate their marital system while successfully, albeit maladaptively, externalizing their individual conflicts in the realm of the marital bond, children are spared elicited involvement.

However, the multitude of experienced unconscious emotions transferred from generation to generation tends to be so intensely and complexly organized that the resulting formation of the emotional climate necessarily encompasses the entire family system. As an integral component of the interlocking configuration inherent in the emotional family climate, each member unconsciously succumbs to the assumption of an assigned role.

Assigned family roles take on a multitude of affective, cognitive, and behavioral presentations and may serve a variety of defensive functions in response to confronted familial tasks or crisis situations. The essence of the sustaining of the family as a stable and balanced system is contingent on the maintenance of both consciously and unconsciously determined roles. It is well acknowledged that families vary in the degree to which they are capable of establishing and maintaining a functionally balanced system—a family system that maintains itself constructively and productively in its evolutionary position within its social context. Familial object-relational role typing assumes a characteristic in which the individual roles synergize to depict certain mythical truths of the family, allegorically played out in the family drama.

The roles are for the most part unconsciously determined and delegated, yet maintained collusively with such inflexible austerity that the family is encapsulated and bound by its own idiosyncratic morality. Inherent in the family drama, there typically ensues a pattern of complementary opposites of stereotyped roles, precariously balancing the system in preservation of its envisioned ideal. There exist the conscientious and responsible family member and the undependable and neglected one; the cool and rational member and the irrational hysteric; the benevolently concerned member and the self-absorbed, dispiteous one; the domineering member and the submissive one; the strong, independent member and the helpless one. One child in the family may be precocious while another is clumsy and backward, another child is perceptively intelligent, still another is ignorantly naive, and so on.

The assignment of roles parallels the assignment of functions with which each member is to service the family system. One member may be expected to direct the family's functioning while the others follow. One member may be selected to represent the family to society. One member may be compelled to disrupt and discombobulate the family while the others struggle unitedly to stabilize the system. In the extreme pathological role assignment, one member may be chosen to play the physically or mentally ill role, facilitating and demarcating the others' wellness. In reciprocation, the family provides services to those solicited individuals. Care and comfort may be provided to the ill member or, conversely, degradation and renunciation may serve a better defensive position. As Framo (1982d) puts it, ''One child in the family may get all the concern and 'love' while another is ignored or subject to unreasoning prejudice'' (p. 27).

Each child in the family may be afforded a specific meaning by the parental couple. Nichols (1984) explains:

The anticipated child may represent, among other things, a more devoted love object than the spouse, someone to succeed where the parent failed, or a peace offering to re-establish loving relations with grandparents. (p. 202)

One child may be assigned the task of regulating the distance between parental, marital partners. Similarly one child may be expected to distance the couple while another is expected to facilitate a merger, in which case both children need to work in coordination. A child may be expected to be the family's decision maker, as in the case of couples who parentify their children. Significantly, all of the aforementioned interlocking coordinations are established and maintained by the collusive participation of each member of the family constellation. The family drama is sustained and processed by the mutually and unconsciously determined, implicit and covert family fantasies and basic assumptions, which are designed in implementation to represent what the family perceives to be its essential truth and morality.

In the functionally impaired family system, Brodey (1959) notes, the family's drama, based on its unconsciously generated and mutually shared fantasies, is in essence a portrait of the various components of psychic conflict inherent in the internal representational world of any one given member of the family. That individual's internalized object relations are, upon internal processing, externalized to be played out collusively by the role confluence of familial interaction.

Brodey (1959) comments further: "Similarly, if we put each of the stereotyped family roles together into one, there is synthesized in this total the major conflictual characteristics of each member" (p. 383). The family, in unity, unconsciously selects the specific internal conflicts that it determines must be acted out defensively and adaptively to sustain the individual members as well as the family as a system. This transactional phenomenon illuminates the interlocking complexity with which the system processes its intrafamilial dynamism in kaleidoscopic fashion. This processing is shaped by redundant yet everchanging interactional patterns in evolutionary formation. The family becomes stuck in its defensively perpetuated array of transactional interchange; however, in subjection to the multitude of intrapsychic conflicts experienced individually and played out interpersonally, the family drama's cast membership maintains its dynamic, progressive or regressive, movement in face of the vicissitudes of individual and familial life development. The family system forever seeks equilibrium; however, it never succumbs to dormancy.

As an adaptive means by which the family can play out its members' intrapsychic conflicts as well as effectively sustain as a system among other family systems, the members collectively coordinate to delineate and present the family as a self-contained psychic entity comprised of its substructures, which are appointed to and assumed by the various members of the family. Zinner and R. Shapiro (1974) explain that specific intrapsychic functions are unconsciously dispersed

among different family members so that specific members come to represent and act on behalf of one psychic structure over a particular period of interaction. Taken as a whole the family appears to constitute a single, relatively complete, psychic entity; taken alone, each individual seems to be psychologically incomplete and over-representative of one mental structure. (p. 179)

Id impulse, superego restriction, and ego functioning are carried out by individual members of the family. The family, in unification, comprises the id-ego-superego structural entity that exists as the internal organizational world of each individual family member but cannot be functionally exercised by any one given member and must therefore be constituted collectively by the entire family membership. Because the particular delegation of specific mental functions alters with the changes of familial context, individual family members are subject to assuming a variety of "as-if" (Deutsch 1942) characterizations and presentations in an attempt to adapt to the particular scenario of the family drama at any given time. Individual members must present themselves in variation to fit the familial context.

Zinner and R. Shapiro (1974) clarify the as-if presentation of the family as a whole:

The family *acts as if* integration of impulse and restraint *within* each member, i.e., intrapsychically, was beyond his capacity. The family as a whole assumes responsibility for this integration by distributing the functions of impulse and restraint among its membership so that at any moment family member A may be involved in relatively unmodulated drive discharge activity while member B is serving as the critic and source of restraint on A's activity. (p. 180)

One member becomes the vehicle through which the family's combined id-instinctual discharge is facilitated, while another member assumes the role of regulating the id impulse to meet the demands of the family's combined super-ego agency. This collusively acted scenario affords both impulse expression and impulse restraint, preventing any one member from having to effect both functions. This preserves the integrity of the individual members and of the family system as a whole. Boszormenyi-Nagy (1965b) notes:

Although the assignment of good and bad roles to certain members may be regarded as attempts at a system-based, complementary self-delineation, these relational patterns serve the members' basic needs for impulse discharge as well. (p. 68)

Insofar as the three structural components of the intrapsychic domain—the id, ego, and superego—are insufficiently organized because of the lack of healthy,

early object-relational internalizations, individuals will be able to function effectively in interpersonal relations only to the extent that close, significant others are available to help them effect the functioning of these structural components (Muir 1975, 1982). Having failed to acquire clear differentiation from
familial objects and thereby having failed to delineate effectively the personality organization of the self, the individuals are rendered incapable of acquiring
the sufficient ego and superego functioning required to modulate effectively
both libidinal and aggressive id-instinctual discharge and to assume a healthy
and integrated position in the external object world.

The emotional climate—as determined by the family drama and played out
within the confining roles unconsciously and collusively delegated to individual
members by the family system in its entirety—is based on the perceived needs
of the family group as it develops a defensive stature in adaptation to the family
context itself as well as the extrafamilial world. Shared and unconscious fantasies and basic assumptions are conjured up by the family to give the system
definition and purpose. What the family discerns as the truth and as the essence
of morality serves as the foundation on which the family constructs its patterning of dynamic interaction. In accordance with the inescapable family drama,
each member is subject to the mandate imposed by the collective family system. Within the confines of the delegated roles, the individual members acquire
and depict meaning, purpose, function, and self-definition.

=14=

Object Relations and the Saliency of the Family Synergism

Understanding the intricacies of familial role typing necessitates an investigation into the shared unconscious fantasies and basic assumptions that govern the system's transactional processes and illuminate the specially designed meaning and purpose of each individual's membership. The dynamic interplay between intrapsychic forces and interpersonal involvement weaves the very fabric with which the family mobilizes its melodramatic venture through the family life cycle. Familial tasks such as the separation and individuation of its members and the concomitant facilitation of ego differentiation and identity formation present the family with potential for either growth, productivity, and constructivity or stagnation, torpidity, and destructivity. At stake here, transcending individual development and welfare, is the ability of the family as a system to sustain in a higher degree of order and to hold viable potential for expenditure of energy in an organized manner. It is only in a negentropic process that the family can yield individuated, ego-autonomous persons who can establish themselves in an integral, contributory position in the social object world. In fact, the two dimensions conjugate in confluence to form a single process: the person necessarily individuates within a context of a social environment, acquiring distinction and existence in comparison and contrast with other objects of that social world; and, likewise, the society evolves in continuous transformation in response to the unique expansion and contribution of each of its members.

Because the individual is naturally embedded in a social context of other persons, the recursive interactional processing inherent in this self-other matrix necessarily dictates the form and direction of the individual person as well as the evolution of the human society. Society evolves through interlocking perceptions and associated actions of its membership, as the development of the individual proceeds in response to the perceptions and behaviors of others. To punctuate an isolated constituent of this circular and global phenomenon, and thereby elucidate its profound yet delicate characteristics, we acknowledge the family as being the most immediate and significant human system to which individuals belong. Individuals first and foremost promulgate and affirm the self in the context of the family of origin. This context of significant others assumes a position of great influence on the declaration of the selves of the family's membership. In this light we will investigate how the perceptions of family members come to bear on the formation of identity and selfhood in its individual adolescent members, and in reciprocity how that formation affects the identities of other family members. It is in this investigation that we encounter the saliency of the family synergism.

As children proceed through the developmental stages, which culminate in the advent of adolescence and the formation of a relatively secure and stable ego-identity, the evolving sense of selfhood is contingent on the parental assessment and appraisal of the children. Because, as Erikson (1956) contended, the psychosocial task of adolescents is to secure a functional position in the adult object world, adolescents are appropriately and acutely in tune with the perceptions and cues of the parents and significant others in critical self-evaluation of progress with this task. The tenuous narcissistic equilibrium of adolescents is acutely vulnerable to the perceptions of others and therefore relies heavily on the mirroring of the self through respected and trusted others such as the parents. Insofar as the parents are capable of providing a holding environment conducive to the facilitation of an accurate, reality-based self-perception, adolescents will, in the normative process, acquire a balance of healthy narcissism and a view of the self as being distinct, unique, and equitable to the surrounding environment of other persons. They will come to acknowledge, like, and respect themselves.

Insofar as the parents are incapable of integrating ego-dystonic aspects of the self and of maintaining a mental representation of their children as being distinct and differentiated persons from themselves, they will develop a distorted reality sense of the children's existence and therewith develop rigidly stylized perceptions of the children conforming to their own defensive needs. E. Shapiro (1982–1983) and R. Shapiro (1967, 1968, 1979) claimed that these "parental delineations" of their adolescent children have their origins in earlier object-relational experiences of the children's lives that resurge during the second separation-individuation process. The family as a whole regresses in shared, unconscious, defensive fantasy in the face of adolescent emancipation to a state wherein the parents are able to constrain maladaptively the children's emerging sense of identity and associated autonomy. By contrast, in the normative process, the healthy, functional family will develop delineations of the children wherewith the parents communicate to their children the perceptions acquired from realistic and actualized characteristics of their children. The defensive needs of the parents will to varying degrees color their delineations of their children and will to varying degrees interfere with empathic responsivity to their children's maturational needs.

The concept of delineation as applied to the psychoanalytic study of interpersonal interaction within the family system implies a communication network of perceptual and behavioral interchange wherein family members overtly or covertly disclose their perceptions of and attitudes about one another. R. Shapiro (1968) explains succinctly:

By delineation we mean the view or image one person has of the other person as it is revealed explicitly or implicitly in the behavior of the one person with the other person. This is behavior which expresses how the one person identifies the other person. It includes behavior which expresses attitudes about the actions of the other person, as well as behavior which reveals expectations of the other person. (pp. 460–61)

How family members "identify" other members is a specific and direct reflection of the quality of the internal object representation that they have formed of the others. Furthermore, the nature of the identification of the other family members is contingent on the self-representation that they have formed in relationship to those significant objects. The quality and nature of this internalized self-object relationship influences primarily the perceptions of and behaviors toward the other family members.

The individual ego organization and functioning of the family members organizes around these internalized object relations. R. Shapiro (1967) elucidates the concept of delineational behavior:

In the language of ego psychology, it is behavior that contains the expression of an object representation and the ego organization mobilized in relation to this object representation. Various ego functions are mobilized in relation to object representation and behavior with an object. For example, the characteristics of autonomous ego functioning or state of ego regression effect the behavior of delineation. (p. 226)

In this light, the inherent reciprocity in which family members communicate experienced perceptual, emotional, and cognitive processing becomes evident. To punctuate but one linear component of this recursive circularity of interaction, the parents' delineations of their adolescent children, insofar as they formulate around reality characteristics of the children, have a great facilitating impact on the emergence of their children's healthy, well-integrated, and consolidated sense of identity and selfhood.

The parents' healthy reality sense of their maturing children will lay the foundation for the promotion of a functional, familial holding environment in which all family members, including the liberating adolescents, can withstand the shifting of the familial organization inherent in the passage from one family life-cycle stage to the next. Conversely, however, should the parental delineations of their liberating adolescent children be dictated by the defensive needs of the parental couple, the perceptions of and attitudes toward the children will to some degree be distorted. Because of the parents' own early object-rela-

tional, developmental failures, rendering them incapable of effectively differ-
entiating self-representation and object representation in current periods of familial developmental stress and crisis, they become subject to the unconscious,
defensive employment of mechanisms whereby they forestall the subjective experience of anxiety as elicited by the adolescent children's age-appropriate quest
for autonomy.

The essence of this phenomenal intrapsychic and interpersonal experience
constitutes what was referred to by E. Shapiro (1982–1983), R. Shapiro (1967,
1968), and Zinner and R. Shapiro (1972) as parental "defensive delineation."
The internal defensive organization of one or both parents becomes manifest in
the interpersonal arena of family transaction. As a result, parental defensive
delineations, according to Dorpat (1985), "are those determined more by their
service in behalf of parental defensive needs than by their capacity for apprais-
ing the adolescent's actual attributes" (pp. 180–81). E. Shapiro (1982–1983)
clarifies this conceptualization:

We observe a complementary use of projective identification of dystonic aspects of their
self-representations by these parents, which blurs their capacity to experience themselves as separate from the particular child in areas of conflict. Through the use of this
shared defense, parents fail to perceive accurately the reality of the child, developing
defensive stereotyped delineations of him. (p. 212)

In this light, the thrust of the conceptualization of the parents' defensive
delineation of their adolescent children lies within the intrapersonal sphere of
the individual parents. What determines the quality of a given parental delineation is the intrapsychic organization of each parent individually. The parents'
own styles of defensive operation coordinate with the quality of the mental
representation of their children to create the framework from which a given
delineation is constructed. The quality of the parents' self-representations and
the quality of the relationship between the self and the object specifically determines, albeit only in part, the perceptions that the parents have of their
developing children. The coordination of unique defensive organization and the
mental representation of the object as being indicative of the intrapsychic domain of each individual parent, creates a dynamic interplay of mutual influence. R. Shapiro (1967) comments:

When behavior of an individual with an object contains evidence of distortion of the
object related to the individual's defensive organization, then defensive delineation exists. The concept of defensive delineation thus represents an integration of two structural
concepts in ego psychology. It includes behavioral referents both of the concept of
object representation and of defensive organization. Defensive delineation is a conceptualization of those situations in which defense alters the behavioral referents of object
representation. It is a response to the behavior of the other person that stimulates anxiety
in the one person and gives rise to defensive operations, which are revealed in the nature
and style of his delineation of the other person. (p. 226)

Inasmuch as the intrapsychic makeup of the delineating parent has direct impact on the perceptions of and attitudes toward the adolescent children, it would be well to recognize that the experiential and observable phenomenon of parental defensive delineation takes effect on the interpersonal field. The salient features of this familial, interactional occurrence are illuminated only by the interchange of intrapsychic and interpersonal phenomena as generated by the both subtle and profound nuances of the family group's common phantasma-goric invocations. Dorpat (1985) comments:

Defensive delineations are the expression at an individual level of family group behavior that is determined more by shared unconscious fantasies than by reality considerations. Family group behavior and subjective experience both are determined to varying degrees by shared unconscious fantasies and assumptions. (p. 181)

The family's shared unconscious fantasies and basic assumptions provide the context in which parental delineations, both defensively and nondefensively organized, acquire their origin and ongoing generation. As previously noted, the family's common fantasies and frame of reference are formulated early in the formation of the family system, often within the marital system before the introduction of children. Therefore, at the developmental stage of adolescence, the children have been subject to the parents' perceptual delineations since the children's conception. These delineations may exemplify the productive and constructive aspects of the functionally differentiated yet integrated systemic organization or, in the perpetuation of family disorganization and dysfunction, may be distorted characteristically to fit the defensive anatomy of the parents' individual personality structures and interpersonal modes of transaction. In the interpersonal modes of transaction, the defensive needs of the parents mitigate the adolescents' maturational expression of age-appropriate needs. The parents' defensively laden perceptual distortions, biases, and prejudices impinge on the adolescents' expression and assertion of the self, skewing the parents' defini-tion of the children and potentially skewing and confusing the adolescents' own self-definition.

Insofar as adolescents are capable—via developed self-object differentiation, integration of contradictory good and bad ego states, and effective ego-auton-omous functioning—of sustaining a healthy narcissistic equilibrium and effect-ing a functional reality sense, the emerging self is likely to withstand the impingement of parental defensive delineations. Capable of surviving the growth-inhibiting impact of the familial context, adolescents are likely to maintain age-appropriate cognitive processing and behavioral display recognizable to the extrafamilial world as being normative to the developmental phase of adoles-cence. In this case, there is an overt discrepancy between the parents' and the outside observer's view of the adolescents, and only by comparison of the adolescents' behavior in the context of the family's shared, unconscious fantasy world with the adolescents' behavior outside the family arena can the discrepancy be illuminated. R. Shapiro (1967) notes that, in recognition of the parents' defensively delineated perceptions of their child, there

may be a clear and obvious disjunction between the view of the adolescent expressed by the parent and that seen by the observer. It may become evident only when the delineation is viewed in the context of a particular reality situation and of the specific behavior in reality of the adolescent. (p. 227)

Parental defensive delineations may be marked in totality by incongruent views of the adolescents, each unique to a given interactional context. Adolescent children, for example, may be perceived by the family as being incapable of functionally autonomous behavior yet concurrently selected to represent the family's perceived strength, stature, and efficacy in presentation of the extrafamilial community. Adolescents are perceived as being alternately weak and ineffective and strong and competent, depending on the contextual needs of the family at a given juncture. Similarly, parents may perceive both realistic strengths and weaknesses of their children yet persistently attend to only one, at the potentially destructive expense of neglecting the other. For example, a child may be recognized and praised for independent behaviors, yet neglected by the parents in response to age-appropriate dependency needs. R. Shapiro (1968) summarizes this conceptualization:

Defensive delineation can also be inferred when despite correct parental perception of the adolescent there is a consistent selection of adolescent characteristics which are perceived and responded to by the parent and others which are not attended to. Defensive delineation may be inferred from contradictions in parental definition of the adolescent, or in behavior or attitudes which contradict explicit definition of the adolescent. (p. 461)

A discrepancy may also be observed from an outsider's perspective in how parents verbally describe their perceptions of the adolescent children within the family and to outside observers, and in how they covertly communicate these perceptions to their children. This discrepancy exemplifies the rigidity with which the intrapsychic and interpersonal defensive operations of the parents sustain. Zinner and R. Shapiro (1972) remind us:

These "defensive delineations" are an expression of parental defensive organization and, as such, the parent is strongly motivated to sustain these perceptions of the adolescent, regardless of the adolescent's behavior which might otherwise alter the parental image. (p. 524)

To maintain their individual psychic stability and the homeostatic balance of the marital system, parents mold their internal object representations of their adolescent children to fit their own defensive needs and to provide hope for the actualization of their unconscious fantasies and wishes. The availability of employable defense mechanisms is steadfastly maintained by the parental couple to ensure against the forthcoming realities of themselves, their children, and the entire family system. R. Shapiro (1968) comments on two available defense mechanisms:

Examples of denial may be seen in a definition of the adolescent that is directly contradictory to the behavior the adolescent is manifesting. Repression can be inferred from characteristic parental delineation which does not acknowledge prominent areas of adolescent behavior. (p. 461)

Splitting, introjection, projection, projective identification, and idealization complement and expand the defensive armamentarium. Potentially imperceptible to family members as well as to extrafamilial observers, the salient components of the family systemic organization synergetically configurate to illuminate a confusing picture from which emanates perhaps only a vague, mystical aura of contortion and obliquity. Stierlin (1977) summarizes the aforementioned conceptualization of parental delineation:

[P]arental perceptions and expectations—and this seems crucially important—must be inferred from a total transactional gestalt. They are complex and ambiguous and not necessarily identical with what parents say or believe at any given moment. (p. 176)

. . .

Because parental perceptions must be inferred from an often inconsistent behavioral gestalt, we frequently deal with an ambiguous situation. What on the surface looks like a separation-inducing expectation may have a covert inhibiting dimension, and what appears as an inhibiting perception may, in effect, promote an adolescent's autonomy. In order to do justice to this complexity, we must . . . differentiate between *overt* and *concealed* perceptions and expectations. (p. 178)

The effects of parental delineation on identity-forging adolescents is of great significance. Individuation and the striving for ego autonomy render adolescents susceptible to the parents' implicitly and explicitly communicated perceptions that either enhance and foster the process of emancipation or impede its facilitation. R. Shapiro (1968) suggests that "there is a significant relationship between parental delineation of the adolescent and adolescent identity formation" (p. 460). Should the inherent vicissitudes of adolescent separation and individuation elicit anxiety in the parental couple, two dynamic processes will subsequently initiate: (a) the children will sensitively cue into the parental experience of anxiety that subsequently reverberates throughout the family system, and (b) the parents will shore up their defenses to shield their vulnerability. Because the parents mirror their children's emerging sense of self, and because it is in their reflection that the children see an image of the self and therewith formulate an internal self-representation, the children are subject to whatever perceptual shadings the parents may interject into the quality and nature of the parent-child relationship in face of forthcoming self-object differentiation.

Also, as previously noted, the children internalize certain aspects of the external objects of the parents as well as the relationship that transpires between the self and these significant objects. In this process of internalization of external objects and object relations, the children come to form identifications with these significant persons and relationships, and incorporate these identifications into the structuring of the internal world and the formation of an ego-identity. Characteristics attributed to adolescents by the parents as they communicate their perceptions to the children contribute to the ongoing modification of the children's self-representation (R. Shapiro 1979). Parental delineations formulated in defensive postures in face of their children's maturing object relations affect the family's emotional climate and directly inhibit the liberation of the child from the family orbit into the adult world of object relations. Zinner and R. Shapiro (1972) explain that "the adolescent does identify with defensively distorted parental images of him, and in this fashion, his own subjective self-experience is likely to be affected by his parents' efforts to diminish their own anxiety" (p. 524).

Adolescent children are also likely to aid the parents in relinquishing the shared, experienced anxiety. Because parental anxiety is dispersed among the membership of the family and contributes to the family's common emotional experience, all members mobilize to counteract the force. R. Shapiro (1979) comments on the adolescent's participation in this anxiety-laden familial experience:

Delineations of the child and adolescents *[sic]* which serve a defensive function for the parent are particularly coercive, in that behavior in the child incongruent with these parental delineations lead to *[sic]* anxiety in the parent. The child is then motivated to behave so as to mitigate this parental anxiety. Internalization by the child of the parent's projections into him moves the developing child and adolescent into a role which is complementary to parental defensive requirements, with which the parent unconsciously identifies. (p. 191)

R. Shapiro noted further that in the effort to allay the parents' anxiety experience, adolescents may comply with the role assignment that defensive delineations serve to determine and within which they will restrict behaviors and attitudes. Compliance with the assigned role and the reinforcement of parental perceptions strengthen the parental defensive stature. Shapiro comments on the function of role assignment and how it affects the adolescent's emerging sense of identity as facilitated by parental delineation:

The dynamics of role allocation operate in a broader framework of unconscious assumptions of the family as a group. These, over time, establish a pattern of internalizations within the self-representation. Unconscious assumptions within the family and related

experiences of projective identification impinge upon the reorganization of internalizations required by ego-id maturation during adolescence. These influences may interfere
significantly with individuation and the consolidation of identity in the adolescent. (p.
191)

Adolescent children's bid for autonomy and engagement in extrafamilial object relations, along with their experienced modifications in instinctual drive,
are thwarted by the unspoken demands generated by the transmission of emotional experience within the family arena. Anxiety generated by the phase-
appropriate task of separation-individuation in adolescence permeates the very
essence of the family emotional climate.

Because of the circular and interdependent nature of systemic interaction
within the family, and because the family's emotional climate is necessarily the
result of its own internal processing, adolescents and other children in the family are not observed as mere passive recipients of parental delineation. In particular, the stunted attempt of adolescents to liberate the selves from the infantile object ties of the family circle, to form more expansive and mature object
relations with the extrafamilial world, is not a simple reflection of a linear
cause-and-effect relationship. Parents do in fact influence the development of
their children, as has been noted, and, in recursive circularity of influence, the
children affect the subjective experiences of the parents as well as the quality
and nature of the parent-child relationship.

Just as the parents hold potential for defensively molding the internal object
representations of their children, adolescent children are similarly capable of
defensive utilization of the family in the service of ameliorating their own experienced fear and anxiety and of disavowing certain undesirable aspects of the
self. In reference to the available employment of the projective-identificatory
defense mechanism, R. Shapiro et al. (1975) explain this transactional experience:

This phenomenon is observed in behaviors in which the individual adolescent projects
conflictual aspects of himself into other group members with whom he then identifies.
In this way, he need not suffer the anxiety of taking responsibility for these characteristics in himself with, however, important consequences for his own personality functioning and evolving identity. He may then continue to disown significant components
of his impulse life or conscience, rather than achieving internalization and integration
of these needs and controls into a stable ego identity during adolescence. (p. 88)

Along with the capacity for utilizing the parents as recipients of externalized
id-impulse desires and superego sanctions, and the disavowed, split-off, and
projected aspects of the self, adolescents are capable of inducing, through attitudes and behaviors in relationship with the parents, modifications in the self-
representation of the internal worlds of the parents. In face of expanded and
mobilized id-impulse drive experiences, adolescents defensively project super-

ego sanctioning onto the parents, who subsequently are anticipated to play out the critical demands on the adolescents to curtail such id-impulse desires, leaving the adolescents free to some degree to act out the experienced instinctual drives without subjecting the self to the internal turmoil of id-superego disparagement.

Insofar as the parents are able to assume the superego functions attributed to them by their defensively statured adolescent children without disrupting the stability of their own identities, as determined by the quality and nature of their respective internal self-representations, this transactional phenomenon can functionally strengthen the family system's shared identity—a family ego—along with the individual ego systems of the family members. Insofar as the parents' ego-identities are so tenuously formed that they fall prey to the projections and projective identifications of their adolescent children, the children are confronted with the reality that the selves of the parents are vulnerably subject to the manipulations of the adolescents. Even in cases of healthy, stable parental ego systems and a unified parental system, adolescents who are newly forming extrafamilial object relations, and are thus providing alternative contexts for self-assessment, leave the parents more vulnerable to the modified views that the adolescent children have of themselves in relationship to the increasingly less intensely cathected parental objects. Stierlin (1977) clarifies:

The child at adolescence is becoming less dependent on his parents; through school and peer contacts he makes available to himself alternative models for forming his self-image and identity. He can now more effectively bring his own perceptions of his parents to bear on the latter. With new cognitive tools at his disposal and increasing claims for the merit of his judgments, he can now play powerfully on his parents' vulnerabilities by labeling them as bad parents or failures in life. He can thus shape their own image of themselves. (p. 174)

Adolescent children are thus faced with the necessity, ideally, of taking a look at how their view of their parents is equally influential in the reciprocity of parent-child relational perceptions and delineations. As R. Shapiro (1967) suggests, "His conceptual capabilities are also directed toward self-reflection and toward an examination of his behavior toward his parents and the ways in which this provokes particular directions of response in them" (p. 236).

The facilitation of ego-identity formation in each and every member is the shared task of the family system. Individuals' identities are necessarily formed within the context of significant others who mirror the emergence of the self to foster the formation of their self-definition in comparison and contrast with the self-definitions acquired via the same process by each and every other family member. What transpires and perpetuates throughout the family life cycle is a vast and both subtle and profound array of a mutually influential self-delineation and other delineations with which the members demarcate their self-bound-aries in confluent and dovetailed configuration. The emergence and consolidation of an effective ego-identity and sense of selfhood reflect the saliency of the family synergism.

=15=

Familial Object Relations and the Defensive Menagerie

By preserving the narcissistic equilibrium, ego integration and consolidation, and the general stability of each family member individually as well as of the family as systemic whole, the family coordinates in interdependent and synergetic configuration to sustain the patterns of object relations conducive to the maintenance of the integrity of its individual and collective membership. The family's kaleidoscopic quality of interaction and transaction is generated and governed by the interchange of individual, intrapsychic defensive organizational patterns and the means by which such patterns are manifested in the emotional, cognitive, and behavioral interplay in the interpersonal context of the family. The nature of the resulting familial object relations and defensive menagerie typifies and exemplifies the desperation and austerity characteristic of the family's struggle to define, affirm, and declare its existence.

The shared unconscious fantasies and basic assumptions underscore the family's attempts to embody and pronounce the cohesion and unity to which it desperately clings. The normative progression of the family life cycle presents the family with phase-appropriate developmental tasks potentially perceivable by the family as a direct threat to the sustenance of the system and of the members individually. Separation and individuation is one such family task inherent in the productive and constructive evolution of the family group; yet it is frightening to the group in its inherent requirement of the family to shift to a higher level of systemic organization wherein the familial context transforms in response to the modified, maturational needs of the family members. Adolescents' bid for ego autonomy and expansion of object relations is but one such need. The phase-appropriate need of the parents to be recognized both by themselves and by their emancipating adolescent children as continued significant objects in the maturing children's lives must be established as being necessary to the facilitation of a smooth and functional evolution of the family life cycle.

As a means of confronting the perceived imminence of familial disorganization in face of separation-individuation, the family shores up its defensive armamentarium and faces the onslaught of adolescent "rebellion." The specific defensive organization is determined by the shared unconscious family fantasies and basic assumptions underlying the system's interactional modalities. One such fantasy and assumption is that individual autonomy and independence are indicative of a member's rejection of the family group, and in effect constitute an act of aggression and pose a direct threat to the integrity of the system. Berkowitz (1981) comments:

In contrast to providing a facilitating environment, and despite heartfelt avowals to the contrary, many of these families often resort to a variety of counter-separation attitudes and behaviors under the impact of the adolescent period. To varying degrees, these parents attempt to hold their . . . adolescent close, to possess their child, and to prevent individuation. . . . Occasionally . . . they may admit their wish to have been able to stop the passage of time when their children were small. (p. 190)

Parental perceptions of their adolescent children's bid for autonomy as a hostility-laden act of aggression and explicit rejection of the family unity directly influence the defensive stature that the family as a whole will assume to counteract the perceived denunciation of the group's shared perpetuity of mutual concern, caring, and, above all, love. The separation and individuation of the family's adolescent members is seen by the remaining membership, and often by the liberating adolescents as well, as defiance of this encompassing sense of "goodness." The family group in response rejects the "badness" that is permeating its circle and threatening the family unity. The family's conceptualization of goodness and badness is derived from the uniquely intrapsychic defensive organization of its individual members. The familial task of separation and individuation of its adolescent members, as a recapitulation of the first separation-individuation process of toddlerhood, elicits emotional, cognitive, and behavioral responses from the parents as they experience the resurgence of ambivalence and anxiety associated with earlier object-relational experiences revolving around separation aand individuation from their parents. E. Shapiro et al. (1977) elucidate this phenomenon:

Parents . . . because of critical interactions with their own parents during separation-individuation, have unconsciously associated either autonomous or dependent behavior with either libidinally or aggressively tinged self-object representations (i.e., autonomy is associated with "good" experience and dependency with "bad," or vice versa). (p. 79)

In this light, the parents have come to integrate into their internal self- and object-representational worlds perceptions of their selves as being possessed of either goodness or badness as associated with their drives for ego autonomy.

The internalized representations of the objects of their parents have also been colored with good and bad qualities, depending on the parents' response to the autonomy-seeking behavior of their children, which provides either gratifying facilitation or ungratifying impediment of separation-individuation. The parents' rekindling of these early object-relational experiences and associated ego states directly influences their perceptions of their adolescent children's quest for ego atuonomy as being either an appropriate expression of maturation or an undesirable act of aggressive repudiation. E. Shapiro et al. further explain:

> Because of an unstable integration in each of the parents of positive and negative ego states, each has resolved his original conflict about issues of autonomy and dependency, by an identification with the libidinally influenced self perception (i.e. each sees himself as "lovingly dependent" or "strong and autonomous") and a denial and projection of the aggressively tinged alternative. (p. 79)

In identification with the good self as desiring either dependence or independence, the parents will perceive their liberating adolescent children in like fashion; the children are just like parents as adolescents, either good or bad for striving for ego autonomy. Adolescent children are likely, though not necessarily so, to internalize this parental perception and therewith identify the self as libidinally good or aggressively bad.

The adolescent members of a family system that is incapable of providing a holding environment within which the family group is able to facilitate the separation and individuation of its maturing members are subject to the regressive pulls of infantile object-relational experience, wherein in the separation-individuation phase of toddlerhood, and again in the second separation-individuation phase of adolescence, the children experience internal and interpersonal conflict in face of normative drives for ego autonomy and an interpersonal context that prohibits the undertaking of the separation and individuation.

The adolescents recapture the experience of infancy and toddlerhood wherein, in response to experienced ambivalence and anxiety in face of conflicting object-relational experiences of drive and wish gratification and drive and wish ungratification, they split the internalized object representation into the good, gratifying object and the bad, ungratifying object, and form a concomitant split of the ego into a good, deserving self and a bad, undeserving self. The defense mechanism of splitting enables the children to tolerate the conflictual ego states of goodness and badness in relation to the goodness and badness of the significant external objects. Zinner and E. Shapiro (1975) comment on the nature and quality of the individual's experiences of goodness and badness of the self and of the object:

> These terms are attributes defined . . . by the affective quality of the relationship at a given moment. "Good" and "bad," therefore, connote not moral evaluations or judgments made by a mature superego but affective states of pleasure and "unpleasure." (p. 108)

Internal states of pleasure and "unpleasure" are the direct results of the quality of object relationship and constitute very primitive forms of emotionally based self-experience.

The confrontive task of adolescent separation-individuation triggers within the emotional climate of the family experienced states of conflicting goodness and badness. The "bad" adolescent children who wish to repudiate the family unit and stake a claim to self-sufficiency introduce an anomaly to the goodness of the family. To defend against the perceived existence of conflicting emotional states of goodness and badness within the system, the family may resort to the defense mechanism of splitting of good and bad experiential states in an attempt to adapt to, if not to master and alleviate, its undesirable, anxiety-producing presence. E. Shapiro et al. (1977) explain the phenomenon of splitting in the family that is incapable of facilitating the emancipation of its adolescent members:

Within the family group, attributes of "goodness" (providing, gratifying, loving) and "badness" (depriving, punishing, hating) are separated one from the others and reinvested in different members so that each family member appears relatively preambivalent and single-minded in relation to the troubled adolescent. The family group, taken as a whole, appears to be a single, ambivalent entity, loving and hating, giving and withholding, rewarding and punishing. (p. 79)

The family as a group regresses into shared unconscious fantasy of an early infantile experience wherein the splitting of objects enables the family to delineate various members as the embodiment of either goodness or badness. As Zinner and E. Shapiro (1975) put it, "In these families, sources of gratification and of deprivation of oral supplies are not perceived as emanating from the same family member" (p. 108). Rather, by means of alleviating the struggle of ambivalence toward a given object as the source of needed and desired ministrations, individual family members are selected to play out in coordination the inherent goodness and badness of the family system. The individual members are perceived by the family in restricted form as being of a given dimensionality and the embodiment of a given characteristic.

Splitting within the family may take a variety of forms. The children of the family may assume the roles of the good and the bad, dissociating the caring and concerned from the selfish and indifferent. Zinner and E. Shapiro (1975) provide an example:

[T]he various children within the family may be delineated in an unambivalently polarized manner. In one family two siblings were explicitly experienced by their parents as "night" and "day." "Day" was seen as caring about the family and giving unselfishly, while "night" was perceived as exploiting the parents, stopping at nothing to provide pleasure for herself at their expense. (p. 109)

The parents in this case can maintain an illusion of a complete and encompassing circle of love exclusive of the bad and disconcerting child. Yet, in another form of splitting within the family, dichotomous reflections of goodness and badness may take the form of parent-child collusion against the badness of the other parent. The child may perceive one parent as being the source of all gratification, free of all bad characteristics that must therefore be attributed to the other parent, who is perceived as dispiteously withholding of supplies. In yet another pattern of defensive splitting, the family may view itself as the container of all goodness, while the extrafamilial world is perceived as being cold, hostile, and impinging. The family unites against the dangers of the external world. Zinner and E. Shapiro (1975) conclude that

The family, as a whole, for example, may experience itself as all-good, as the sole competent and caring provider for its adolescent; the outside world, in complementary fashion, is viewed as hostile and dangerous to the adolescent. (p. 109).

In this case the parents may capitalize on the real potential dangers of the community (e.g., crime, corruption, drugs, and sex) to subjugate and entrap their children within the confines of the family circle. The adolescent children may, in counteraction, split the harsh, controlling, dominating parents from the gratifying, confirming, and promising world of the peer group. Adolescents may idealistically attribute an unrealistic characteristic of nurturance and support to the group of friends, thus attributing an equally unrealistic proportion of misunderstanding to the parents.

The variations in defensively patterned splitting within the family exemplify the shared unconscious fantasies unique to each family system; however, the universal purpose of such splitting lies within the family's desperate and misguided attempt to maintain the essence of the family group function—to provide a system conducive to the growth, productivity, and constructivity of each of its members and of the group as a whole. Zinner and E. Shapiro (1975) summarize:

There are, therefore, a variety of configurations that dissociated attributes of "goodness" and "badness" may take within the family group and its social context. Despite this variability, however, there remains a common denominator in these families: the shared unconscious fantasy of the family group that hostile feelings will destroy the loved anaclitic object. The fantasy generates, then, the defensive imperative for the family to split the loving and hating self- and object representations in order to protect the paramount libidinal ties. (p. 109)

Self-representations and object representations that are imbued with libidinal qualities must be separated defensively from those self-representations and object representations that are aggressively laden. The price that the family pays for such a benevolently yet maladaptively erected defensive stature is its inability to delineate realistically the characteristics of the individual members, establish a functional position in the extrafamilial world, maintain a reality sense, and constitute a stable context within which individual members can differentiate and individuate.

The splitting mechanism of defense with which the family colludes in a desperate attempt to preserve its unity and integrity, and deny any evidence of hostile and aggressive intrasystem experience is analogous in concept to what Richter (1976) called a "dissociative mechanism." Mechanisms of dissociation are defensively employed by families in which "clear internal devisive *[sic]* processes" operate in both overt and covert collaboration of the family's membership. The family system is fragmented into dual or multiple segments wherein each divisional component is complemented and balanced by another component of equal validity and influence. Through interdependence of the system's carefully yet mostly unconsciously chosen elements, the family amalgam assembles in synchronicity to effect a family system in which all perceived conflictual and intolerable experiences of emotion, cognition, and behavior are defensively contained and appropriated. Richter explains:

> The family divides itself up into one part which is permitted to be strong, healthy and good, whereas another part, by way of compensation must be weak, sickly and bad. Sometimes several children or even adult members of the family function in turn as "masochistic victims," since a family of this kind knows no other pattern of organization than permanent division into a hypomanic, denying section and an abject, masochistic section, whereby there is always mutual unconscious participation by both sections. (p. 389)

This type of intrasystemic processing is perpetuated by the regressive forces by which the family as an entire unit is thrust into a defensive stature in an effort to maintain the stability of its system. Negative emotional, cognitive, and behavioral experiences (e.g., hostility, aggression, and refutation of values and ideals) inherent in the family climate of interaction are perceived by the family as threatening to this stability. The family as a whole succumbs to the defensive employment of projective mechanisms by which the group makes unconscious, maladaptive attempts to acquire control and mastery of the negative experience that pervades its existence. Insofar as the family is successful in its primary desire to rid its essence of such negative experience by projecting its "badness" onto the familial world, it is likely, though at great growth-inhibiting expense, to equilibrate its system in functionability. However, the potency of adolescent age-appropriate drives for the expansion of ego autonomy and object relations is generally more than sufficiently strong to impede the family's attempt to project the children's perceived aggression and repudiation onto external others. In this case, the family is subject to the self-perpetuated operation of intrafamilial splitting and projections.

Defensive splitting serves to locate the threat to the family's unity and integrity specifically in a given member or members of the group, where it can be more easily controlled. However, as previously noted, since badness of a variety of meanings can be in essence the manifestation of one family member's disavowed, split-off aspects of the self projected onto another member (e.g., parents' perceived aggressiveness and hostility of their selves experienced during their earlier adolescent striving for autonomy), the problem becomes one of intrapsychic stability of the family's individual members as well as the stability of the system as a whole. Berkowitz (1981) speaks of this intrafamilial regressive phenomenon characterized by enmeshment of individual ego systems:

In this regression, boundaries between individuals are weakened, and primitive defensive functioning is increased, including projection of disavowed parental aspects into the adolescent, and the adolescent's collusive participation in this process. In this family regression, in response to revived, unresolved issues of adolescence, family members may take unrealistic, stereotyped positions with prominent use of denial and distortion. (p. 191)

The perpetuity of the fluidity of ego boundaries and interchange of recursive introjections and projections holds the regressive and defensive force in place as the family strives collusively to equilibrate the narcissism of the individual selves and to balance the systemic whole. The example of the parents who perceive the aggressive liberation of their adolescent children as being equivalent to the virulence and abomination revolving around their own unresolved separation-individuation issues, illuminates this degenerative familial transactional phenomenon. The tenuous stability of ego boundaries and the resulting fusion of ego systems facilitate the operation of the projective defensive mechanism. The disavowed aspects of the self, which are defensively projected onto another family member, are not completely disowned by the projector. The fluidity of ego boundaries and fusion of egos render the projecting subject unable to escape in totality from the confines of subject-object interaction; and therewith the subject continues to experience to variable degrees the emotional content of the projections in vicarious identification with the object of recipience. Projective identification is a more expansive, complex, and interpersonally involved defense mechanism than is projection, and it requires the unconsciously collusive and reciprocal participation of subject and object.

As Zinner and R. Shapiro (1972) suggested, parents tend to identify with their adolescent children in comparison with themselves and, because the merger of individual ego systems ensues to a variable degree, the parent-child interactional quality becomes imbued with and identifiable by the circularity of potentially increasing transactional introjections and projections. All parties involved may experience difficulty in disengaging themselves from this potentially iniquitous circle of captivity. The degree to which this familial transactional phenomenon assumes the quality of psychopathology is determined by the unique interplay of individual defensive organizations and the gestalt of this multifaceted interplay as generated by the family as a systemic whole.

Inherent in this interchange of intrapsychically and intrasystemically defensive organizations is the outside observation of myriad introjected and projected elements of the participating personalities. Aspects of the self that are deemed ego dystonic, be they good or bad elements, are subject to candidacy for participation in the intrafamilial defensive process. Dorpat (1985) explains:

Clinical reports in the literature reveal that a wide range of unconscious contents, conflicts, and affects may be denied and then projected. When the object is idealized, the "good" parts of the self are projected, and when the object is denigrated, it "receives," as it were, the "bad" parts of the self. Thus whole objects, part objects, self objects, introjects, conflicts, affects, functioning, ego ideal, superego elements, drive representations, and many other contents have been identified as the projected elements of the personality. (p. 181)

Dorpat further notes that the commonality of vicarious experiences between the subject and the object of projective identification may be characterized by qualities of bad object-relational experiences such as rejection, impingement, and the withholding of supplies as well as those good experiences of acceptance, gratification, and the provision of supplies.

Zinner and R. Shapiro (1974) asserted that even those good, ego-syntonic aspects of the self cherished by a given family member may be projected onto another and therewith identified. The projection of a split-off, good aspect of the self onto another family member (e.g., a parent's attributing a cherished aspect of the self to a child) serves the potentially healthy function of providing the child with a healthy internalization by means of selective identification, and concomitantly serves functionally as a vehicle for the intergenerational transmission of parental values, ideals, and goals. This familial phenomenon is effective insofar as the parental projections remain congruent with the actual personality of the children and can thereby become ego syntonic to them.

The projection of one family member onto another—a projection that is incongruent with the actual personality organization of the recipient—creates a schism with which the only means of dealing defensively is for the projecting subject to negate or outright deny those emotions, cognitions, and behaviors of the object that do not attend to the subjects' perceptions. Dorpat (1985) comments:

In projective identification the object is perceived and related to as a distanced but not separate part of the self, and any behavior of the object that does not fit the subject's projection is frequently ignored or discounted. The reality of the object that cannot be used to verify the projection is not consciously perceived, and . . . the subject has a negative hallucination for whatever it is about the object that is discordant with his or her expectations and wishes. (pp. 181–82)

Brodey (1959) defined the relationship between the projecting subject and the recipient object in the intimate context of the family group as that of a "narcissistic relationship," wherein an aspect of the self is mirrored in the emotional, cognitive, and behavioral experiences of another family member. Brodey notes that "the inner world is transposed to the outside with little modification, and the part of the outer world attended to is selected *only* as it validates the projections, *other impinging realities being omitted*" (p. 385). Accepted as the only means by which the family can function as its own system of organization and in the context of other families, the family rigidly maintains the splitting, projective, and projective-identificatory defensive stature in which it by necessity separates and draws distinction between the internal subjective worlds of its members and the external reality of the object world. External reality can therefore be used subjectively and defensively, in both acceptance and denial, to support the contrived internal reality sense of the family's individual members and of the family as a unified whole. Brodey expands on this conceptualization:

[E]xternal reality is used in a special way. External reality is used, primarily, to rationalize the unintegrated primary process manifest in the action language (what actually happens) and to prevent the usual form of integration between internal and external reality. It has been noted that only the segment of reality that verifies projection is attended to, and even powerful impingement of asymmetric reality is omitted. Fragmentation, altered perspective, and omission—these, all unspoken and out of awareness, would compromise the rules to be mastered for socialization within this family culture. (p. 395)

The family group's coordinated establishment of a functional reality sense, however distorted that may be, is organized by the mandates of the family's shared unconscious fantasies and basic assumptions, and is therefore contingent on the maintenance of an intrafamilial process of defensive interchange. The defensive employment of splitting enables the family to circumvent the fear of its fragmentation and dissolution that it dreads and anticipates in confrontation with a perceived intrasystem schism such as that posed by the threat of emancipating adolescents. The family's emotional, cognitive, and behavioral climates dare not allow invasion by hostile, aggressive, rejective, or otherwise bad experiences, lest it be paralyzed or destroyed.

Subsequent and complementary to the process of defensive splitting, projection of disavowed or cherished aspects of the self onto another family member allows the projector to purge the self of ego-dystonic qualities or strengthen and illuminate treasured, ego-syntonic elements of the self by attributing them to another family member who collusively embodies such projected personality characteristics. Because the projecting subject cannot completely disown the disavowed aspects and would not desire to disown the treasured aspects, the subject necessarily maintains a vicarious relationship with the object of the recipient of the projections. Unable or unwilling to dissociate fully from the projected aspects of the self, the projecting subject, through this sustained vicarious relationship, forms an identification with the recipient. Projectors thus secure a part self. This process constitutes the essence of the projective-identificatory defense mechanism. The sustained identification entangles the participating family members in a self-constructed web of defensive and adaptive interdependence.

=16=

Familial Narcissistic Object Relations

To understand thoroughly and absorb the full flavor of the synergetic quality of familial organization, and thereby explain the dynamic motivational force behind the unconsciously employed mechanisms of splitting, projection, and projective identification, we will investigate the intricacies of the collusively interlocking participation of the entire family membership characteristic of the family's desperate attempt to maintain a systemic, narcissistic equilibrium as well as the balance of self-esteem and self-definition of the parents in face of their unresolved, early object-relational conflicts.

Maintaining a functional narcissistic balance is a struggle to some degree for even the healthiest of individuals. The threat of periodic onslaughts and blows to one's self-esteem renders one vulnerable to the inherent vicissitudes of the experiences of ever-expanding and maturing object relations. As noted previously, the unconscious subjection of children to the stereotypical roles attributed to them by the unique dictates of the parents' internal world of object relations creates a dynamic, interpersonal interplay formulated by introjective and projective defensive transactions. These transactional patterns re-create, through intergenerational transmission, the unresolved aspects of the previous parent-child object relations internalized and sustained within the intrapsychic of the parents only to be regenerated in current parent-child interaction. Because these early object relations and their internalization significantly affect their self-concept, in adulthood individuals will unconsciously and benevolently attempt to repeat the early object-relational experiences in an effort to master such relationships and either improve or sustain their effectivity in attaining and maintaining a healthy sense of personal esteem.

Splitting off and projecting disavowed and/or cherished aspects of the parents' personalities onto their children serves the purpose of either altering the parents' poor self-esteem or strengthening their high self-esteem, reflecting the parents' narcissistic vulnerability. Berkowitz, R. Shapiro, Zinner, and E. Shapiro (1974a) explain:

Frequently the relationships between parents and split-off aspects of themselves projected into their offspring serve to recapture lost nuclear family relations that bore on the self-esteem of the parent when he was a child. Parental dependence on the adolescent, we have found, derives significantly from the parents' own relationships (now internalized) with primary objects which led to early narcissistic fixations. In these families, a basic function of the child is to maintain parental self-esteem by colluding in reenacting with the parent these unresolved relationships from the parents' families of origin which significantly affected the development of their self-esteem. (p. 382)

The parents depend on their children to provide, through collusive relationship with the children, unyielding narcissistic supplies in support of the parents' sense of worthiness as individuals in their own right. In the process, the children's sense of worthiness and value becomes inescapably tied to the services that they collusively provide their struggling parents. The children's collusively bound attempts to free their parents from their fixation in self-esteem development subjugates the children in the process, rendering them arrested in their own striving for functional narcissistic equilibrium. This phenomenon becomes a primary and integral element of shared family regression and can take a variety of formations, all defensively and adaptively as well as unconsciously designed and implemented. A parent may identify a child as the parent's own parent, for example, of the previous generation of parent-child object relations, leaving any emotionally laden, unresolved conflicts to be played out on the current interpersonal field between parent and child.

Meissner (1984) provided a clinical example illustrative of this relational phenomenon, wherein a mother dispossesses experienced conflict and associated ambivalence in relationship to her own father and attributes the hostility to her rejected son upon birth. The child internalizes its mother's projections and becomes the very embodiment of the anger and rejection that the mother experienced with her own rageful, alcoholic father. Meissner (1984) clarifies:

To keep the lines of connection clear, it was not simply that this infant became the object of a displaced perception on the part of the mother, but that, more accurately, he was the object of the projection of her own aggressive and violent impulses that had been internalized, that is to say, introjected from her violent and abusive father. Thus, it is frequently the case that the rejection of the child can mirror the parents' own sense of rejection by their parents. (p. 410)

In this example, the mother externalizes through projective mechanism that which she had in early object-relational experiences internalized through the introjective process from her father. Sustaining as an introject within the internal object world of the mother and maintaining as an ego-dystonic characteristic, the hostile, punitive introject poses a consistent threat to the precarious self-esteem of the mother. The advent of parenthood provides the narcissistic-ally vulnerable individual with a defensive means of projectively dispossessing those feared, anxiety-producing, and otherwise ego-dystonic aspects of the self, thereby relieving injury to the ego's disposition.

Maintaining a functional sense of adequacy and confirmation of the self is a struggle inherent in all individuals throughout the life span. Therefore every context in which individuals find themselves inherently presents the individual with potential opportunities for either the maturation or the debilitation of self-esteem, and it is the nature and quality of object relations comprising the variable context, including primarily the family circle, that determine the narcissistic development of all individuals. Berkowitz, R. Shapiro, Zinner, and E. Shapiro (1974b) noted that, within the familial organization and interaction family members tend to share in their narcissistic vulnerability and defensively maintain their tenuous self-esteem by projecting disavowed and split-off aspects of the self and the internal conflicts therewith onto other family members, and then attempt to attain mastery over these conflicts by identifying with the family member who introjects the projected elements. Berkowitz et al. (1974b) clarify this phenomenon as it epitomizes the individual's unending struggle to maintain a narcissistic balance:

The precarious narcissistic equilibrium of the family as a whole is reflected in the projection by one family member into another of dissociated and conflicting aspects of self-regard. In such a fashion each individual attempts to resolve in an interpersonal sphere intrapsychic conflict concerning contradictory valuations of the self, by projecting one or the other disowned estimation of the self and attempting to locate it within another family member. (p. 356)

The emotional patterning of interaction and transaction evolving within this familial defensive and adaptive organization is characterized by what Boszor-menyi-Nagy (1962) conceptualized as "pathologic need complementarity." The reciprocation of need gratification among family members provides the family members with a sense of object relatedness to which they attribute significant meaning, though it is regressive in nature, as they collusively fall prey to the regressive pulls of infantile dependency and associated wishful fantasies. Brodey (1959) describes this reciprocation and complementarity of needs in punctuating the parent-child relationship with its narcissistic nature:

The narcissistic relationship established is reinforced by reciprocal projection and verification. This role casting and role taking is not one sided. By incorporating the ego-dystonic "irrational" side of the parent, the child not only gives to the parents a way to avoid inner anxiety and to maintain equilibrium, but receives in return (1) a pseudo-identity, (2) the narcissistic relationship attached to these ego-dystonic pseudoidentities, and (3) relief of his task of dealing with reality beyond these limits (he externalizes this by projecting responsibility to the parents who recognize it as their own, leaving and allowing for the child the irresponsible position and thus confirming the projection). (p. 397)

Brodey (1959) further suggests that through the child's relieving the conflict and associated anxiety between parental, marital partners by assuming the parents' projections, the child facilitates the narcissistically tinged endowment granted by the vulnerable parents. He explains:

By focusing the parents' energy and attention on himself, the symptomatic member thus keeps the narcissistic investment received from the parents at a maximum. [Reciprocally, Brodey (1959) continues:] The parents, too, retain maximally the narcissistic investment from the child, for upon the parents has been externalized by the child his image of the parents as the omnipotent ones. (p. 400)

The family is intertwined in a collusively defensive pattern of projective and introjective interchange in the benevolent attempt to maintain the narcissistic equilibrium of its individual membership as well as of the group as a systemic whole.

The role assigned unconsciously by the family to the child to relieve and/or rechannel parental and familial conflict not only subjugates the child and effects a precarious self-definition, but also exemplifies the fixation in which the family group as a whole regresses into a narcissistic withdrawal. This narcissistic fixation and withdrawal encapsulates the family in a fused and enmeshed organization of relationship, wherein ego boundaries remain blurred and diffuse. Individual family members become extensions of each other's psychic structuralization, preventing functional differentiation of ego systems. In such a familial, organizational typology, family members by necessity attempt to coerce and control their self-extensions in order to sustain their already tenuous narcissistic equilibrium. This subjugation of family members leading to role allocations is unconsciously determined by the family to be a requirement for sustenance of the family system as well as of the individual. The result of this group enmeshment within which introjective, projective, and projective-identificatory defensive engagement ensues is that the family members delineate each other as self-extensions and thereby use one another as narcissistic objects. The delineation and use of narcissistic objects can serve as a functional means of bridging the individual, both child and adult, to the realities of the object world insofar as ego boundaries are well differentiated within the familial organization, leading to the conscious perception of separate, though interdependent, identities comprising the family group.

However, insofar as individual identities remain diffuse as a result of the lack of ego differentiation and overdependence, family members steadfastly maintain a grip on their self-extensions of other members, desperately attempting to coerce the narcissistic object into fulfilling the mostly unconscious ego demands and wishful fantasies encompassing the projecting family members.

The narcissistic object's inability or unwillingness to embody the projections of other family members through introjection of the projected elements produces anxiety and fear within the family members and is perceived to be a threat to the narcissism of the frustrated projector—a personal affront to the integrity not only of the individual members but also of the family as a unique group. The response to this assault on the esteem of the self and the group is, to variable degrees, experienced narcissistic rage at the ungratifying narcissistic object.

Berkowitz et al. (1974a) punctuate the parent-child relationship to explain this common, dysfunctional familial phenomenon:

The parents themselves demonstrate a failure in the development of adequate psychic structure for self-esteem regulation which leads to an overdependence on external objects for the maintenance of self-esteem. This externalization of intrapsychic conflicts around self-esteem in these families results in the use of offspring as narcissistic objects: shortcomings perceived in the child are experienced as reflecting the parents' own inadequacies and are responded to by narcissistic rage and devaluation. The child is then required to maintain parental self-esteem by functioning as a recipient for the parents' unacceptable depreciated estimations of themselves which they project into him. (pp. 393–94)

Berkowitz et al. further noted that the more the children fail to assume the projected elements of the parents' perceived self-inadequacies, the more rageful the parents become in further degradation of the children. Under the increasing pressure of parental projections, the children will succumb to one or the other of two adaptive mechanisms: They will either further resist the subjugating pressure, thereby intensifying the vicious circularity of defensive interplay, or they will futilely comply with the parents' use of them as narcissistic objects, thereby participating in the collusive dynamism by identifying with the parental projections. In either case, the negative-feedback looping serves to perpetuate the problematic process featured by the overinvolved, highly narcissistic family.

Designated as narcissistic objects, children are delegated the arduous responsibility of maintaining the parents' self-esteem. Richter (1976) considered two differing means by which this dynamic, narcissistic relationship transpires. The parents project unclaimed aspects of their own faltering ego-ideal, hoping that their children are both able and willing to actualize these unfilfilled wishes and desires incorporated into the idealization of the parental self. Because ego boundaries are blurred in the narcissistic object relationship, the parents are capable of feeling aggrandized by the accomplishments of the children, as though the achievements were possessed within the parents; they thereby bolster their self-esteem. The other pattern of narcissistic object relationship is characterized by the aforementioned parental projections of disavowed aspects of their selves, which are deemed ego dystonic and injurious to the ego integrity of the parents.

It is possible for both of these dynamic transactions to eventuate simultaneously as one child in the family becomes the narcissistic object imbued with
the good aspects of the selves of the parents while another child assumes the
projected bad elements of the parents' selves. The concept of familial role
assignment makes this phenomenon operational. In an even more dysfunctional
light, and more confusing and potentially growth inhibiting to the child, one
child may serve concurrently as the recipient of both positive and negative
projected elements. The child is expected to, and sometimes does so successfully, live out these contradictory personality characteristics. The child in this
case is more likely to escape this binding interactional process unscathed if the
good projected aspects come from one parent and the bad elements are assumed
from the other. The good parental introject holds potential for outweighing the
bad parental introject, leaving the child capable of making sense, by identification with the good introject, of an otherwise conflictual and confusing experience. Insofar as the projected good aspects of the one parent are realistic
enough to be effectively imbued by the child, a healthy identification can be
formed that can stabilize the child in face of the impingement of the bad introject.

The aforementioned description of the narcissistic object relationship inherent in the family that experiences difficulty in internally maintaining a functional narcissistic equilibrium of its individual members as well as the balance
of the group as a systemic whole is formulated on what Stierlin (1973, 1974,
1976) referred to as "ego-binding," a conceptualization of the family interaction in which the parents "substitute their own controlling ego for the child's
developing ego and subject him to conflicting messages" (Stierlin 1976, p.
282). Stierlin (1974) suggested that the binding parents force children to subscribe to the parents' distorted style of cognition and perception, thereby facilitating in the children the development of a similarly distorted view of themselves and the object world. Children, then, are incapable of developing a sense
of their own discriminating ego.

In contrast with the concept of ego-binding, Stierlin (1976) addressed another type of binding, in which the parents and children are entrapped in overly
narcissistic involvement. "Id-binding" is characterized by the parents who
"overstimulate and infantalize their child and thereby manipulate and exploit
his dependency needs" (p. 282). The children are enlisted by the parents to
perform a reparative function in securing what the parents discover missing in
their own sense of selfhood and self-fulfillment. The parents siphon from the
children the resources with which to fulfill idealized wishes or disavow ego-
dystonic impulses and personality characteristics. These children "then appear
commissioned to provide their parents with desperately needed 'id nutriment' "
(Stierlin 1973, p. 209). The recursive cycle of defensive and adaptive interchange is effected by the child's reliance on the parents, as facilitated by the
parents' provision of an ego-identity, however distorted that may be, and the
child's reception of narcissistic supplies inclusive of a sense of grandiosity.

The engulfing emotional attachment characteristic of the family in narcissistic object-relational engagement renders the members inescapably tied to each other, desperately clinging to what they perceive as the only means by which they can maintain an integrated sense of self—a self balanced in self-definition and self-regard. Bowen (1960) believes that in such a collusively fused sense of relatedness, ego differentiation becomes impossible, and the parents care for their children not as distinct persons but as extensions of the parents' selves. The parents' concern is for the images of themselves, which they project onto, locate, and focalize in their child. In this sense, the object of the child becomes a contrivance of the parents' narcissistic strivings. The narcissistic object, the "self-object" in Kohut's (1977) term, serves to feed the "merger-hungry personality" of the parents, who are unable to perceive their children as independent of themselves and are unable to discriminate their own emotions, cognitions, and perceptions from those of the children. The children in essence live through the parents.

This type of parent-child narcissistic, object-relational configuration can take other forms of transactional patterning. Not only may the parents facilitate an object relationship conducive to the children's acquired, excessive dependence on the parental figures for guidance of the children's ego development, but they may form such an intensified dependence on the children for narcissistic supplies and enhancement that they entertain fantasies of oral gratification and fusion with the children, as if the children were perceived as the parents of the parents. Parentifying the children serves to entrap both the children and the parents in a symbiotic matrix in which all parties experience intense anxiety at the mere thought of physical or emotional separation. The children are forced prematurely to assume functional independence at the expense of failing to develop healthy, age-appropriate dependence on the adult object world. They fail to form object relations characterized by healthy interdependence and in some cases, Modell (1975) suggested, may develop a narcissistic illusion of self-sufficiency wherein they fail to develop the capacity for healthy object relatedness in either a supportive or a supported role. Boszormenyi-Nagy (1965b) added that the more the parents parentify the children by behaving immaturely, the more the children are coerced into assuming the complementary position of "parent" by behaving prematurely adultlike. All parties fail to acquire age-appropriate ego functioning.

In yet another form of narcissistic parent-child, object-relational patterning, the children are delegated the role of actualizing the parents' unfulfilled aspects of the self, which linger in fantasied experience or have been completely repressed into the unconscious realm of the psyche. Unconscious parental fantasies of infantile dependence on their own parents may alter the perception of the parents' developing children as the children are gradually emancipated and seek expansion in object relations. The parents may perceive the children as revolting actively against the unitary authority of the family circle and resent the emancipation while simultaneously attaining vicarious gratification from its enactment (Meissner 1978a). Zinner and R. Shapiro (1972) expanded on this conceptualization by highlighting the dual function of the adolescent children's liberation (perceived as rebellion by the parents) in balancing the parents' narcissistic equilibrium in face of unresolved id-instinctual drives:

Within a family, then, a parent may be free both to experience the vicarious gratification of his own impulse through his adolescent and to repudiate and punish the adolescent for expressing those same impulses. Had this gratification-punishment axis remained internalized one might imagine the parent to be bound by a corresponding neurotic turmoil. With one aspect of a previously internalized conflict now projected on to an interpersonal relationship, one can envisage a diminution of parental anxiety with, for example, the parent speaking for the superego, and the adolescent, as the parent sees him, speaking for the instinctual demand. (p. 526)

The gist of this intrapsychic, object-relational experience, played out in the interpersonal sphere of the family group, is that parents who have failed to develop a well-integrated ego-identity and a functional and effective means of maintaining a stable self-concept, rely defensively and adaptively on the significant objects of the family system to help regulate a balance of self-esteem. Experienced parental anxiety revolving around unconscious, instinctual drives and urges as well as unconscious fantasies of reestablishing infantile dependence, omnipotent control, and fusion with the mothering object may well trigger the erection of a defensive stature conducive to the maintenance of tenuously established ego consolidation and ego differentiation. The associated defensive armamentarium often incorporates the use of family members as the recipients of these unacceptable, unconscious experiences projected onto them. In this light, the children in the family may, upon parental consignment, serve as the moral conscience for the parents who feel, at least unconsciously, incapable of assuming for themselves.

Stierlin (1973) describes one aspect of this interpersonal phenomenon with an example of the child who is allowed to a variable degree to detach from the familial circle while still remaining narcissistically tied to the parental, reparative mandations:

[T]he delegate may become commissioned to become his parent's conscience. . . . This type of delegate is allowed to move, temporarily, away from the parental orbit, i.e. he is not devastated by excruciating unconscious guilt should he leave (i.e. betray) his parents. Such a delegate is allowed to leave his parents—on the condition that he takes it upon himself to atone for their guilt. (p. 209)

In a more generalized and universal vein, Stierlin (1973) further notes that parents may use the narcissistic object of their children as the instrument of their "self-observation." The parents transfer the observation, attention, and affirmation of their selves to their perception and evaluation of their children. "The child might have to provide the constant living contrast of badness or craziness which the parent needs in order to remain reassured about his (or her) inwardly doubted virtue or sanity'' (p. 209). The children serve as an instrument of comparison and contrast as well as the recipients of disavowed parental projections. In this light, the parents' ego-ideals are fortified, albeit at the expense of their children's emotional, cognitive, and behavioral maladjustment as well as the lack of a self-proclaimed ego-identity. Conversely, Richter (1976) believes that the children may be assigned the task of fulfilling the unattained narcissistic strivings of the parents who therewith form a narcissistic identification with the successful children, bolstering their own ego-ideals. Richter also suggests that, in a differing vein, parents who subscribe to puritan morality may alleviate their own experienced anxiety over the failure to attend to such mandated codes by unconsciously assigning such a duty to their children, who are then directed to exercise such mandations for the parents. Richter (1976) explains that these parents

unconsciously try to silence their self-reproaches by making the child achieve a lofty ideal of purity in their place. In keeping with the parental ideal self, which the child is expected to realize, he will be given a perfectionistic training directed towards greatness, strength, success, or towards absolute moral integrity; and through this pressure and through this constraint he experiences difficulties of development which are typical of this role and have been amply illustrated by casuistic examples. (p. 388)

The children in the family are given a position of great power in stabilizing the parents' narcissistic equilibrium as well as, in general, the very sustenance of the parents' sense of the self. The children are compelled to assume this role because it provides not only the forthcoming of narcissistic supplies but also grants the children a relational context in which to formulate and promulgate their identity or sense of self. The relational context thus becomes mutually entrapping and reciprocally generated. Unable to express themselves, the parents as well as the children fail to achieve functional interdependence, and come to form and process a fused sense of oneness wherein differentiation becomes tenuous at best, and assertion of the self is contingent on the collusive participation of the narcissistic object. In this object-relational process, all parties involved regress in collusive coordination to a position of familial torpidity, a state of symbiotic engulfment, and an inability to evolve in maturation either as individuals or as a family group.

=====17=====

Further Study of Familial Narcissistic Object Relations

As mentioned in the preceding chapter, parents may exert a great deal of pressure on their children to perform to the standards established by the parents as a desperate, albeit precarious, means of stabilizing parental self-esteem and self-definition. Contradictory qualities of parental self-representations behoove the parents unconsciously and defensively to project their devalued self-images onto their children or, conversely, to project their cherished self-images as a means of focalizing and containing them in their children and thereby forming an identification with them. In either case, the children are enlisted to serve as narcissistic objects, viewed by the parents as extensions of their selves. Those children who are either unwilling or unable to alleviate parental anxiety over contradictory ego valuations, and who thereby fail to equilibrate their parents' narcissism are subject to the rage directed toward them by their parents in face of their fear of losing control of not only their children's emotional, cognitive, and social development but also of their own sense of self-cohesiveness and self-identity. Meissner (1984) describes the parents' struggle for a stable sense of personhood and personal value:

[T]he parents themselves seem not to have developed adequate inner resources for the relatively independent regulation of their own self-esteem. They frequently demonstrate the typical vacillation between narcissistic extremes: from haughty, entitled grandiosity and inflated self-concepts, even to the point of omnipotence, on the one hand, to a sense of inferiority, inadequacy, worthlessness, and shamefulness, on the other. (p. 404)

Meissner stresses that these parents have failed to establish functional autonomy and independence from objects of early relational experiences, and therefore use their children as current narcissistic objects, in place of their earliest infantile objects, on whom they can become dependent for narcissistic supplies in aid of self-esteem regulation. Berkowitz et al. (1974b) note that such parental reliance on children

for narcissistic sustenance derives from their own relationships with primary objects that resulted in narcissistic fixations. Hence, in these families the child's basic function is perceived as maintaining parental self-esteem by colluding in re-enacting with the parent unresolved relationships from the parents' own nuclear families which significantly affected their self-esteem. (p. 358)

It is not only the perceived good or bad aspects of the selves that the parents defensively externalize in their continued struggle for self-identity and personal value. The fear of the parents' own sense of weakness or inadequacy, perceived as being directly threatening to the sustenance of the self, may become the generated thrust of parental defensive projection onto their children. The parents project onto their children that which is ego-dystonically intolerable to the self: the fantasied wishes of regression to infantile dependence on the parental objects. Richter (1976) explains:

Parents can feel big, strong and active, for example, as long as they can find realized in the child the feelings of smallness, impotence and passivity they have been warding off. The child has to, as it were, actualize the depression which the parents deny in themselves. In this role the child represents the helpless reverse side, by denying which the parents are able to retain a self-image of greatness and omnipotence. (p. 388)

Richter further explains the mutual growth inhibition that this object-relational phenomenon inculcates in both parents and child:

Naturally, for a child of this kind the danger of stunted development is particularly great, since it is only by weakness and wretchedness that he can provide the necessary condition which allows the parents by contrast to assert their narcissistic ideas of grandeur successfully. (p. 388)

In these familial object-relational experiences, the children are expected to fulfill unconscious, regressive needs that were never satisfied in the parents during their early object-relational experiences and that can never be gratified in the current marital relationship. Not only do the children of this familial configuration become used as narcissistic objects, they also—and this is equally influential on psychosocial development—internalize the immature narcissism of their parents and are thereby denied an effective role model with which to engage in later adult object relations at the level of maturity.

The parental experiences of helplessness and depression attributed to the children through projective mechanism, to be vicariously actualized for the parents by the children, do not, however, fully vindicate the parents of these cognitive and affective states. Rather, these states, in only partial disavowal, remain within the experiential realm of the parents through their identification with them in their children subsequent to the children's internalization of such projected qualities. This continued experience of helplessness and depression that the parents have acquired by failing to live up to the mandations of their own ego-ideals (though it is partially disowned by projection onto the children) is left to be further defended against and played out in the interpersonal, familial field. Identifying with their children who have embodied the weak, inefficient selves of the parents, the parents respond to such experience with devaluation and repudiation of the internalizing family members. Berkowitz et al. (1974a) explain:

In this manner, the depression and loss of self-esteem which the parent experiences when failing to live up to his ego ideal is transformed into anger at the adolescent who has come to embody the poorly performing self. The discrepancy within an individual between the actual self and an ideal, aggrandized version of the self has thus been transmuted into interpersonal conflict between family members. (p. 382)

In another pattern of familial narcissistic object relations, Paul and Grosser (1964) described a transactional process wherein the parents, unable to tolerate helplessness and narcissistic injury, attribute to the children not their experienced low self-esteem but, rather, their desired omnipotence. The parents retain their helplessness as a means of complementing the omnipotence and omniscience they attribute to other family members. By this means, the parents retain some hope of making sense of the otherwise hopeless interactional situation and acquiring some means of controlling its effects. Projecting such omnipotent, controlling powers onto the children only intensifies the perception and use of the children as narcissistic objects. The fear of losing, in essence, a desperately-clung-to part of their selves elicits intense anxiety and conflict within the parents. Paul and Grosser further noted that the experienced helplessness on the part of the parents is the result of a partial awareness of the symbiotic attachment that they and their children have continually struggled to resolve and relinquish. With this fear of helplessness and experienced ambivalence concerning object attachment and loss, the parents dread the perceived imminence of loss of the loved object, and the resulting fragmentation and dissolution of the self.

In a similar vein, an interactional process may ensue in which the parents again project images of their selves in opposition to those reflecting their ego-ideal. Parents who may have a strong wish, for example, to be strong, autonomous, and independent, whether or not they may be so in actuality, may attribute projectively to their children such personality characteristics that are oppositional yet complementary to their own. Delineating their children as weak, needy, and dependent permits the parents to present themselves as being consistent with their ego-ideals as well as being effectively loving and caring in their parenting efforts. However, because the parents retain an element of the projected self and identify with it in the recipients of the projection, in the

recipients' perceived, unduly clinging dependence the parents are likely simultaneously to resent their children in anger and disgust. E. Shapiro et al. (1977)
expand on this conceptualization:

In other words, if each parent sees himself in his own way as "lovingly dependent,"
the . . . child is seen in a shared unconscious manner as ruthlessly independent. If each
sees himself as "strong and autonomous," without dependent needs, the designated
child is perceived as ravenously demanding and totally dependent. (p. 79)

In the example of parents' viewing their children's age-appropriate dependency needs as draining the parents in a manner laden with hostility, Berkowitz
(1981) suggested that they may resort to either of two defense mechanisms at
their disposal: They may capitalize on their children's perceived dependency,
punctuating their children's hostile motives as proof of their (the parents') need
to counter the aggression with applied love and generosity consistent with their
ego-ideals; or, conversely, they may transfer their own feelings of dependency
experienced in their earlier object relations, which were never fully met, to the
current parent-child relations and negate the humiliating affect of the experiences by subduing the dependency needs of their children. "Then [in Berkowitz's words] the disowned needs of the parents seen in the child may be thwarted
by the parents who had felt those same needs thwarted in their own development'' (p. 191).
   The regressive force to which the entire family succumbs in the face of
autonomy-versus-dependence issues is characterized by the blurring of ego
boundaries and the lack of individuated and differentiated ego-identities. The
enmeshment characteristic of this familial organization renders the individual
members dysfunctionally reliant on the others for support of their ego functioning and regulation of their narcissistic balance. The family system equilibrates
in stability only insofar as the members are able and willing to meet the narcissistic demands and elicitations of one another. The separation and individuation
of any one member, and the resulting emancipation from the family circle,
present a remarkable threat to the narcissistic sustenance of the other members
individually as well as of the family group as a whole. The narcissistically
vulnerable parents perceive the emancipation of their adolescent children as a
blow to their self-esteem and integrity, disrupting their tenuously established
narcissistic equilibrium. The resulting parental experiences of anxiety and rage
subject the parents to defensive repudiation of their children and the projection
and projective identification of split-off, disavowed aspects of their narcissistically injured selves onto their bad, "disrespectful" children. The family in
regressive and defensive stature as a whole clings to the only perceived hope
available—the further intensified solicitation of remaining family members as
narcissistic extensions of their selves and targets for disavowed projections.
   The narcissistic injury to the parents and the repudiation of their children
may become so intense that the parents will defensively extrude their children

from the family circle. This defensive ploy may assume a characteristic similar to what Stierlin (1974) referred as the "mode of expelling," wherein the parents reject their children whom they perceive to be an impediment to the collusively shared ideal of the family group. "A strong centrifugal force pushes many of these children into premature separations" (p. 170).

It is more out of neglect, however, that these parents abandon their children or expel them from the family confines. In response to narcissistic injury at the hands of emancipating loved ones, on the other hand, the parents, in conjunction with projecting devalued estimations of themselves onto the children, are more likely to expel them prematurely from the family unit not only out of the anxiety over separation and feared abandonment but even more so out of the pain and shame of being, from their perspective, rejected by their children. Berkowitz (1981) explains:

Many . . . parents of . . . adolescents who appear at first glance to be simply rejecting parents are, in fact, responding out of their enormous vulnerability to separation anxiety and dread of abandonment by defensively rejecting and abandoning their adolescent child before the child can abandon them. This same dynamic can operate in possessive parents when the loss of the separating adolescent appears irretrievable and inevitable. (p. 191)

Often the mere threat of parental rejection is enough to subdue the liberating children in their quest for autonomy and more expansive object relations, and pull them back into the family orbit of collusive interaction conducive to the facilitation of the misguided family ideal of togetherness and mutual dedication.

Within the confines of this familial narcissistic object-relational organization, ego boundaries remain permeably weak and individual identities remain diffuse. Family members engage one another not as whole objects in differentiated, interdependent interaction but as part objects, using one another for the fueling of narcissistic supplies and as containers of disavowed projections. Individual ego systems as well as the family ego system fail to flourish within this field of narcissistic objects. On the contrary, their ego systems deplete as the individuals acquire a faulty sense of selfhood and personal value through their defensively perpetuated interactional organization. The family fails to facilitate the mirroring of the self-definition and self-assertion of its membership as differentiated, autonomous persons, each of whom seeks an identity reflective, ideally, of the interdependent functioning and purposeful striving of the family group as a social unit. Ego boundaries remain blurred as individual identities diffuse and the family group regresses in collusive interplay to a state of perpetual dependence on one another for the very sustenance of the precariously perceived individual selves and the family group as a unit. Individual family members do not facilitate mutual ego support; rather, they unempathically impinge on one another in the desperate attempt to acquire narcissistic supplies and/or project disavowed personality characteristics and cognitive and affective experiences. Individual and collective ego impoverishment is the result of familial narcissistic object relations.

Ego-depleted individual family members inherently assume an overdependence on the spoken and acted approval of others both within and outside the family circle to confirm their tenuous sense of personal worthiness and self-affirmation. For the individual family members, the narcissistic object serves a regulatory function of balancing intrapersonal self-esteem. Incapable of sustaining an intrasubjectively acquired regulation of functional narcissism, family members desperately cling to one another as self-extensions that serve to replenish their depleted ego systems. Within this interlocking transactional experience of the family group, the members collusively assume full responsibility for each other's subjective experiences and welfare; members maintain a powerful function of such potential intensity that they are able not only to live for one another but also to anticipate accurately the emotional, cognitive, and behavioral experiences that transpire within the family group. Brodey (1961) comments:

[I]n the narcissistic system of [family] relationships the unexpected is so reduced that each family member can predict how the other will behave within the family constellation. This being so, each member takes on a responsibility that most of us happily to large measure escape. Ordinarily, one can act for oneself—and leave to the other person the responsibility for taking his own position. But as the unexpected is removed and the system closed, each move would bring a known balancing and expected move from the other; then *one possesses a power of anticipation,* which gives one's acts new meaning as controlling the total balance. Operationally one becomes responsible for balancing others. (p. 72)

Within this emotionally constricting familial atmosphere family members must fend for themselves, so to speak, as they defensively struggle to maintain some sense of self-cohesion and ego-identity. Assuming responsibility for one another's intrasubjective experiences and for the unity and sustenance of the family group, individual members desperately attempt to locate and assume an adaptational position conducive to meeting the prescribed mandates of the family social group as well as those of individual biopsychosocial development. Boszormenyi-Nagy (1965b) speaks of the inherent complexity of this wholehearted effort:

Any family member who becomes caught in an object role in the network of relational systems is at a considerable disadvantage. It is at the whim of the Other's internal need templates, a motivational field which is basically inaccessible to his own needs. Perhaps his best countermove is to make the Others the relational objects of his needs and selectively to perceive only the ego-syntonic aspects of the transaction, but the result can be a mutually paranoid and defensive attitude on the part of both sides. (p. 60)

Thus is set into perpetual motion the defensive array of mutual introjections, projections, and projective identifications characteristically applied by the family interactional system comprised of undifferentiated, excessively dependent individuals who lack the fully developed capacity to maintain a healthy sense of self-constancy and object constancy.

=18=

Familial Object Relations and the Entrapping Emotional Process

Unable wholly to own their own conflictual self-representations of both "good" and "bad" qualities, the family members rely on defensive employment of projective, projective-identificatory, and introjective mechanisms as a precarious means of protecting their self-dignity as well as of attempting to establish their own self-definition and thereby form a stable, internal self-representation. Thus is established what Bowen (1960) referred to as the family's unique "emotional process." In this process, family members are unconsciously and collusively dictated to assume an integral position sustaining the transactional interchange by projecting disavowed aspects of the self onto others and reciprocating by introjecting others' projections. Inherent in this defensive and adaptive interplay is the understanding that no members are permitted to leave the field in an attempt at differentiation and separation, lest all family members involved experience separation anxiety and fear of dissolution of the self and the family group.

Since the family members involved in the emotional process live both with and for the others, they are compelled to embody and actualize each other's projections and help facilitate mutual identifications. Entrapped in their own systemic organization, enmeshed in each other's sense of being, the family group evolves as a tightly enclosed and highly constricted system suppressing its own growth and contributory position in the social world as well as stifling the individual psychosocial development of its membership. Slipp (1973) expands descriptively on this familial phenomenon:

Without a stable, integrated, and internalized system of introjects, the parents remained stimulus-bound and needed external objects upon whom to project certain split introjects. In turn, other family members were required to introject, incorporate, and act out these split introjects. However, in order to stabilize the *internal* system of the parents, the entire family became locked into a rigid, mutually controlling *external* system of interaction in which each one's self-esteem and survival was dependent upon the other member's participation. (pp. 384–85)

The symbiotic involvement characteristic of this familial emotional process reflects the sense of self-object undifferentiatedness characteristic of the earlier object-relational, mother-infant matrix. Subject to regressive pulls in this direction of merger, individual family members, while unconsciously obliging their regressive, fantasied wishes with the provision of blissful experiences, simultaneously defend against such wishes for fear of engulfment. They thus become entrapped in a push-pull, object-relational engagement. The vacillating and reciprocating exchange of introjections and projections exemplifies and plays out this ambivalence as it becomes not strictly a dyadic interchange reminiscent of the earlier mother-child bond but spills over to incorporate the intrafamilial object relationships inclusive of a dyadic, triadic, and other multicomponent relational configurations. Bowen (1960) describes this emotionally binding and constricting familial process:

I have used the terms "emotional demand" and "emotional process" to describe the emotional responsiveness by which one family member responds automatically to the emotional state of another, without either being consciously aware of the process. . . . This "emotional process" is deep and it seems somehow to be related to the *being* of a person. It runs silently beneath the surface between people who have very close relationships. It operates during periods of conflict and periods of calm harmony. (p. 368)

The thrust of this strong motivational force that encapsulates its participating members in its perpetuating whirlwind and dictates the daily interactional experiences, as well as the longitudinal, evolutionary development of both the family group and its individual members, hinges on the uniquely interconnecting array of regressive transferences characteristic of all family systems. The family's emotional process evolves from its inception with the initiation of its system by the forging of the marital bond through the family's developmental life cycle. To punctuate the evolutionary process in terms of developmental phases, each phase, incorporating its inherent familial object-relational experiences, emanates from and builds on the relational experiences of the previous phase. Thus any object-relational configuration at any given juncture in the life cycle has its roots in the very earliest object-relational experiences of the family system.

As Meissner (1978a) suggests: "The family emotional process is a natural outgrowth of the earliest dynamic interactions within the family which has its own inherent continuity and history" (p. 82). Meissner further notes that, because the family life cycle is continuous, the vicissitudes of ongoing object relations originate not directly from any given parent-child generation; rather, the relational dynamics carry over transgenerationally to incorporate elements of transference patterns transpiring in reflection of significant object relations and internalizations of previous generations.

A family interactional pattern exemplary of the aforementioned entrapping emotional process is that characterized by the term used by Wynne et al. (1958), "pseudo-mutuality." This pattern of familial object relations serves to confine the family members within the flexible yet impermeable boundaries encircling its self-perceived self-sufficient social system. The family group interacts collusively to prevent divergence of any one member from its constrictive delineations, though in the process it further encloses the system:

In short, the pseudo-mutual relation involves a characteristic dilemma: divergence is perceived as leading to disruption of the relation and therefore must be avoided; but if divergence is avoided, growth of the relation is impossible. (p. 207)

It is a false sense of mutuality that the family collusively engenders, the established outcome of which is a stabilizing force that traps family members into assuming a complementary and contributory position in the family's on-going emotional process. Wynne et al. (1958) explain:

In pseudo-mutuality emotional investment is directed more toward maintaining the *sense* of reciprocal fulfillment of expectations than toward accurately perceiving changing expectations. Thus, the new expectations are left unexplored, and the old expectations and roles, even though outgrown and inappropriate in one sense, continue to serve as the structure for the relation. (p. 207)

Wynne et al. further suggest that this intrafamilial, relational position holds firm—neither faltering nor developing, holding the family system in entropic dormancy, disseminating nothing but intense emotional discharge and impeding the formation of mature, genuine object-relational experiences.

This type of constrictive and entrapping process is conducive to the facilitation of what Avery (1982) conceptualized as "family secrets." Family members collusively and covertly agree to refrain from revelation within and outside the family circle of a given family secret "which, if openly expressed, would clash violently with the family's ego ideal and threaten its object ties" (p. 471). Avery contended that a shared family ego-ideal of perpetual togetherness and empathic concern may functionally bind a family in spite of their excessive object hunger and manipulative, transactional interchange because it gives the family a sense, albeit misguidedly, of respectable identity. Should the secret be expressed openly and the family's ego-ideal obliterated, the family would be left to face the resultant pain, guilt, and shame.

Stierlin (1977) found that such an overly cohesive family unit, guided by its ideal of maintaining a sense of togetherness and solidarity, is generated primarily by the guilt that the family would experience should the ideal be shattered by intrusive outsiders or family members attempting to age-appropriately liberate themselves from the circle of harmony. Guilt is very easily transmitted from family member to family member in the intensely emotional family process, and all share in recognizing its motivational source and eliminating any intrafamilial emotional, cognitive, or behavioral expression perceived to be oppositional to the family unity.

Because, as previously noted, family members are not able to flourish in their intrafamilial and extrafamilial object relations as a result of the restrictions of the family's entrapping emotional process, the family members relate to one another as mere part objects, never grasping fully the sense of wholeness of the others or of themselves. What intrasubjective experience is acquired is readily disseminated for the mutual sharing of the collective group, and family members relate to one another as one collective, shared psychological agency, as part of which each member assumes a complementary and contributory role in its structure and organization. Boszormenyi-Nagy (1965b) expands on this conceptualization:

The nature of part-object role assignments in symbiotic systems differs fundamentally from the dialogic role relationships of differentiated individuals. Moreover, the multiperson, *intersubjective sharing* quality makes these object-role assignments differ even from immature, partial object-role assignments on a one-to-one basis. . . . Further, since in these families no one is ever fully committed to relate to other members as a whole person, and no one is ever able to offer himself as one whole object to any other member's strivings, no reciprocal relationship can ever be formed. The resulting, deficient relational and emotional development becomes fixated by the fact that all members contribute unconsciously to the maintenance of the state of intersubjective sharing. (pp. 63–64)

The family members' individual senses of the self emerge from this engrossing, object-relational context and take form around the perceptions and delineations each has of the others and the mandates set forth by the shared family ego-ideal. Within this emotional vortex, family members necessarily become acutely sensitive to and aware of the emotional, cognitive, and behavioral manifestations of the others. Highly responsive to these manifestations, the family members coordinate with precision because it is for the collective welfare of the family group that the individuals live, and dissolution of the family's purpose and ideal means dissolution of the individual members' selves.

Within this undifferentiated, conglomerated mass of ego systems, individual egos, insofar as they can be definitively demarcated, assume a characteristic more adequately and accurately described as pseudo egos. The pseudo ego develops in organization, structuralization, and functionability under the auspices and in validation of the other family members' projections. The family members' internal psychic worlds are reflective of the family's emotional process and the perceptions and delineations the others have of them. The internal sense of reality thereby formed is reinforced only insofar as it continues in congruence with and reinforcement of others' expectations. Individual family members will manipulate their own reality sense and modify their subjective experiences in accordance with the family's projections. The family's reinforcement of this distorted and externally derived reality imposes on the self-definitions of its membership.

Family members assume these prescribed definitions of the self lest they be without an ego-identity—the result of perceived imminent fragmentation and dissolution. The family members are prone to develop "as-if" (Deutsch 1942) characterizations or "false self" (Winnicott 1965) organizations, wherein they, as a means of functional adaptation to their environmental context, vicariously assume whatever positional role is deemed necessary to facilitate the familial complementarity. Family members learn to adapt to the familial context, organize their subjective reality around it, and reciprocate the delineations and externalizations transpiring within this context.

In this pattern of interpersonally derived intrapsychic experiencing, there is established an object-relational configuration that is analogous to Brodey's (1959) conceptualization of the infant in adaptation to its mother's externalizations:

The infant perhaps would learn that survival within this relationship depended on expressing its own needs in a way and at a time conforming with the mother's projected expectation. The long-term reinforcement of the needs that happened to match the mother's, and the frustration of the needs omitted by the mother, would then alter the child's behavior in the direction of validating the mother's projections. (p. 385)

Brodey (1959, 1965) adds that family members involve themselves, in this light, not in relationships among genuine, whole objects but in relationships among the individual selves and their internal representations of others. Family members relate to each other insofar as the others are perceived as being extended parts of their selves.

The family members are not, however, powerless in this entrapping emotional process; they maintain the capacity either to validate or to invalidate the others' delineations and projections, both of which put leverage on and thereby strongly influence the others. Assuming the projected elements and thereby verifying their efficacy, members contribute complementarily to the facilitation of the recursive pattern of defensively reciprocating interplay in which all involved parties perpetuate the introjective-projective transactional patterning inherent in its regressive positioning, in a desperate and benevolent search for individual and collective identities.

The object-relational patterning is set, and the regressive force of its procession entrenches the involved family members within its constrictive parameters. The family becomes stuck in its very systemically contrived pattern of defensive and adaptive interchange. Should any given family member fail to assume the externalized elements of others via introjective mechanism, and thereby fail to embody and actualize the split-off, disavowed elements of the others' selves, the resulting anomaly presented to the system breaks its circular motility, alters its interlocking coordination, and results in a shift to a new organizational level of interactive experience. This new level of familial organization holds potential for either progressive movement in the direction of more age-appropriate, developmental phase-appropriate, and mature object relations or, conversely, for further regressive entrenchment in growth-inhibiting defensive transaction.

Because the family group as a system has so much invested in maintaining its carefully, yet mostly unconsciously, devised emotional process based on its basic shared, unconscious fantasies and assumptions and their associated delineations, it may become difficult, and sometimes inconceivable, for the family to modify its intrasubjective and intersubjective experiences in continuous reorganization of and advancement to higher orders of interpersonal relations. The family group, insofar as it clings to defensive interaction as a means of preserving its precariously and tenuously established sense of existence, is subject to the fixated perpetuation of regressive interpersonal transactions. As noted previously, the advent of adolescence and its inherent biopsychosocial vicissitudes presents the family as a group with the arduous and challenging task of providing a holding environment conducive to the facilitation of separation-individuation and expansion of object relations of, for example, its liberating adolescent members. This developmental phase of the family life cycle provides the family with the prime opportunity either to advance in individual and familial growth, productivity, and constructivity or to stagnate in regressive fixation. Clinical experience indicates that all too often the regressive force of defensive interplay strongly dictates the family's course of evolution during this trying period of time. Further investigation is therefore warranted into the involved factors of its phenomenology.

One contributing factor to the effectiveness of adolescent separation and individuation for both the children and the family group is the degree of ego differentiation, autonomous functioning, and ego consolidation afforded the children up to the pubertal phase. This is of course directly correlational to the ego development and self-definition of the entire family membership, in particular of the parents. To the degree that the adolescent children's ego system is functionally differentiated and integrated, the children will be capable of selectively internalizing and identifying with the familial externalizations that are more ego syntonic and enriching to the development of the self and to dismiss those perceptions, delineations, and projections inhibitory of ego autonomy and ego expansion. The inherent vicissitudes of adolescent development do, however, make this maturational acquisition a trying experience for the children that can be either facilitated or impeded by the quality of the holding context of the familial organization.

Meissner (1984) pointed out that what adolescent children internalize from the familial organization becomes inextricably tied to the idiosyncratic dynamics of the children's internally processed drives, fantasies, and associated defensive needs. Insofar as the children struggle with unresolved symbiotic attachment, clinging to such attachment will be necessary to maintain self-cohesion in face of impending separation and autonomy; and the children's introjections will be shaded in nature and quality by both object dependence and defensive struggle against such dependence. Meissner explains that what the children internalize through projective mechanism from the family relational system

is excessively colored by infantile dependence on or defenses against the attachment, excessively colored with infantile narcissistic needs and its [sic] attendent vicissitudes, whether of narcissistic grandiosity or devaluation or narcissistic rage; the attachment thus becomes contaminated by the intense ambivalence of the tension between the need for increasing autonomy and independence and the impediment of continuing dependence, the failure to achieve a sense of differentiated self. (p. 390)

Meissner further maintains that children therefore fail to integrate potentially healthy, constructive introjections and identifications therewith, leaving their internal sense of selfhood under great influence of pathogenic introjects shaded by narcissistic attachment, oral dependence, and defensive conflict. Further results of these internalizations are the failures of the children to establish healthy self-esteem, stable and differentiated internal self-representations and object representations, and a cohesive and consolidated sense of personal identity.

With a precarious sense of ego-identity, an inability to maintain a healthy narcissistic equilibrium, contradictory experiences of the self and of the object, and a continued struggle with infantile object ties, it is easy to understand how children, in face of the inherent vicissitudes of biopsychosocial development characteristic of the adolescent developmental phase, can become enthralled by the family's entrapping emotional process. One may wonder why emancipating adolescents do not simply refute the familial perceptions, delineations, and projections, and traverse the extrafamilial world with their own sense of selfhood, identity, and esteem.

The answer to this lies in the necessarily intertwining connection of adolescents' intrapsychic structure and organization with the nature and quality of the emotional process of the family system to which the children contribute and in which they participate. The entrapment of the family process of emotional, cognitive, and behavioral interaction and transaction, in conjunction and mutual influence with the hitherto developed intrapsychic world of its adolescent members, subjugates the adolescent children into assuming their designated role within the family group and experiencing the self and object relations within the confines of the family circle. Should the children defy these familial mandations and venture beyond the family group, the result is both an externally and an internally derived threat of loss of narcissistic supplies from and the abandonment of the family group. The children's intrapsychic and intrafamilial experiences are dominated by this fear. Brodey (1965) explains:

The narcissistic intensity and its corollary abandonment become an important prototype. The child's mode of structuring experience parallels this intrapsychic organization. It is repeatedly reinforced—reach [sic] out to discover the unknown is penalized; fear of separation is extreme in the child who is specifically trained *not* to find his way beyond the family circle. The struggle is to hold onto what is known. Nothing must be lost or abandoned except by *complete* loss of cathexis. There is no mobility in these relationships—one is either continuous or abandoned. (pp. 189–90)

The normative developmental task of adolescence of separating and diverging from the familial orbit is fraught with fears of intense subjective experience of aloneness, detachment, and alienation—all of which are intensified by the family's associated experiences of feeling rejected, renounced, and therefore rageful. The entrapment is set, as Boszormenyi-Nagy (1965a) illustrates:

The inner abhorrence of loneliness, object-loss, or lack of dialectical Self-delineation . . . makes one comply with the role demands of a "pathological" family system even when there is little chance for a reciprocal dialogue of give and take. (p. 123)

Feared loss of the loved and needed objects of the adolescents' world stifles the children in the bid for autonomy and self-expansion. Family members cling to each other and their circumscribed unity because their polarized cognitive processing dictates that self-expression in any form is equivalent to complete alienation and refutation of the family group. This fear, according to Stierlin (1973), "makes for excessive interpersonal intensity insofar as the child, his will to separate sapped, has no other object than his parent on which to channel, and hence diffuse, his instinctual and other needs" (p. 207).

This familial phenomenon forms the essence of what Zinner and E. Shapiro (1975) referred to as the "carrot and stick" dilemma. The family presents the adolescent members with a carrot and a stick, implicit of an all-or-none option. Zinner and E. Shapiro explain:

The carrot is the implicit promise of an all-gratifying idealized object relation with certain family members who are purged of all hateful qualities. These "bad" attributes, in turn, have been projected into other family members or into the outside world, which is then seen as hostile and uninviting. (p. 111)

. . .

The stick, on the other hand, represents the family "becoming" the "bad mother" in reaction to their child's attempts to separate. This is a potent retaliatory sadistic group behavior that threatens the total cutoff of supplies and oral ostracism, which is terrifying to the youngster who then equates psychological growth with alienation and starvation. (p. 112)

Should the children attempt to proceed with the normative bid for ego autonomy and expansion of object relations, the price is to face abandonment by the family and withdrawal of all supplies, leaving the children with the fear of isolation and detachment, resulting in perceived fragmentation and dissolution of the self. Should the children choose to maintain the idealized, good object relationship with the family group, it comes at the expense of failure of ego autonomy and self-definition.

The result of this familial occurrence is the internally disruptive experience of the adolescents in face of this no-win dilemma. In defensive organization, the children are subject to the regressive pulls of the residues of infantile dependence, recapitulating the struggles with dependence versus independence of earlier object-relational experiences. Just as in the case of infantile experience, adolescents experience a threat to the sustenance of the self. Mandelbaum (1977) explains:

What triggers off his inner chaos is often a chain of direct or subtle cues of a most confusing nature, but which are in essence threats of abandonment which reawaken dim memories of threats to survival in the early months of life. Such memories lead to rage reactions blaming one primary figure while idealizing another, confusions about identity, and regressions to earlier modes of behavior. (pp. 431–32)

Conflicts over separation and individuation not only emerge in children with the advent of adolescence, as they did in the first separation-individuation phase of toddlerhood; they also elicit parental anxiety and the recapitulation of their (the parents') experiences with their toddlers during this first separation-individuation phase. Experienced rage at the hands of frustration and fear in both the adolescent children and the parents spurs the family group in its entirety to engage in defensively generated regressive interaction reminiscent of earlier intrafamilial object-relational experiences.

The sustenance of the selves of the entire family membership and the group as a systemic whole is contingent on the contributory participation of all members in the entrapping emotional system. Maintenance of the already tenuously established selves of the family requires the collusive perpetuation of the emotional intensity characteristic of this enmeshing familial pattern of relationship. Should the family be deprived of this emotional closeness, symbiotic in character, it feels that it lacks the generated thrust not only to hold itself together as a unified group but also to maintain the personality integration and consolidation of each of its members.

From the adolescent children's perspective, Slipp (1984) stresses, "disruption of the symbiotic relationship is experienced as a loss of the self, as an inability to survive intact alone, and as an act of destruction of one or both parents" (p. 92). The parents likewise entertain the fantasy that they too would be subject to annihilation of the self at the hands of the emotional experiences of fear, pain, anger, aloneness, detachment, and alienation. All of the family members feel compelled to control such subjective experiences by controlling each other in the perpetuation of the entrapping emotional process. Loss of control means loss of the family and its individual selves. Slipp (1982) further contends that the individual is compelled to comply to the family pressure, since by preserving the group, his or her own survival is felt safeguarded. The individual is fixated or functioning at a primitive symbiotic level where one's survival is experienced as merged with the group's survival. (p. 224)

Within this symbiotically enmeshed pattern of object relatedness, the family members do not converge in closeness in a unified, collective effort to advance the family group in generativity; rather, they conglomerate out of desperation to cling to their own survival as individuals by means of preserving the emotional intensity of the object-relational process. It becomes clearly evident why the loss of one of its members is perceived as being threatening to the survival of the group. Boszormenyi-Nagy (1965b) speaks of the contrast in the experience of object loss for the healthily integrated and the emotionally entrapping families:

Members of a differentiated family system have to cope with object loss and mourning, but members of an amorphous family system have to fight the felt self-disintegrative threat inherent in the separation of any member. They do not seem to be able to partake of that type of growth of the ego which is said to proceed via abandoned object relationships . . . because of the intersubjective fusion, rather than subject-object demarcation quality of their relatedness. (p. 66)

The "amorphous family system" has no definitive character or organizational form; it simply exists as a group of individuals imprisoned in their self-created desperation and clinging for mere survival as individuals and as a group. The primary purpose of the group is formulated solely on a very implicit and covert agreement by all involved to maintain the family's precarious integration at the accepted expense of denying individual definition and expression of age-appropriate needs. Boszormenyi-Nagy (1965b) comments further:

In our terms the captive aspect of the object-role assignment becomes apparent when the person who is "caught up" is, by definition, unable to act as a subject, i.e., to reciprocate according to his own needs by assigning object roles to others. For instance, he may be made to listen to or care about others without being able to make the others comply with his own needs. The captive of a relationship can be made to "give" without himself being given to. (p. 62)

From this perspective, the welfare of the individual is contingent on the welfare of the group. As the price for the maintenance of the family as a systemic group, the family members must suppress, if not deny, individual needs. The system must survive!

The intensity with which the family group clings steadfastly to the maintenance of the homeostatic balance of the system is evident in, once again, the example of the adolescent children's age-appropriate bid for ego autonomy and expansion of object relations. The family group will react to the children's emancipating efforts with countermoves desperately designed and implemented to draw the defying, "disrespectful" youths back into the family circle. Threats of abandonment and withdrawal of gratifying supplies are perhaps most influential in retaining the children's family involvement. The family may attempt to bribe the children with further oral and narcissistic supplies as well as material goods. In more extreme cases, the family may instill guilt and anxiety in the children by feigning mental or physical illness within the family membership or threatening suicide in the despair of losing a family member. In the ultimate pathological case, incest, life threats, or murder may serve to prevent the children from repudiating the unity of the family.

Stierlin (1973) noted that even those adolescent children who feel compelled to escape the constriction of the family by running away often do so with such guilt that they sabotage their own efforts; thus they are forced to return with the summoning of expected punishment. Confinement to the family's entrapping emotional process does not, however, render the individual members fully helpless and powerless. Indeed, the children of the family may hold great leverage on the parents who maintain so much narcissistic investment in them. Stierlin (1976) reported a case wherein the parents bound their child into serving as an exploited delegate for their gratifications: "And in thus being owned and even enslaved, he was given meaning, a task, and perhaps most important, he was given *power*" (p. 286).

The power may come in the form of narcissistic omnipotence—the feeling of grandiosity through the acquired ability to regulate functionally the self-experiences and self-esteem of the parents. Meissner (1984) explains:

The child, on his part, is the object of particular narcissistic investment from the parents and becomes so vital to the parents' existence and figures so prominently in the maintenance of their self-esteem that his involvement in this emotional system tends to maintain and reinforce his sense of omnipotent grandiosity. (pp. 414–15)

The gratification that the child acquires from such a vital parent-child object relationship reinforces the child's participation in the regressive narcissistic relationship.

Slipp (1973) pointed out that just as infants having primary-process cognition and an unattained sense of self-object differentiation believe that they have magical control over external objects that are perceived to have no existence independent of the infants' thoughts and actions, so children of this type of narcissistic familial relationship likewise continue in some quality and to some degree to believe in this magical, omnipotent functionability. They believe that they possess mystical, manipulative control of the functioning and welfare of significant external objects. Thus their wish for disengagement from the family circle not only elicits threats of parental abandonment and withdrawal of supplies through narcissistic investment in the children but also threatens the loss of experienced narcissistic grandiosity that accrues an elemental sense of identity for the children.

Rubinstein and Timmins (1979) remark on the consequences for both the child and the parents of the child's urge to separate and individuate:

Whenever growth occurs, particularly during adolescence, it is experienced by the parent as a threat to his or her self-esteem and as a narcissistic self-injury. This may lead to the enactment of hostile patterns that will be regressive in attempting to maintain the preexistent narcissistic dyad between parent and child. Every hostile act initiated by either one brings about a consequent regret, with feelings of guilt, and renegotiations, which tend to reestablish the narcissistic contract they have shared up to that phase of maturation. (p. 128)

The strong binding that the family's emotional process engenders provides the means by which this enveloping systemic organization sustains in its regressive, crippling position. Unable to facilitate the functional maturation of its membership, the family as a group succumbs to the regressive pulls of infantile dependence, narcissistic object relationship, and internal conflict, rendering the group stuck in its defensively motivated yet benevolent attempts to hold on to the very existence of its unified group and its individual members, both of which are enmeshingly perceived to be one and the same. The lack of acquired ego differentiation and ego integration and consolidation renders the family paralyzed in confrontation with the inherent vicissitudes of developmental progression. Maturation means disengagement, and disengagement means total object loss to the family of highly intense emotional involvement. To this family, object loss means fragmentation and dissolution of the family group as well as of the selves of its individual members.

=19=

A Synthesis of the Marital and Family Object Relations Model

The concept of "object" as formulated within the framework of evolving psychoanalytic theory has assumed a quite varied position of significance to the development of the human personality. In the early stages of Sigmund Freud's theoretical formulations, the essence of but one constituent of a three-component structure of the instinctual drive was attributed to the object. For Freud, the instinctual sexual drive was the organizational gist of the person. During early postnatal human life, the infant's acquisition of nourishment at the object of the mother's breast comprises its sexual activity. The instinctual drive, as manifested by the infant's sexual activity, consists of the experiencing of the sexual source, the activation of the sexual aim, and the sexual object of its attraction (S. Freud 1953b). Freud's early focus was on the instinct as biologically predetermined, and the object of the instinct's aim as variable and of only secondary significance to the instinct itself. Rangell (1985) notes:

[S]ince objects for Freud served not a subject as a personality but, at that stage of the development of theory, a sexual drive and a mental function, such objects could also not be a personality. The wish stemming from the need associated with the function was for an object which could establish a perceptual identity with a mnemic image formerly associated with the achievement of satisfaction. The object in this model is not necessarily a person and is only incidentally linked to the need satisfaction by being an associated percept. (p. 302)

Later in Freud's theoretical formulations, he conceived of the object in a more expansive and significant light. The original cathexis of the object, upon the loss of the object, subsequently became an identification with that object, processed through the introjection of the object into the ego. In 1923 Freud (1961) remarked:

[T]he process, especially in the early phases of development, is a very frequent one, and it makes it possible to suppose that the character of the ego is a precipitate of abandoned object cathexes and that it contains the history of those object-choices. (p. 29)

By identifying with the introjected object, the infant is capable of maintaining libidinal cathexis of its soothing, gratifying functions, which therewith renders the loss more palatable to the infant. The object and the infant's interaction with it are of primary significance in the characteristic development of the .as yet weak ego. Subsequent psychoanalytic theory follows that of Freud in crediting the nature and quality of object relations with the evolving construction not only of the ego but also of the superego; the ego-ideal, which spans the two structures; and the whole of the self—all of which transpire via the internalization of significant, early object relations.

As Kernberg (1976) saw it, the essence of Freud's tripartite structural model of the mind—the id, ego, and superego—is contingent in formation on the internalized object-relational experiences that are contained and preserved in the component structures and serve as tools for their creation. General psychoanalytic theory and object relations theory are essentially one and the same, and object relationships are the gist of our study of human development and nature. Kernberg's theory was formulated in significant part on the framework laid down by Fairbairn's (1954) theoretical constructs concerning the infant-ego's object that will provide the infant and the person throughout the life span with the gratification, love, and security for which a person forever longs.

Fairbairn was among the first of the psychoanalytic theorists and clinicians to postulate the ego's internalization of significant external objects, objects of both "good" and "bad" qualities. He further hypothesized that the ego, on internalization of the object, splits the object into separate good and bad objects and forms a concomitant split of the ego into good and bad selves, which continue to cathect their respective good and bad objects. The split-off, matched, good self-object relationships and the similar bad self-object relationships become dynamic structures of their own, capable of generating and processing energy, and therewith constitute ongoing internal object relationships.

Ogden (1983) comments on Fairbairn's conceptualization:

[T]hat which is internalized is an object relationship consisting of a split off part of the ego in relation to an object which is itself, at least in part, a dynamic structure. The split off aspect of the ego retains the capacity to function as an active psychological agency, albeit functioning in a primitive mode due to its relative isolation from other aspects of the developing personality. (p. 233)

The internal object relation is isolated in the sense that it is repressed by the central, conscious part of the ego. It is in the current interpersonal field that the dynamic activity of such repressed object relations continues to be manifest and to influence the nature and quality of, for example, current marital and familial interaction and transaction. Fairbairn (1954) summarizes this conceptualization:

[T]he nature of the personality is determined by the internalization of an external object, and the nature of group relationships is in turn determined by the externalization or projection of an internal object. In such a development then we detect the germ of an "object-relations" theory of the personality—a theory based upon the conception that object-relationships exist within the personality as well as between the personality and external objects. (p. 153)

Within this conceptual frame of reference psychoanalysis has deepened its theoretical and clinical investigations into the nature and quality of the relationship prevalent, initially, in the mother-infant bond and, subsequently, in the father-toddler matrix and later in the child-sibling involvement. Ultimately, to further understand the development of human nature, we would do well to investigate the myriad interlocking, coordinated, multicomponent, and multifaceted object relationships that exist within the familial organizational system. In this light, we necessarily recognize that the "object" in our study of interpersonal relationships is in essence analogous to a "self." The object is another person who is subject to the same internally and externally mandated vicissitudes of biopsychosociological maturation. Just as there exist objects to the subjects of ourselves, so we are simultaneously objects to the selves of others. Rangell (1985) remarks:

Whatever is said of the subject holds automatically and reciprocally for the object. Wherever there is integration, there are parts that have been fused. The object consists of the same structures and clusters of function as the subject. Any or all of these may be reacted to singly or in combination, in accordance with the proclivities and preferences of the subject, or based on the reciprocal interactions of both. (pp. 304–05)

In this light, the nature of object relations theory of the person within the context of like persons assumes a very humanistic flavor. The conceptualization of the human being flowering from the initially undifferentiated self-mothering object matrix, maturing into increasingly expanded and sophisticated object relations, culminating in the achievement of genital primacy and the biopsychological capacity to effect reproduction and facilitate functional life-cycle procession is the very essence of humanism. The natural outgrowth of this maturational process is the gradually acquired concept of the self as being distinct from other persons and as a person in one's own right. Relationship in the normative process sustains; however, according to Loewald (1978), "relationship, in contrast to sameness, identity, or 'symbiotic fusion,' implies difference, presupposes differentiation" (p. 502). Loewald further explains object relations theory:

If we use the term object relations for any and all psychic interactions of objectively distinguishable human beings, regardless of whether or not instincts and ego are differentiated from object, then the primary datum for the genetic, psychoanalytic psychology would be object relations. This relatedness is the psychic matrix out of which intrapsychic instincts and ego, and extrapsychic object, differentiate. (p. 503)

The process by which the self emerges from the self-object matrix of the mother-infant bond, and thereby conceptually differentiates the self from the object, is arduous and precarious for the young child. The infant's experienced ambivalence toward the significant mothering object at the hands of the mother's inevitable failure to answer the infant's every wish and need, renders the infant in a quandary as to how to adapt to this conflictual presence of vacillating gratification and ungratification, pleasure and unpleasure. Subsequent splitting of the object into good and bad objects, concomitant to splitting of the ego into good and bad selves, enables the infant to adapt functionally, albeit tenuously, to this conflict. As the toddler's maturing ego system allows the child to tolerate experienced ambivalence through the internalization of mother's soothing functions, it relies less on the employment of the defense mechanism of splitting and is capable of integrating conflicting good and bad aspects of the object as well as good and bad aspects of the self in relationship to the object.

Dicks (1963) suggested that the young child internalizes the good object relationships and forms an identification with them, thereby equipping itself with the capacity to establish and maintain mature love in a variety of object relations throughout the life span. Children learn to diffuse aggression once they acquire the capacity to integrate functionally the good and bad qualities of the object as well as of the self into a cohesive, stable ego-identity capable of relating effectively to significant objects of the external world.

Individuals who have not acquired the autonomous ego functionability and ego differentiation required to achieve mature object love, are subject to excessive, growth-inhibiting reliance on internal object-relational models to dictate their current modes of interpersonal relations. Relations with external objects are thus neither effective nor strong enough to modify correctively the internal models, leaving the individuals stuck in the redundant repetition of dysfunctional early object-relational experiences. Malone (1979) explains:

When separation-individuation is incomplete, the individual cannot differentiate himself sufficiently from his inner models and tends, or is compelled, to repeat them. In addition, the models internalized include maladaptive and pathological relationship experiences with parents and significant others which usually are not modified or corrected by experience. This ultimately sets the stage for the kinds of inadequately differentiated maladaptive personal-interpersonal motivations, behaviors, defenses, and relationships that profoundly affect marital choice, marriage, parental functioning, and family life. (p. 15)

Thus the stage is set for the formation of defensive process within the marital and family relationships. Entrapped within this defensive array of mechanistic and maladaptive interaction, a couple will forge the marital bond in initiation of a new family system, advancing the evolution of the family life cycle. The marital partners seek one another in an acutely selective, though mostly unconscious, benevolent attempt either to avoid the anxiety and pain of early object-relational experiences or to effect correction of and mastery over such experiences, both of which serve unconsciously to preserve the individual's desire to seek comfort, solace, and security in relationship to the external, potentially gratifying, and needed love object. It is in the face of the lack of pleasure from the ungratifying aspects of the libidinal object that the young, underdeveloped infant-ego splits off its relationship to the object and sends part of its own structure along with the object into repression into the unconscious.

Sutherland (1963) addresses this universal phenomenon:

These subsystems have been split off because their aims were incompatible with the preservation of the ego-syntonic relationship with the needed person. The conflict gives rise to "pain" (fear, anxiety, guilt, depression, etc.) associated with their activity.

They are excluded from the conscious self by forces of varying resistance. Their dissociation from consciousness means that little or no adaptation or learning occurs within them. (p. 117)

Stuck in the continuous processing of redundant object-relational patterns, the couple struggles in the attempt to adapt to one another and the relational context that they constitute.

Because the repressed object relations return in varied manifested forms (e.g., dreams, cognitive processing, and individual symptoms) and in comprehensive form through interpersonal transaction, the individual is subject to the resurgence of conflictual pain and anxiety, albeit manifested in disguised configuration such as marital object relationship dysfunction. Sutherland (1963) comments on the inevitable return of repressed ego-dystonic object relations and the repressed needs associated therewith:

A particularly important feature of these needs is that, though there is a defensive tendency for the person to take them to other people than those he wishes to maintain his close good relationship with, nevertheless, there is an even more powerful trend for them to come back into any close relationship with one person. That is to say, *the repressed not only returns, but it tends to return to the representative of the more comprehensive relationship from which it was originally split off.* (p. 118)

The marital partner is the primary representative of the original mothering object and the one with whom the individual desperately and benevolently attempts to actualize long-standing wishful fantasies. Sandler and Sandler (1978) note:

Although our behaviour does not, of course, consist only in repeating past object relations, it is certainly true that a great deal of our life is involved in the concealed repetition of early object relationships in one form or another. This includes those patterns of relationship which have developed as safety-giving or anxiety-reducing manoeuvres, as well as those which satisfy instinctual wishes. (p. 287)

Sandler and Sandler also suggest that the means by which the repetition of both good and bad early object relations is facilitated in disguised form in the marital relationship constitutes the essence of the transference phenomenon. Based on the mostly unconscious wish-fulfilling needs of the individual marital partners, each partner will establish a preconceived role expectation of the other, which will to a great measure determine object choice and the process of the marital relationship. Insofar as each partner is able to coerce the other into assuming the role of wish fulfiller and oral-need supplier, a workable, though potentially and probably maladaptive and destructive, marital relationship will transpire.

In this light, Boszormenyi-Nagy (1965b) notes that the relationship between the "Self" and the "Other" in marital interaction transcends the two persons' purely conscious and real-life transactional desires:

The relational world of the dyad, thus, is more complex than merely an encounter of two subjects' competing assertions. The structure of a relationship apportions subject and object positions to the relating partners, and as long as one remains "in relationship," the Other's needs become one's secondary needs through one's becoming an object to the Other's strivings and a ground for his assertiveness. (p. 50)

. . .

Yet the Self, while becoming the object of certain interactions, nevertheless remains the motivational source. Being the object in the true relational sense, on the other hand, connotes an action sequence that stems from the Other's motivations. (p. 51)

Interdependence and mutual influence underscore the gist of this relational phenomenon.

In speaking of the potentially healthy and functional aspect of role attribution and role assumption, Sandler and Sandler (1978) suggested that the individual's search for the loving and loved object and the quest for fulfillment of unconscious, primitive needs and wishes may be conducted effectively through the same relational process:

[T]he traditional distinction between the search for objects on the one hand and the search for wish-fulfilment or need-satisfaction on the other fades into insignificance. *The two can be regarded as being essentially the same.* If a person creates stable object relationships, then he creates, through his interaction with his objects, through their mutual affectively significant communication, both a constantly recurring source of wish-fulfilment and a constant object relationship. (p. 289)

Insofar as the couple is able mutually to facilitate a marital process wherein the two partners can acknowledge and affirm both themselves and the other, and consolidate a differentiated ego structure as an integral component of a marital system ego, they are likely to proceed through the developmental phases and the inherent vicissitudes thereof in mutual growth, productivity, and constructivity. The introduction of a child into the evolving family system presents the marital couple with mandates for intrasystem organizational modification. The marital system must shift to a higher order of organization, wherein the couple not only must sustain the marital bond but also must establish and identify themselves simultaneously as a parental couple. Parenthood becomes not only a phase of the family life cycle but also a developmental phase of each parent individually, with potentially profound, and always significant, effects on the personality development of each parent (Benedek 1959).

The formation of a parent-child relationship wherein members are inherently mutually influential provides a framework from which the child's personality and sense of selfhood will emerge. Reciprocally, the influence of the child provides an opportunity for the parents either to adapt to or to correct conflicts of their internal representational worlds, as derived from early object-relational experiences with their parents, and thereby achieve growth in personality organization. Insofar, however, as parents as a marital couple become entangled in their own defensive, interlocking array of transactions and remain stuck in their self-perpetuated, maladaptive relational processes, they are likely to play out the same relational patterns in the parent-child dyad and the parent-parent-child triangulation. The advent of parenthood as a developmental phase can present the parents with the opportunity to achieve the phase-appropriate psychosocial task of "generativity" (Erikson 1956), or it can facilitate and expand on the continuance of intrapsychic and interpersonal psychopathology inherent in the family system.

The process wherein the parents and the children become enthralled in the morass of introjective and projective defensive interplay, fostering continued dysfunctional intrasystemic transaction, is elucidated by the transference phenomenon in which the parents unconsciously perceive their children as they did their own parents in early childhood, or they perceive the children in a way corresponding to how they felt during the same developmental phase of their childhood. Schwartz (1984) adds that children, in reciprocation, are also subject to transference reaction in perceiving and responding to the parents during a given developmental phase in a way analogous to how the children viewed their parents during preceding childhood developmental phases. The children's transition from one phase to the next will, in the normative process, elicit similar perceptions and attitudes toward the parents, as derived from the nature and quality of the children's internal parental-object representations, reflecting both real parental attitudinal and behavioral attributes and the children's actual, past object relational experiences with the parents. Normal and transient regressions can and do elicit transference reactions toward the parents. The parents have the challenging task of recognizing and responding to these reactions in their children with empathy and support.

Schwartz (1984) comments on the psychosocial consequences for both the parents and the child, should the parents not be capable of empathically responding to their child in face of these transference phenomena:

The parent who is unable to empathically understand these transference repetitions will respond in what may be considered a countertransference reaction which is nonfacilitating of the child's development in the phase in which it transpires. For example, the parent who does not comprehend the regressive transference attitudes of the child in the course of his/her progressive maturation will reengage the child as if they were again in that earlier, and for the most part, superseded phase. The results will be a transference-countertransference transaction which will pathologically influence the child's (and parent's) resolution of developmental issues and conflicts pertaining to the present ongoing phase. (p. 370)

The developmental phase of adolescence is a particularly arduous time for both puberty-age children and the family group as a whole. The maturation of the adolescent children is subject to impediment in response to the regressive pulls of infantile dependence and the longing for nurturance and support, which leaves the children with experienced ambivalence regarding concomitant desires for both dependence and independence. The parents who, for a variety of reasons, are unable to provide a holding environment conducive to the facilitation of the children's ego autonomy and identity consolidation, also are subject to regressive pulls wherein family members engage one another in interactive emotional, cognitive, and behavioral patterns characteristic of earlier familial organization.

Because the parents retain unresolved, conflictual experiences revolving around their own separation and individuation, they are incapable of comprehending the normative process of adolescent emancipation and autonomy-seeking conducive to the growth and development of the entire family membership. The threat of narcissistic injury and disequilibrium of both the parents individually and the family system as a whole coerces the parents into delineating their children, as deemed appropriate, to foster and facilitate the dispersal of and adherence to the family's shared unconscious fantasies and basic assumptions. The family clings to such foundational fantasies and assumptions for fear that otherwise individual and familial disorganization, and possibly disintegration, will ensue.

One such commonly held fantasy is that individual striving for ego autonomy and object relations expansion of its membership is analogous to and proof of hostile and aggressively tinged devaluation and repudiation of the family unity. Unable to tolerate the blow to the narcissistic balance of the family membership, the family in its entirety regresses to a state characterized by primary-process cognition and adherence to the pleasure principle. In this collusively bound state of affairs, the family succumbs to the defensive employment of splitting, projective, introjective, and projective-identificatory mechanisms wherewith it haphazardly attempts to overcome its experienced helplessness. In this regression, they lose sight of reality, conjuring their own and becoming inattentive to the normative phase-appropriate needs of the members and of the family as a systemic whole.

Insofar as the parents have organized their new family system around the hub of a healthy, well-integrated marital relationship, with the ability and willingness to identify themselves and one another as fully differentiated and autonomous individuals, coalesced in a circular emotional pattern of ego interdependence, they will be able to maintain a functional reality sense conducive to the recognition of age-appropriate needs and the growth and maturation of the entire family group. The family in its entirety coordinates to provide a relational configuration conducive to its effective provision of a holding environment in which members appropriate the resources with which to effect the internal regulation of self-esteem and self-affirmation. Berkowitz, R. Shapiro, Zinner, and E. Shapiro (1974b) describe this operative familial process:

[A]n important work task of the family, regulated by the reality principle and mediated through secondary-process thinking, is to facilitate the mastery of life tasks at each phase of development of each of its members. With regard to the evolution of healthy self-esteem regulation in the developing child, the family as a group must provide an empathic context in which the child is permitted to experience tolerable disappointments and gradually to separate and differentiate himself from the family without being devalued or threatened by a withdrawal of supplies. This facilitates the internalizations and structure formation allowing integration of grandiose omnipotence and helpless inferiority. (p. 355)

Within this facilitating context all family members participate in the group task of providing a supportive environment in which each member is empathically and appropriately encouraged to break from the family circle and seek a contributory position in the extrafamilial, adult object world.

Reality testing in this process of familial interaction assumes the characteristic of normative secondary-process cognition. The family's perceptions and the both verbal and nonverbal communication thereof strengthen and facilitate the expansion of individual ego-identities in both intrafamilial and extrafamilial object relations. Individual family members formulate and maintain modifiable, yet stable and functional, internal self-representations and object representations, promoting experiences of good object relationships and rendering the inevitably, though variably, experienced bad aspects of those otherwise growth-producing relations more palatable and contributive to the learning process. Mutually and collusively determined delineating perceptions of family members, based on the dictates of individual and familial defensive operations and magical primary-process cognitive organization, render the family entrapped in its uniquely designed and perpetuated style of maladaptively redundant and regressive transaction.

This emotional, cognitive, and behavioral transactional patterning subsumes the essence of individually derived and mutually processed defensive mechanism wherewith the family unconsciously and collusively splits its membership into an array of sectors, each imbued with a given characteristic contributing to the family systemic collection of good and bad, productive and nonproductive, capable and incapable, well and sick, and the like—qualities perceivably contained within the family group. Provided with the misguided security of maintaining closer scrutiny of its both positive and negative internal elements, the family feels better equipped to handle a feared, potentially destructive development within the confines of its internally loving, caring, and concerned circle of goodness. Insofar as the family process is defensively incapable of sustaining this fountain of love, it may resort to the externalization of all badness into the extrafamilial world, imbuing the world with the evil temptations of life, viciously draining the family unity of its protectiveness and existence.

The projective and introjective defensive process reinforces the familial splitting mechanism. The kaleidoscopic quality of the interlocking, yet continuously modifying, configuration of mutually processed introjections and projections illuminates the intricacy with which the family members actualize their shared unconscious fantasy. Meissner (1978b) explains:

We have only begun to realize that the inner psychological reality of families has to do with the complex interplay of projections and introjections. To the extent that family members are caught up in the emotional matrix of the family . . . they are involved in the process of projection and introjection, they contribute to the projective elaborations which play upon all the involved family members and they internalize the projective matrix that is set up and sustained by the family interaction. What is introjected, and thereby becomes part of the inner world of each member, is the complex of interpersonal projections and introjections—the stuff of psychoanalytic personality formation which is based on and derived from object-relations. (pp. 789–90)

Meissner further stresses that the individual family members internalize the family system as a whole, inclusive of the family's modes of transaction, codes of self-expression, styles of perception and cognition, and means of coping with negative emotions. Individual members' identification with the objects of their projections, insofar as the objects accommodate the projections via the introjection of the projected elements, solidifies the fusive bonding by which individual ego structures mesh. The resulting "undifferentiated family ego mass" described by Bowen (1978) necessarily renders the individual family members acutely sensitive to the emotional experiences of each other, subjecting them to the impinging and smothering capacity actually to feel what the others feel.

This meshed family system, constricted within the formidable confines of its self-prescribed delineations, stifles its otherwise expansive progression, falling prey to an entropic stalemate. Guided strictly by the dictates of the interlocking array of defensively propelled projections and introjections, family members ultimately amalgamate to effect a potentially self-destructive systemic whole—a whole identified and characterized by the mutuality of symbiotic dependence. The family does not grant itself the facilitating context in which individual members are supportively encouraged to individuate through self-definition and self-affirmation. Family members are first and foremost, in negation of interdependent constituency, travestied caricatures of the family conflict.

In this light, there is a reciprocation of influence in which the intrapsychic development and the external, interpersonal relations of the individual coexist in simultaneous formation. The internal self-representational and object-representational world and the external field of marital and family relationships mirror one another in an inextricably tied vortex, from the cavity of which the uniquely characterized person or self formulates and emerges. The internal and external worlds are experienced reflections of one another. Boszormenyi-Nagy (1965b) adds:

If we assume that one's discrete Self-experience depends on the vicissitudes of one's Self-Other encounters, the intrapsychic and interpersonal relational realms assume interconnected causal significance. The internalized relational patterns will, to a certain extent, predetermine the external relational preferences and the fate and level of involvement. External relationships, on the other hand, can contribute to the content and quality of what evolve as building stones of the endopsychic structure of Self and Other representations. (p. 74)

Internal-world object representations and associated self-representations take shape as directly reflective of the individual's actual relations with external, real objects. In turn, the internalized relationship has direct impact on the quality of subsequent real-world object relations. Both expand in spiral configuration as the organizational development of the self complements the social organization of the family.

Slipp (1984) descriptively expands on this conceptualization:

[E]xternal reality shapes internal fantasy. External real objects modify and shape the child's internal world of objects through the processes of projection and introjection to approximate reality more closely. In the terms of general systems theory, external reality is seen as a more differentiated organization that is internalized through positive feedback in order to facilitate adaptation. (p. 55)

Slipp contends that the interpersonal relations within the family system in effect serve as either positive or negative feedback loops that generate the functioning of the internal world. He provides a clinical example of a family enthralled in regressive transaction, wherein the observable patterns of intrasystem transaction directly correspond to the internal fantasied, object relations world of one of its child members. Because of the lack of differentiation between internal, fantasied object relations and the reality of external, familial object relations, the system stalemates in collusive deadlock wherein the child and the family as a whole complement one another in the employment of defensive mechanisms. Intrapsychic functioning and interpersonal interaction serve in mutually dependent, recursive reinforcement to create reciprocating negative feedback loops. Slipp (1984) continues:

Not only is the fixation initiated by this process, but it is perpetuated by negative feedback in the here and now of the ongoing family interaction. Thus, the family interaction, when it parallels the child's unconscious fantasy, serves as a deviation-correcting, negative feedback loop to sustain the child's primitive internal world of objects. In turn, the child's participation perpetuates the existing form of family interaction. Later, as an adult, the patient will attempt, through the use of projective identification, to shape significant others to parallel their internal fantasy. Thus the process is repeated and this shaped external reality is then internalized, as a negative feedback loop, to perpetuate the fixation. (p. 56)

In this scheme of things, one can use as a theoretical framework a complementary and mutually enhancing integration of psychoanalytic conceptualization of intrapsychic formation and function, with general systems interpretation of the family systemic process. The two models of the intrapersonal and the interpersonal in combination and mutual affirmation by no means effect a duplicity of constructivity. As Slipp (1984) maintains,

individual and family dynamics were viewed as interactive and interdependent forces, each influencing the other. The intrapsychic dynamics of each individual and the processes of the family were seen as isomorphic, not as separate and polarized from each other. (p. 11)

One might take this postulational stance one step further and firmer: Insofar as each theoretical and hypothetical position is legitimate and useful in its own right, the two, it is suggested, by necessity are valid yet incomplete without the acknowledgment and utilization of one another. The thesis hitherto set forth, this writer believes, serves in an effort to dispel the false dichotomy of intrapsychic and interpersonal phenomena.

═══20═══

Epilogue

Contemporary thought within the psychoanalytic paradigm progressively expands to include conceptualizations regarding the structuralization of the developing psyche as it unfolds from the matrix of relations with significant external others. The evolution of conceptualization is moving, albeit slowly, in the direction of what Balint (1950) referred to and made a plea for: a "Two-Body Psychology," an idea recognizing the fact that a newborn infant is innately embedded in a matrix of relatedness to its mothering object and matures through the experiential events inherent in this relationship. Modell (1968, 1984) has been convincingly instrumental in supporting Balint's claim that traditional psychoanalytic theory has remained within the one-body, or what Modell (1984) preferred to call a "one-person," psychology, inhibiting the conceptualization of an individual personality forming within the encircled setting of a person-to-person relationship. Modell (1984) comments:

Traditional psychoanalysis has not yet acquired the theoretical language that would enable it to describe a process occurring between two separate personalities in terms of encompassing the events in both individuals. We are forced to describe the actual object as a "representation" in the mind of the subject. That is to say, traditional psychoanalysis is a one-person psychology. (pp. 11–12)

In concurrence with this writer's hypothetical proposition that the object-relations model be inclusive of both the internal and the external spheres of object relations, Modell (1984) suggests:

I have focused on the problem of the internal object as it is, I believe, a failed attempt to retain an object-relations theory that is consistent with a one-person psychology. . . . Psychoanalysis is both a one-person and a two-person psychology. I am not proposing that this "new" context replace traditional psychoanalysis, but merely that the limits of a one-person psychology be recognized—that the addition of a two-person context is intended not to replace classical theory but to extend it. There is a persistent and sustaining duality through much if not all of the subject matter that comprises the body of psychoanalytic knowledge. (p. 20)

As presented throughout this volume, the concept of internalization represents a metaphorical bridge between real, external relationships and the structuralization of the intrapsychic system. This connection serves an elemental function in the coalescence of the internal and external worlds. As Modell (1984) says: "The importance of a two-person context is not to be taken as a depreciation of the central significance of internalization and structure formation. Such concepts are indeed indispensable for us" (p. 21). The construction of the psyche is contingent on the internalization of significant self-sustaining functions provided by specific mother-child relations, just as the maintenance and expansion of object relations with external others is contingent on the evolving maturation of the intrapsychic organization and the resulting materialization of the self. Meissner (1986) explains:

The infant is embedded in a matrix of object relations (object related) from the very moment of birth, if not before. . . . From the very beginning, then, internalization processes are taking place and result in the laying down of building blocks of structural aspects of the infant psyche and components of the emerging self.

If we return to our working definition, our focus here is on those specific processes by which the infant subject transforms the regulatory interactions with his environment and particularly with the caregivers in his environment into inner regulations and characteristics. From the very beginning of this process, the infant is interacting with his environment and assimilating from it as well as accommodating to it. (p. 60).

The self, in this light, not only is accrued through internalization of the supporting and life-sustaining external object but also, in ongoing formulation, is molded by the nature and quality of relations with other significant external objects. The efficacy of the self is determined by and determinative of the efficacy of external interpersonal relationships. The two are recursively bound. Modell (1984) speaks of this element of his "two-person psychology":

The self is both a psychic structure, colored by the process of internalization, and also an endopsychic perception, exquisitely dependent upon the immediacy of the response of the other. The self is a permanent structure, but also something always in the process of being reshaped. This is testimony to the fact that we remain forever social animals; the sense of ourselves is constantly molded by the responses of loved ones, friends, as well as the anonymous members of a group. (p. 22)

Internalization, via the process of introjection of external objects and the relationship of the self to these objects, is but one side of the coin. Externalization, via projection and projective identification, is the counterpart of internalization. It is precisely the quality of introjective-projective propensity that transpires between personalities that provides the object-relational framework from which we can explain the interconnection between the internal-world and the external-world relationships. Introjective-projective defensive and adaptative processing forms the essence of interpersonal involvement. Meissner (1978a) elaborates on this phenomena, which is inherent in all social relations and is specifically illuminated by the complexities of family process:

Further, the family emotional system and the transference are analyzed in terms of components of the organization of the individual personality which derive particularly from an object relations frame of reference. In these terms, the complex interaction between the individual and his objects can be conceptualized as based on a continual commerce carried on through complex interactions of introjection and projection between the individual and the object world which surrounds him. Through the use of the related concepts of introjection and projection, the reader can gain a theoretical continuity which extends from the intrapsychic level through the interpersonal to the level of social and familial analysis. (p. 84)

The dynamically reciprocal interplay of introjective and projective mechanisms is inherent in both functional and dysfunctional marital and family systemic groups. The degree to which these mechanisms are defensively perpetuated and the degree to which the marital and family members can maintain a clear and stable sense of self-object differentiation determine the quality of the group interaction in terms of functionability. Modell (1985) states that even in the healthiest of individuals, marriages, and families, *"issues concerning autonomy and self/object differentiation are carried forward and are worked through symbolically during the entire life cycle"* (p. 90). Ambivalence prevails as individuals, to variable degrees, struggle continuously with simultaneous desires for dependence and nurturance, and independence and self-sufficiency.

Where ego boundaries are blurred and ego differentiation is tenuous, introjective and projective defensive mechanisms in perpetual array subjugate the involved marital and family members, and increase dependence on the entrapment in the system's emotional process. The relative strength of ego structures determines the path that individuals take in relations with significant objects (i.e., progressive and regressive movement). Modell (1968) stresses this point in his bid for scientific study of interpersonal relationships in regard to ego development:

The area of clinical experience that awaits better conceptualization is that of disturbed human object relationships. What is now needed is a model that would better conceptualize the ego's relationship to the environment and would encompass progressive and regressive alterations in object relations. (p. 125)

As has been noted, when one member of the family regresses, the entire family unit regresses in conjunction with that individual to a state of infantile dependence and an intrafamilial world dominated by primary-process cognition. The family becomes stuck in its own growth-inhibiting, defensive, and regressive processing. In this light, it becomes evident that individual intrapsychic development and interpersonal familial relations unfold in concurrence. Lidz, Fleck, and Cornelison (1965) support this view as they stress the significance of the familial environment in individual ego maturation:

The emphasis upon the intrafamilial object relationships is not inconsistent with other analytic or dynamic approaches. It includes an interest in causes of ego weakness, of blurring of ego boundaries, of narcissistic withdrawal after object loss, of regression to infantile omnipotence and security, of withdrawal to a world free from the confines of reality testing, and so forth. However, it is considered that the ego develops in relation to objects—particularly to the parental figures—and in a world of the family created largely by the interaction of the parental figures. (p. 81)

To extend this explanation, the progressive and regressive movement of the family's systemic evolution is contingent on the nature and quality of the individual ego systems and the unique and variable interface of these interdependent, intrapsychic systems.

Marital and family theorists and clinicians offer no apology for the complexity inherent in this schematic view of the family, since it is only with this multifaceted dimensional perspective that objective observers can make sense of the family dramatization. This perspective does indeed necessitate a shift in the epistemological framework from which we view man's ability to *know*—to perceive, cognicize, construct ideas and concepts, and engage in decision-making processes.

Traditional psychoanalysis has been formed with a linear epistemology, one that views the individual apart from its natural environment and as comprising an entity distinct on its own. The contemporary object relations theoretical model, as presented here, views the individual as innately embedded in a context of other people. The shift in epistemological assumption necessitates the recognition not of the individual discretely but of the ecological field of which the individual is an integral component. The theory of human nature thus incorporates new basic premises on which we observe and intervene with individuals or with individuals within their ecological context. A marital and family object relations model consists of such premises. Meissner (1978a) elaborates:

Consequently, the intrapsychic organization of the patient's sense of self through the configuration of introjects is one level of analysis that is characterized by its own inherent properties and principles. As soon as one moves to the level of interpersonal interaction, with the interplay of projections and their derivation from the intrapsychic introjects as well as from the patterns of response and interaction set up within the interpersonal context, one has entered a different realm of understanding and analysis in which one may expect different properties and principles to manifest themselves. (p. 85)

The significance of the intrapsychic, unconscious dynamic process is not renounced in this scheme; rather, the internal world of unconsciously processed object relations is affirmed only in the recognition that such psychic organization is the result of the internalization of the external world of object relations that it represents and, similarly, directly affects the nature and quality of subsequent interpersonal relations. Ackerman (1958), a pioneer in the field of the psychoanalytic theory of the family, remarks on the significance of "the realities of the social environment" (p. 30) to the understanding of the unconscious, intrapsychic domain:

I believe that an accurate understanding of the unconscious is possible only when one interprets unconscious dynamics in the context of the conscious organization of experience, the total integrative patterns of personality, and the prevailing interpersonal realities. (p. 30)

The result of this comprehensive study of the intrapsychic in confluence with the interpersonal is a picture of the marriage and/or family in a dynamically processed modality of interaction and transaction reminiscent of an abstraction in ongoing kaleidoscopic configuration. The variegated changing of relational patterns and vistas characterizes the idiosyncratic intricacies inherent in any social system as deeply involved and intimate as the family group. To conceptualize the complexity of this panoramic panoply, we might do well to pursue the solutions to problems in accordance with Bateson's (1979) contention that it is in the classification of processes, and not of individuals, that we secure knowledge. Interaction between observed processes within the family circle generates the synergetic quality inherent in the emotionally laden experience of family life. The primacy of the familial process is that it entails, in full, person-to-person relationships, and it is the experience of these relationships that provides the impetus for—indeed, the very essence of—personal and relational maturation and progression.

Bibliography

Abelin, E. (1975). Some further observations and comments on the earliest role of the father. *International Journal of Psychoanalysis, 56,* 293–302.

Ackerman, N. (1958). *The psychodynamics of family life.* New York: Basic Books.

Arlow, J. (1980). Object concept and object choice: Symposium on object relations theory and love. *Psychoanalytic Quarterly, 49,* 109–33.

Avery, N. (1982). Family secrets. *Psychoanalytic Review, 69,* 471–86.

Balint, A. (1949). Love for the mother and mother-love. *International Journal of Psychoanalysis, 30,* 251–59.

Balint, M. (1950). Changing therapeutical aims and techniques in psycho-analysis. *International Journal of Psychoanalysis, 31,* 117–24.

————. (1953). *Primary love and psycho-analytic technique.* New York: Liveright.

————. (1958). The concepts of subject and object in psychoanalysis. *British Journal of Medical Psychology, 31,* 83–91.

————. (1960). Primary narcissism and primary love. *Psychoanalytic Quarterly, 29,* 6–43.

————. (1968). *The basic fault.* London: Tavistock.

Bateson, G. (1979). *Mind and nature: A necessary unity.* New York: Bantam Books.

Becvar, R., and Stroh Becvar, D. (1982). *Systems theory and family therapy: A primer.* Lanham, MD: University Press of America.

Benedek, T. (1959). Parenthood as a developmental phase: A contribution to the libido theory. *Journal of the American Psychoanalytic Association, 7,* 389–417.

Berkowitz, D. (1981). The borderline adolescent and the family. In M. Lansky (Ed.), *Family therapy and major psychopathology* (pp. 183–201). New York: Grune & Stratton.

Berkowitz, D., Shapiro, R., Zinner, J., and Shapiro, E. (1974a). Concurrent family treatment of narcissistic disorders in adolescence. *International Journal of Psychoanalytic Psychotherapy, 3,* 379–96.

————. (1974b). Family contributions to narcissistic disturbances in adolescents. *International Review of Pychoanalysis, 1,* 353–62.

Bertalanffy, L. von. (1968). *General systems theory.* New York: George Braziller.

Bierley, M. (1951). *Trends in psychoanalysis.* London: Hogarth Press.

Blatt, S. (1974). Levels of object representation in anaclitic and introjective depression. *Psychoanalytic Study of the Child, 29,* 107–57.

Blos, P. (1967). The second individuation process of adolescence. *Psychoanalytic Study of the Child, 22,* 162–86.

Boszormenyi-Nagy, I. (1962). The concept of schizophrenia from the perspective of family treatment. *Family Process, 1,* 103–13.

———. (1965a). Intensive family therapy as process. In I. Boszormenyi-Nagy and J. Framo (Eds.), *Intensive family therapy: Theoretical and practical aspects* (pp. 87–142). New York: Hoeber Medical Division, Harper & Row.

———. (1965b). A theory of relationships: Experience and transaction. In I. Boszormenyi-Nagy and J. Framo (Eds.), *Intensive family therapy: Theoretical and practical aspects* (pp. 33–86). New York: Hoeber Medical Division, Harper & Row.

Bowen, M. (1960). A family concept of schizophrenia. In D. Jackson (Ed.), *The etiology of schizophrenia* (pp. 346–72). New York: Basic Books.

———. (1978). *Family therapy in clinical practice.* New York: Jason Aronson.

Bowlby, J. (1969). *Attachment and loss: Vol. 1. Attachment.* London: Hogarth Press.

———. (1973). *Attachment and loss: Vol. 2. Separation.* New York: Basic Books.

Brodey, W. (1959). Some family operations and schizophrenia: A study of five hospitalized families each with a schizophrenic member. *Archives of General Psychiatry, 1,* 379–402.

———. (1961). The family as the unit of study and treatment-workshop, 1959: 3, Image, object and narcissistic relationships. *American Journal of Orthopsychiatry, 31,* 69–73.

———. (1965). On the dynamics of narcissism. I. Externalization and early ego development. *Psychoanalytic Study of the Child, 20,* 165–93.

Burgner, M., and Edgcumbe, R. (1972). Some problems in the conceptualization of early object relationships: The concept of object constancy. *Psychoanalytic Study of the Child, 27,* 315–33.

Cooper, A. (1985). A historical review of psychoanalytic paradigms. In A. Rothstein (Ed.), *Models of the mind: Their relationships to clinical work* (pp. 5–20). New York: International Universities Press.

Deutsch, H. (1942). Some forms of emotional disturbance and their relationship to schizophrenia. *Psychoanalytic Quarterly, 11,* 301–21.

Dewey, J. (1929). *Experience and nature.* Chicago: Open Court.

Dicks, H. (1963). Object relations theory and marital studies. *British Journal of Medical Psychology, 36,* 125–29.

———. (1967). *Marital tensions: Clinical studies towards a psychological theory of interaction.* New York: Basic Books.

Dorpat, T. (1981). Basic concepts and terms in object relations theories. In S. Tuttman, C. Kaye, and M. Zimmerman (Eds.), *Object and self: A developmental approach* (pp. 149–78). New York: International Universities Press.

———. (1985). *Denial and defense in the therapeutic situation.* New York: Jason Aronson.

Edgcumbe, R., and Burgner, M. (1972). Some problems in the conceptualization of early object relationships: The concepts of need satisfaction and need-satisfying relationships. *Psychoanalytic Study of the Child, 27,* 283–314.

Eidelberg, L. (1956). Neurotic choice of mate. In V. Eisenstein (Ed.), *Neurotic interaction in marriage* (pp. 57–64). New York: Basic Books.

Elson, M. (1984). Parenthood and the transformations of narcissism. In R. Cohen, B. Cohler, and S. Weissman (Eds.), *Parenthood: A psychodynamic perspective* (pp. 297–314). New York: Guilford Press.

Erikson, E. (1956). The problem of ego identity. *Journal of the American Psychoanalytic Association, 4,* 56–121.

Fairbairn, W. R. D. (1954). *An object-relations theory of the personality.* New York: Basic Books.

———. (1955). Observations in defence of the object-relations theory of the personality. *British Journal of Medical Psychology, 28,* 144–56.

Ferreira, A. (1963). Family myths and homeostasis. *Archives of General Psychiatry, 9,* 457–63.

Framo, J. (1982a). Marriage and marital therapy: Issues and initial interview techniques. In J. Framo (Ed.), *Explorations in marital and family therapy: Selected papers of James L. Framo* (pp. 123–40). New York: Springer.

———. (1982b). Marriage therapy in a couples group. In J. Framo (Ed.), *Explorations in marital and family therapy: Selected papers of James L. Framo* (pp. 141–51). New York: Springer.

———. (1982c). Rationale and techniques of intensive family therapy. In J. Framo (Ed.), *Explorations in marital and family therapy: Selected papers of James L. Framo* (pp. 61–119). New York: Springer.

———. (1982d). Symptoms from a family transactional viewpoint. In J. Framo (Ed.), *Explorations in marital and family therapy: Selected papers of James L. Framo* (pp. 11–57). New York: Springer.

Freud, A. (1958). Adolescence. *Psychoanalytic Study of the Child, 13,* 255–78.

Freud, S. (1953a). *On aphasia.* New York: International Universities Press. (Original work published 1891.)

———. (1953b). Three essays on the theory of sexuality. In J. Strachey (Ed. and Trans.), *The standard edition of the complete psychological works of Sigmund Freud* (Vol. 7, pp. 125–243). London: Hogarth Press. (Original work published 1905).

———. (1961). The ego and the id. In J. Strachey (Ed. and Trans.), *The standard edition of the complete psychological works of Sigmund Freud* (Vol. 19, pp. 3–66). London: Hogarth Press. (Original work published 1923).

Furth, H. (1969). *Piaget and knowledge: Theoretical foundations.* Englewood Cliffs, NJ: Prentice-Hall.

Gedo, J., and Goldberg, A. (1973). *Models of the mind: A psychoanalytic theory.* Chicago: University of Chicago Press.

Giovacchini, P. (1984). *Character disorders and adaptive mechanisms.* New York: Jason Aronson.

Goldberg, A. (1981). Meaning and objects. In S. Tuttman, C. Kaye, and M. Zimmerman (Eds.), *Object and self: A developmental approach* (pp. 129–48). New York: International Universities Press.

Goldberg, D. (1985). A reexamination of the concept "object" in psychoanalysis. *Journal of the American Psychoanalytic Association, 33,* 167–85.

Gordon, R. (1983). Systems-object relations view of marital therapy: Revenge and re-raising. In L. Wolberg and M. Aronson (Eds.), *Group and family therapy, 1982* (pp. 325–33). New York: Brunner/Mazel.

Greenberg, J., and Mitchell, S. (1983). *Object relations in psychoanalytic theory.* Cambridge, MA: Harvard University Press.

Guntrip, H. (1961). *Personality structure and human interaction.* New York: International Universities Press.

―――. (1969). *Schizoid phenomena, object-relations, and the self.* New York: International Universities Press.

―――. (1971). *Psychoanalytic theory, therapy, and the self.* New York: Basic Books.

Hartmann, H. (1958). *Ego psychology and the problem of adaptation.* New York: International Universities Press.

Hendrick, I. (1951). Early development of the ego: Identification in infancy. *Psychoanalytic Quarterly, 20,* 44–61.

Horne, H. (1927). *The philosophy of education.* New York: Macmillan.

Horner, A. (1975). Stages and processes in the development of early object relations and their associated pathologies. *International Review of Psychoanalysis, 2,* 95–105.

―――. (1979). *Object relations and the developing ego in therapy.* New York: Jason Aronson.

Jacobson, E. (1954). The self and the object world. *Psychoanalytic Study of the Child, 9,* 75–127.

―――. (1964). *The self and the object world.* New York: International Universities Press.

Joffe, W., and Sandler, J. (1965). Notes on pain, depression, and individuation. *Psychoanalytic Study of the Child, 20,* 394–424.

―――. (1967). Some conceptual problems involved in the consideration of disorders of narcissism. *Journal of Child Psychotherapy, 2,* 56–66.

Kernberg, O. (1976). *Object relations theory and clinical psychoanalysis.* New York: Jason Aronson.

Klein, M. (1946). Notes on some schizoid mechanisms. *International Journal of Psychoanalysis, 27,* 99–110.

―――. (1948). *Contributions to psycho-analysis.* London: Hogarth Press.

―――. (1975). *Envy and gratitude and other works, 1946–1963.* New York: Delacorte Press.

Kohut, H. (1971). *The analysis of the self.* New York: International Universities Press.

―――. (1977). *The restoration of the self.* New York: International Universities Press.

Kolb, J., and Shapiro, E. (1982). Management of separation issues with the family of the hospitalized adolescent. In S. Feinstein, J. Looney, A. Schwartzberg, and A. Sorosky (Eds.), *Adolescent psychiatry: Developmental and clinical studies* (Vol. 10, pp. 343–59). Chicago: University of Chicago Press.

Kuhn, T. (1962). *The structure of scientific revolutions.* Chicago: University of Chicago Press.

Lansky, M. (1980–1981). On blame. *International Journal of Psychoanalytic Psychotherapy, 8,* 429–56.

―――. (1981). Treatment of the narcissistically vulnerable marriage. In M. Lansky (Ed.), *Family therapy and major psychopathology* (pp. 163–82). New York: Grune & Stratton.

Lichtenberg, J. (1979). Factors in the development of the sense of the object. *Journal of the American Psychoanalytic Association, 27,* 375–86.

Lidz, T., Fleck, S., and Cornelison, A. (1965). *Schizophrenia and the family.* New York: International Universities Press.

Loewald, H. (1973). On internalization. *International Journal of Psychoanalysis, 54,* 9–17.

———. (1978). Instinct theory, object relations, and psychic-structure formation. *Journal of the American Psychoanalytic Association, 26,* 493–506.

———. (1980). *Papers on psychoanalysis.* New Haven, CT: Yale University Press.

Mahler, M. (1963). Thoughts about development and individuation. *Psychoanalytic Study of the Child, 18,* 307–24.

———. (1968). *On human symbiosis and the vicissitudes of individuation: Vol. 1. Infantile psychosis.* New York: International Universities Press.

Mahler, M., Pine, F., and Bergman, A. (1975). *The psychological birth of the human infant: Symbiosis and individuation.* New York: Basic Books.

Mahler, M., and Rabinovitch, R. (1956). The effects of marital conflict on child development. In V. Eisenstein (Ed.), *Neurotic interaction in marriage* (pp. 44–56). New York: Basic Books.

Malone, C. (1979). Child psychiatry and family therapy. *Journal of the American Academy of Child Psychiatry, 18,* 4–21.

Mandelbaum, A. (1977). The family treatment of the borderline patient. In P. Hartocollis (Ed.), *Borderline personality disorders: The concept, the syndrome, the patient* (pp. 423–38). New York: International Universities Press.

Meissner, W. (1978a). The conceptualization of marriage and family dynamics from a psychoanalytic perspective. In T. Paolino (Ed.), *Marriage and marital therapy: Psychoanalytic, behavioral and systems theory perspectives* (pp. 25–88). New York: Brunner/Mazel.

———. (1978b). *The paranoid process.* New York: Jason Aronson.

———. (1979). Internalization and object relations. *Journal of the American Psychoanalytic Association, 27,* 345–60.

———. (1984). *The borderline spectrum: Differential diagnosis and developmental issues.* New York: Jason Aronson.

———. (1986). The earliest internalizations. In R. Lax, S. Bach, and A. Burland (Eds.), *Self and object constancy: Clinical and theoretical perspectives* (pp. 29–72). New York: Guilford Press.

Mendez, A., and Fine, H. (1976). A short history of the British school of object relations and ego psychology. *Bulletin of the Menninger Clinic, 40,* 357–82.

Modell, A. (1968). *Object love and reality: An introduction to a psychoanalytic theory of object relations.* New York: International Universities Press.

———. (1975). A narcissistic defence against affects and the illusion of self-sufficiency. *International Journal of Psychoanalysis, 56,* 275–82.

———. (1984). *Psychoanalysis in a new context.* New York: International Universities Press.

———. (1985). Object relations theory. In A. Rothstein (Ed.), *Models of the mind: Their relationships to clinical work* (pp. 85–100). New York: International Universities Press.

Muir, R. (1975). The family and the problem of internalization. *British Journal of Medical Psychology, 48,* 267–72.

————. (1982). The family, the group, transpersonal processes and the individual. *International Review of Psychoanalysis, 9,* 317–26.

Nichols, M. (1984). *Family therapy: Concepts and methods.* New York: Gardner Press.

Novey, S. (1958). The meaning of the concept of mental representation of objects. *Psychoanalytic Quarterly, 27,* 57–79.

Ogden, T. (1983). The concept of internal object relations. *International Journal of Psychoanalysis, 64,* 227–41.

Paul, N. (1967). The role of mourning and empathy in conjoint marital therapy. In G. Zuk and I. Boszormenyi-Nagy (Eds.), *Family therapy and disturbed families* (pp. 186–205). Palo Alto, CA: Science & Behavior Books.

Paul, N., and Grosser, G. (1964). Family resistance to change in schizophrenic patients. *Family Process, 3,* 377–401.

Paul, N., and Paul, B. B. (1975). *A marital puzzle. Transgenerational analysis in marriage counseling.* New York: W. W. Norton.

Phillipson, H. (1955). *The object relations technique.* London: Tavistock.

Piaget, J. (1952). *The origins of intelligence in children.* New York: International Universities Press.

————. (1954). *The construction of reality in the child.* New York: Basic Books.

Quadrio, C. (1982). The Peter Pan and Wendy syndrome: A marital dynamic. *Australian and New Zealand Journal of Psychiatry, 16,* 23–28.

Rangell, L. (1985). The object in psychoanalytic theory. *Journal of the American Psychoanalytic Association, 33,* 301–34.

Richter, H. (1976). The role of family life in child development. *International Journal of Psychoanalysis, 57,* 385–95.

Rubinstein, D., and Timmons, J. (1979). Narcissistic dyadic relationships. *American Journal of Psychoanalysis, 39,* 125–36.

Sandler, J. (1976). Countertransference and role-responsiveness. *International Review of Psychoanalysis, 3,* 43–47.

Sandler, J., and Freud, A. (1985). *The analysis of defense: The ego and the mechanisms of defense revisited.* New York: International Universities Press.

Sandler, J., Holder, A., Kawenoka, M., Kennedy, H., and Neurath, L. (1969). Notes on some theoretical and clinical aspects of transference. *International Journal of Psychoanalysis, 50,* 633–45.

Sandler, J., and Sandler, A. M. (1978). On the development of object relationships and affects. *International Journal of Psychoanalysis, 59,* 285–96.

Sarason, S. (1981). *Psychology misdirected.* New York: Free Press.

Schafer, R. (1972). Internalization: Process or fantasy? *Psychoanalytic Study of the Child, 27,* 411–36.

Schwartz, D. (1984). Psychoanalytic development perspectives on parenthood. In R. Cohen, B. Cohler, and S. Weissman (Eds.), *Parenthood. A psychodynamic perspective* (pp. 356–72). New York: Guilford Press.

Segal, H. (1974). *Introduction to the work of Melanie Klein.* New York: Basic Books.

Shapiro, E. (1978). Research on family dynamics: Clinical implications for the family of the borderline adolescent. In S. Feinstein and P. Giovacchini (Eds.), *Adolescent Psychiatry. Developmental and clinical studies* (Vol. 6, pp. 360–76). Chicago: University of Chicago Press.

————. (1982–1983). The holding environment and family therapy with acting out adolescents. *International Journal of Psychoanalytic Psychotherapy, 9,* 209–26.

Shapiro, E., Shapiro, R., Zinner, J., and Berkowitz, D. (1977). The borderline ego and the working alliance: Indications for family and individual treatment in adolescence. *International Journal of Psychoanalysis, 58,* 77–87.

Shapiro, R. (1967). The origin of adolescent disturbances in the family: Some considerations in theory and implications for therapy. In G. Zuk and I. Boszormenyi-Nagy (Eds.), *Family therapy and disturbed families* (pp. 221–38). Palo Alto, CA: Science & Behavior Books.

————. (1968). Action and family interaction in adolescence. In J. Marmor (Ed.), *Modern psychoanalysis. New directions and perspectives* (pp. 454–75). New York: Basic Books.

————. (1979). Adolescents in family therapy. In J. Novello (Ed.), *The short course in adolescent psychiatry* (pp. 185–204). New York: Brunner/Mazel.

Shapiro, R., Zinner, J., Berkowitz, D., and Shapiro, E. (1975). The impact of group experiences on adolescent development. In M. Sugar (Ed.), *The adolescent in group and family therapy* (pp. 87–104). New York: Brunner/Mazel.

Skynner, R. (1976). *Systems of family and marital psychotherapy.* New York: Brunner/Mazel.

Slipp, S. (1973). The symbiotic survival pattern: A relational theory of schizophrenia. *Family Process, 12,* 377–98.

————. (1982). Interface between psychoanalysis and family therapy. *American Journal of Psychoanalysis, 42,* 221–28.

————. (1984). *Object relations: A dynamic bridge between individual and family therapy.* New York: Jason Aronson.

Spitz, R. (1965). *The first year of life. A psycho-analytic study of normal and deviant development of object relations.* New York: International Universities Press.

Sternbach, O. (1983). Critical comments on object relations theory. *Psychoanalytic Review, 70,* 403–21.

Stewart, R., Peters, T., Marsh, S., and Peters, M. (1975). An object-relations approach to psychotherapy with marital couples, families and children. *Family Process, 14,* 161–78.

Stierlin, H. (1973). Interpersonal aspects of internalizations. *International Journal of Psychoanalysis, 54,* 203–13.

————. (1974). Psychoanalytic approaches to schizophrenia in the light of a family model. *International Review of Psychoanalysis, 1,* 169–78.

————. (1976). The dynamics of owning and disowning: Psychoanalytic and family perspectives. *Family Process, 15,* 277–88.

————. (1977). *Psychoanalysis and family therapy.* New York: Jason Aronson.

Stolorow, R. (1978). Review: Object-relations theory and clinical psychoanalysis. *Contemporary Psychology, 23,* 32–33.

Sugarman, A. (1977). Object-relations theory: A reconciliation of phenomenology and ego psychology. *Bulletin of the Menninger Clinic, 41,* 113–30.

Sutherland, J. (1963). Object-relations theory and the conceptual model of psychoanalysis. *British Journal of Medical Psychology, 36,* 109–24.

————. (1980). The British object relations theorists: Balint, Winnicott, Fairbairn, Guntrip. *Journal of the American Psychoanalytic Association, 28,* 829–60.

Tuttman, S. (1981). A historical survey of the development of object relations concepts in psychoanalytic theory. In S. Tuttman, C. Kaye, and M. Zimmerman (Eds.), *Object and self: A developmental approach* (pp. 3–51). New York: International Universities Press.

Willi, J. (1982). *Couples in collusion. The unconscious dimension in partner relationships*. Claremont, CA: Hunter House.

Winnicott, D. (1965). *The maturational process and the facilitating environment. Studies in the theory of emotional development*. New York: International Universities Press.

———. (1969). The use of an object. *International Journal of Psychoanalysis, 50,* 711–16.

Wolff, P. (1960). The developmental psychologies of Jean Piaget and psychoanalysis. *Psychological Issues, 2,* 7–181.

Wynne, L., Ryckoff, I., Day, J., and Hirsch, S. (1958). Pseudo-mutuality in the family relations of schizophrenics. *Psychiatry, 21,* 205–20.

Zinner, J. (1978). Combined individual and family therapy of borderline adolescents: Rationale and management of the early phase. In S. Feinstein and P. Giovacchini (Eds.), *Adolescent psychiatry. Developmental and clinical studies* (Vol. 6, pp. 420–27). Chicago: University of Chicago Press.

Zinner, J., and Shapiro, E. (1975). Splitting in families of borderline adolescents. In J. Mack (Ed.), *Borderline states and psychiatry* (pp. 103–22). New York: Grune & Stratton.

Zinner, J., and Shapiro, R. (1972). Projective identification as a mode of perception and behaviour in families of adolescents. *International Journal of Psychoanalysis, 53,* 523–30.

———. (1974). The family group as a single psychic entity: Implications for acting out in adolescence. *International Review of Psychoanalysis, 1,* 179–85.

Index

ABOUT THE AUTHOR

RANDALL S. KLEIN was born on March 26, 1954, in Belleville, Illinois. In 1976 he received a Bachelor of Arts degree from Southern Illinois University in Carbondale; in 1978, a Master of Science degree; in 1979, an Education Specialist degree from Southern Illinois University at Edwardsville; and in 1987, a Doctor of Philosophy degree from St. Louis University. Dr. Klein is formerly a psychiatric counselor with the department of psychiatry at St. John's Mercy Medical Center, St. Louis. Currently, Dr. Klein is in private practice of the psychoanalytic psychotherapy of individuals, couples, and families in Sierra Vista, Arizona.

Class Tape Request Form

Reserve Video Late Fees:
$1.00 per hour per tape

Limit 3 Reserve Items

Course Number or
Channel/Block Letter

EEG598333

Class Date(s):

1. 2/10/03
2. _____
3. _____

Checkout period will be
48 hours or 4 hours
depending on tape
availability.

Nadesan~1
shafie

(M)